ASSASSINATIONS, THREATS, AND THE AMERICAN PRESIDENCY

ASSASSINATIONS, THREATS, AND THE AMERICAN PRESIDENCY

From Andrew Jackson to Barack Obama

Ronald L. Feinman

ROWMAN & LITTLEFIELD
Lanham • Boulder • New York • London

Published by Rowman & Littlefield
A wholly owned subsidiary of The Rowman & Littlefield Publishing Group, Inc.
4501 Forbes Boulevard, Suite 200, Lanham, Maryland 20706
www.rowman.com

Unit A, Whitacre Mews, 26-34 Stannary Street, London SE11 4AB

British Library Cataloguing in Publication Information Available

Library of Congress Cataloging-in-Publication Data

Feinman, Ronald L.
Assassinations, threats, and the American presidency : From Andrew Jackson to Barack Obama / by Ronald L. Feinman.
p. cm.
Includes bibliographical references and index.
ISBN 978-1-4422-3121-4 (cloth : alk. paper) -- ISBN 978-1-4422-3122-1 (electronic)
1. Presidents--Assassination--United States--History. 2. Presidents--Assassination attempts--United States--History. 3. Presidents--United States--Biography. I. Title.
E176.1.F39 2015
973.09'9--dc23
2014044057

™ The paper used in this publication meets the minimum requirements of American National Standard for Information Sciences Permanence of Paper for Printed Library Materials, ANSI/NISO Z39.48-1992.

Printed in the United States of America

Dedicated to my brother, Morton Feinman, who was always there for me throughout my life

CONTENTS

ACKNOWLEDGMENTS

No author can ever say that he has produced a work all on his own. Without the support and backing and cooperation of others, this work could not have been published.

I want to begin by thanking David Glauber, a former student of mine from Florida Atlantic University and professor at Broward College, who has always been one of my best friends and supporters in my long teaching career. David provided keen insights throughout the writing process and worked with me to produce the charts and the index, which add so much to this work. Without his critique of the first and second drafts of this book, it would not have been as good a book, and I cannot thank him enough for his commitment.

I also want to thank Peggy Mitchell, who has become a great friend of mine in the past few years, having first come to know each other through her reading of my political and historical blog, *The Progressive Professor*, since its inception in August 2008. As an experienced nurse and educator she is an expert on medicine, and her knowledge of gunshot wounds provided me with a greater understanding. She also offered a critique of the first and second drafts of this book.

I also wish to thank two colleagues, Dr. Stephen Engle of Florida Atlantic University and Professor Eleanor McCluskey of Broward College, for their expert reading of the third draft of the book, and their profound knowledge and wisdom. This book is better for their willingness to examine the manuscript.

Also, my best friend, Alan Borisman, gave me encouragement and support during the time of my writing and revising of this work. He has always been there for me in every way possible.

I also wish to thank Kathryn Knigge, my editor, who has been extremely cooperative and supportive of my efforts in producing this manuscript.

My son David Feinman, who amazes me every day with his intelligence, knowledge, and insights on so many topics, made a major difference with his reviewing and formatting of the second draft, and being so proud of his dad.

His wife and my daughter-in-law, Stephanie Levy, also gave her support and encouragement to the project. I am glad to have her as part of my family, and she is astute and brilliant in so many ways.

Also, my younger son, Paul Feinman, has been an inspiration and has provided great moral support in the creation of this work.

David, Stephanie, and Paul know how much I love them, and how nothing matters more than family.

INTRODUCTION

Since the dawn of civilization, individuals and groups in every society have held grievances toward their nation's leaders. Sometimes, they express themselves in terms of verbal protests, but other times their hostility turns violent. Assassination attempts against leaders have significantly shaped the course of world history and that of the United States.[1]

One of the earliest assassinations from antiquity, Julius Caesar in 44 BCE, led to the fall of the Roman Republic and the rise of the Roman Empire.

The assassination of Archduke Franz Ferdinand, the heir to the throne of the Austro-Hungarian Empire, in 1914, set off the powder keg that became the disastrous World War I. This war transformed the world in many ways, including the rise of the Soviet Union, Fascist Italy, and Nazi Germany; long-term turmoil in the Middle East with the fall of the Ottoman Turkish Empire; the rise of nationalism in the British and French Empires in Africa and Asia, leading to massive changes; and the resentments built up by the war and the Great Depression, leading to World War II, and then the Cold War after that.

The assassination of Czar Alexander II of Russia in 1881 ended the quest for reform within the Russian government, led to further deterioration of the monarchy, and eventual overthrow of the Czarist government by Nikolai Lenin and the Bolshevik Revolution in 1917.

The assassination of Abraham Lincoln in the mid-nineteenth-century United States had a negative impact on the future of America over the next century, and the assassinations of John F. Kennedy and Robert F.

Kennedy a century later transformed the second half of the twentieth century.

Political assassination has been one of the major themes of American history. Eleven presidents and three presidential hopefuls have been directly threatened by assassins. Mental illness or political and economic grievances have influenced these threats. A total of six of these fourteen incidents led to the death of the victim, with three others wounded, and five remaining unhurt, as a result of the assassination attempts.

Also, all five presidents still alive in 2015 have faced assassination threats both in and out of office. Finally, when one adds that Andrew Johnson was targeted to be killed when Abraham Lincoln was assassinated, but the potential assassin became intoxicated instead and Johnson remained unharmed, it means a total of seventeen presidents, and three presidential hopefuls, faced assassination threats or dangers. That means about 40 percent of our presidents can be documented as having been targeted by assassins.

The purpose of this book is to provide information and insight on all of the known facts of assassination threats and dangers for these seventeen presidents, plus the three candidates seeking the presidency who came under attack. One chapter will be devoted to each of the eleven presidents and three presidential aspirants who directly faced threats. Additionally, a careful study and analysis of the five living presidents and the threats they faced in the late twentieth and early twenty-first century will also be discussed.

It is interesting to note that all presidents from Franklin D. Roosevelt onward, except for Dwight D. Eisenhower and Lyndon B. Johnson, have faced assassination threats. While it is possible that Eisenhower and Johnson may have faced assassination incidents or threats, any such attempts have not become public. Knowledge of assassination threats have come through the news media or the Secret Service, which uses modern technological methods to quell the growing number of such threats, including White House intruders and "fence jumpers" since the 1970s.

Through 1901, five presidents faced a perceived threat that we are aware of, while since then twelve presidents and three presidential candidates have faced such threats, reflecting the violent nature of America's political culture. Since the death of Robert F. Kennedy in 1968, all serious presidential candidates, even in the stage of seeking the nomination, gain Secret Service protection and coverage for their own safety, with

Barack Obama gaining it shortly after announcing his candidacy in 2007, 21 months before the election, the earliest in an election cycle that any presidential contender was provided protection by that agency.

The subject of potential presidents, the "Might Have Beens," will also be covered, with the indication that fifteen people might have become president if fate had been different, including ten vice presidents; two secretaries of state; one Speaker of the House of Representatives; one President Pro Tempore of the Senate; and one U.S. senator. Background on these fifteen men, and judgment as to which would have been positive forces or negative forces in the White House, will be offered.

Additionally, the assassins who tried, and sometimes succeeded, in killing presidents or presidential aspirants will be studied, analyzing the motivations for their misdeeds. The forthcoming chapters will discuss that nine of the sixteen assassins of the fourteen potential victims were in their twenties, while five were in their thirties, and two were in their forties, with all being white males, except for two white females.

Conspiracy theories will also be touched upon, with the understanding that they cannot be proved to be factually accurate, but add mystery to the question of why these presidents and presidential candidates faced assassination threats.

The charts provided in the appendix will add insights to the whole subject. Within the bibliography, readers can find significant sources about the presidents who faced assassinations and attempts.

1

ANDREW JACKSON AT THE U.S. CAPITOL

Andrew Jackson, our seventh president (1767–1845), served in the presidency during the tumultuous years of 1829–1837. He was the first president not born to the aristocracy, not related to the Founding Father generation, and hailed from neither Virginia nor Massachusetts. Instead, Jackson spent most of his life in the "frontier" state of Tennessee, becoming wealthy, owning the plantation known as the "Hermitage," and acquiring a substantial slave population, similar to earlier Virginia aristocracy presidents George Washington, Thomas Jefferson, James Madison, and James Monroe.

Jackson was a combative person throughout his life and became the hero of the American West's frontiersmen, as well as the spokesman for the working class in the eastern urban areas of the nation. Journalists characterized him as the spokesman for the "common man," the image of the average American, and he gained his fame through his military exploits in the War of 1812. Weeks after the signing of the Treaty of Ghent ending the war, he won a major psychological victory over the British at the Battle of New Orleans.

Soon after, Jackson gained greater fame and notoriety in the invasion of Spanish Florida in 1817, creating a major controversy within the James Monroe cabinet over his arrest and execution of two British nationals, and the excessive killing of Seminole Indians, while fulfilling the goal of seizing Florida, which had become a problem for the United States because of Indian raids and boundary disputes with the state of Georgia.

Jackson then became the territorial governor of Florida and also served as a congressman and senator from Tennessee before running for president in the election of 1824. This was the first national election in which all white male citizens could vote, regardless of their economic station. Jackson ended up first in popular votes with 153,000 votes, and first in electoral votes with ninety-nine, in a four-man race against Secretary of State John Quincy Adams, Speaker of the House Henry Clay, and Treasury Secretary William Crawford.

But since no one had won a majority of the electoral votes, as required under the Constitution, the election was thrown to the U.S. House of Representatives. Henry Clay was not eligible, because of the guidelines of the 12th Amendment to the Constitution, having ended up fourth in the electoral vote total. Clay then threw his support to Adams, guaranteeing him the vote of thirteen of twenty-four states, and therefore, elevation to the presidency, even though Adams was second in both popular and electoral votes. The situation became more politically toxic when Adams gave Clay the position of secretary of state in his administration, which up to that time seemed a guarantee of elevation to the White House. Jefferson, Madison, Monroe, and Adams had held that position before becoming president.

Jackson claimed that Clay and Adams brokered a "corrupt bargain," and a four-year campaign ensued to remove Adams from the White House. Partisanship increased as the preceding Era of Good Feelings that manifested itself after the War of 1812 shifted to the creation of two new parties, the National Republicans led by Adams, and the Democrats led by Jackson. Both Adams and Jackson clashed again in the bitterly divisive campaign of 1828, from which Jackson emerged victorious.

The tumultuous campaign of 1828 forecast what was to come during Jackson's eight-year presidency—constant conflict and confrontation—and this became the environment for the first president to face threats to his life.

Jackson reflected a new political culture, which encouraged confrontation and aggressiveness, as Jackson himself had killed several men in gun duels earlier in his life. His policies caused tremendous polarization. Jackson promoted the spoils system to benefit his own Democratic Party over the opposition Whigs, which replaced the National Republicans by 1832–1833. He demonstrated willingness to invade South Carolina and hang former Vice President John C. Calhoun, if necessary, in the Nullification Crisis. His decision to destroy the Second National Bank of the United States, helping to cause the Panic of 1837 as he left office, became highly contentious. His policy of a forced removal of Native Americans through the Indian Removal Act to Oklahoma, caused thousands of deaths in what is known as the "Trail of Tears" (occurring under both Jackson and successor Martin Van Buren), and disturbed Clay and others in Congress. His condemnation of abolitionists and defense of slavery caused tremendous opposition among those committed to end "the peculiar institution" of slavery. No earlier president generated as much vehement opposition as Jackson did in his eight years as the nation's chief executive.

Jackson received volumes of hate mail and death threats during his presidency, something new in America, but sadly becoming a norm for future presidents who challenged the status quo and promoted change. It is known that Jackson had two physical threats against his life, and also had a notable death threat by letter, and the story of these incidents is both fascinating and revealing. It is interesting that all three death threats occurred after he had been reelected to his second term, suggesting that his personality and policies were inciting.[1]

As far as is known, the first physical threat against Jackson occurred on May 6, 1833, months after being inaugurated for his second term. Robert B. Randolph, who had served in the U.S. Navy, had been removed by orders of the president on charges of embezzlement. Randolph seethed over the dismissal and was determined to assault the president, a startling event, as no such situation had ever occurred before in presidential history. Jackson was en route to Fredericksburg, Virginia, for a dedication ceremony to honor the life of Mary Ball Washington, the mother of George Washington.

As President Jackson was passing through Alexandria, Virginia, Randolph confronted him. Randolph appeared without warning or notice, and struck the president while he was on a steamboat. Randolph was unarmed, but in a rage, he punched Jackson in the face, causing the elderly president's nose to bleed. Members of the crowd aided Jackson and subdued Randolph. Jackson refused to press charges, but it was a shock that this direct assault on the president of the United States had actually occurred.[2]

A much more intriguing event was the apparent death threat by written letter of Junius Brutus Booth, the father of future Abraham Lincoln assassin John Wilkes Booth. This letter's legitimacy was confirmed by the Andrew Jackson Papers Project at the University of Tennessee, and publicized on PBS's *History Detectives* series in 2009.

Booth had been born in London and was, like his sons John Wilkes and Edwin, a famous actor, specializing in Shakespearean theater. He also was known for his mercurial personality, and he was extremely demonstrative and emotional.

According to the University of Tennessee Jackson project, Booth was very disturbed by Jackson and his policies in office, and on July 4, 1835, penned a letter, threatening the life of Jackson in a very dramatic fashion. Booth was furious over two prisoners that he wanted Jackson to pardon, who had been convicted of piracy, men named De Ruiz and De Soto, in a high profile trial of the time period. Addressing the president as "You damn'd old Scoundrel," he threatened Jackson, stating: "I will cut your throat whilst you are sleeping."

The Jackson project confirmed that the letter was not a forgery or a joke, but a real threatening document, and the only time there was any correspondence between Booth and Jackson. Proof that it was authentic was based on Booth's staying at a hotel in Philadelphia and writing on stationary of the hotel in that city. The handwriting of Booth from other surviving correspondence confirmed that he was the author of the threatening letter. Also, Booth wrote an apology for having written such a threat to "authorities of the country."[3]

While these two incidents are of great interest, the most significant threat against Jackson occurred a few months before the Booth letter, on January 30, 1835, in Washington, D.C., and at the U.S. Capitol of all places, the only time that such an incident took place in the legislative building of the U.S. government. The first serious presidential assassin to go down in American history, an infamous list, was an English born house painter named Richard Lawrence. Lawrence migrated to the United States at about age twelve with his parents, and his life seemed uneventful as a child and early adult. His occupation as a house painter perhaps poisoned him in some manner, possibly lead poisoning, and affected his mental and emotional being by his early thirties.

Evidence of his odd behavior emerged in 1832, when he, seemingly without any reason, left Washington, D.C., on the way to England, but then quickly returned, and then planned again to go to England, but soon claimed he was being prevented from traveling by the U.S. government.

He also claimed that journalists wrote stories critical of his travel plans, certainly very odd behavior. These signs of disorientation were worrisome to his family, but they seemed unable to figure out what to do about Lawrence's mental and emotional state. This behavior should have been reported to authorities, but because there was little understanding of mental illness at the time, nothing was done.

Lawrence quit working, but claimed the U.S. government owed him a large sum of money, as he was King Richard III of England and owned two estates in England. He told his sister and brother-in-law, with whom he lived, that he was being denied the money he was owed, due to Andrew Jackson's campaign to destroy the Second National Bank of the United States, an event that was ongoing from 1833 until the time of the assassination attempt. Totally delusional, Lawrence now came to believe that *if* Jackson was assassinated, then Martin Van Buren would become president, and he would guarantee that Lawrence would be paid the money that the government supposedly owed him.

Lawrence had become paranoid, and his relatives noticed that he wore expensive clothing that drew odd attention to himself, and gazed at people for long periods of time, sometimes smiling in a strange manner. At other times, he was hostile to everyone he met. At one point, he threatened a maid who he thought was ridiculing his strange behavior, as well as family members, including his sister. Lawrence's bizarre behavior included laughing hysterically, cursing vehemently, and often just talking to himself.

Increasingly, Lawrence monitored Jackson's activities in the nation's capital, and seemed to talk to himself about, and complain about, the wrongs Jackson had done to him. On January 30, 1835, his illness got the better part of him and he decided to take action, walking to the U.S. Capitol, where Jackson was attending the funeral of South Carolina Congressman Warren R. Davis. Apparently, Lawrence had planned to shoot Jackson as he arrived at the Davis funeral, but he was not close enough to carry through with his plan.

Lawrence lingered near a pillar at the East Portico of the U.S. Capitol, waiting for Jackson to pass as he was leaving the funeral. Lawrence suddenly emerged, firing a pistol at Jackson's back, but the Derringer misfired. Armed with two guns, he pulled out the second Derringer pistol and aimed again at Jackson, but fortunately, again, the second gun misfired as well. These firearms were susceptible to being affected by moisture, and the winter weather, therefore, made them damp and less effective. Both weapons worked perfectly during the ensuing investigation, with the odds of both misfiring being highly unlikely, so we can say that the weather conditions saved Jackson's life.

Jackson noticed what was happening, and his gut reaction was to combat the challenge, as he had done so many times in his younger years. In retaliation, he became the only president to react directly to his attempted assassin, proceeding to use his walking cane (Jackson was sixty-seven at the time) to hit Lawrence over the head mercilessly, until bystanders (including Tennessee Congressman Davy Crockett) interceded and wrestled Lawrence into submission.

This was an extremely fortuitous event, and one that no one could have predicted. To have two weapons fired in a successive, rapid fashion and have neither accomplish its purpose was seen as a divine event by many and added to the heroic image of the "common man" president.

After being arrested for his attempted assassination of Jackson, Richard Lawrence was brought to trial in the nation's capital just twelve days later, something unheard of in modern times. He was prosecuted by Francis Scott Key, who famously authored the lyrics to America's national anthem, "The Star Spangled Banner." In the quickest trial on record, Lawrence was judged insane and, therefore, found not guilty. He was institutionalized in a series of facilities and hospitals, and last was housed in what became known later as St. Elizabeth's Hospital in Washington, D.C., known at the time as the Government Hospital for the Insane. Lawrence finally passed away in custody, apparently of natural causes, on June 13, 1861, at approximately age sixty.

The concept of conspiracy arose, with John C. Calhoun, Jackson's first-term vice president and his mortal enemy, having to deny on the Senate floor that he had plotted against the president. Jackson believed to the end of his life, however, that somehow, Calhoun had been engaged in a conspiracy to kill him.

Additionally, some suspicion arose over a former supporter of Jackson, Mississippi Senator George Poindexter, who had become a major critic and was shown to have hired Richard Lawrence as a house painter just months before the attempted assassination of the president. While Poindexter vehemently denied such a plot, he was defeated for reelection, with Jackson's strong suspicions, which had an effect on many, convincing many people of a conspiracy, something easy to claim, but impossible to prove.

Still, most independent observers concluded that Lawrence took part in his action all by himself, and the evidence of him being a paranoid schizophrenic, a deranged and delusional man, stands out in history as the ultimate conclusion. Thankfully, the first presidential assassination attempt had led to no harm to the president, and Jackson finished his second term and would live on in retirement for the next eight years, still the center of controversy and conflict, as he had been most of his life.

Had Jackson been assassinated in 1835, one can speculate that Martin Van Buren, becoming president two years before his actual election, might have chosen a different chief justice than Roger Taney, who became a very divisive chief justice over the next twenty-eight years into the Civil War era. Also, possibly, Van Buren might have tried to reconstitute the Second National Bank that Jackson had destroyed, and possibly would have, therefore, prevented the Panic of 1837, which took seven years to achieve full economic recovery. Van Buren might have been seen as a better president than he was, having to deal with the economic damage that Jackson had promoted, and might have calmed the tension between North and South, which had occurred during the Nullification Crisis. But then, again, Van Buren later was the presidential nominee of the Free Soil Party in 1848, opposed to the expansion of slavery, which might have ended up causing a rift between North and South, as he was a native New Yorker. As always, one can never be certain of what *might* have happened, but it is interesting to consider a scenario such as this one discussed here.

2

ABRAHAM LINCOLN AT FORD'S THEATRE

Abraham Lincoln (1809–1865), the sixteenth president of the United States (1861–1865), has been rated by most scholars as the greatest American president since around the turn of the twentieth century. An estimated fifteen thousand titles have been published on Abraham Lincoln and his presidency. Only Confederate sympathizers, of which there are many even after 150 years since the Civil War, would argue against his greatness.

As president of the Union during the Civil War, who waged war against the Confederate States of America and whose whole time in office was consumed by the conflict, Lincoln was subjected to numerous death threats on a regular basis. At least three incidents stand out in the time he was at the center of American government.

As president-elect, on his way to the inauguration, one plot was to kill him in Baltimore in 1861. While president in 1864 and traveling by horse to the Old Soldiers Home, his haven away from the White House, he was subjected to a second assassination attempt. The third major assassination attempt succeeded in killing the sixteenth president of the United States at Ford's Theatre in Washington, D.C., just days after the Civil War ended and transformed American history for all time. In the process of planning the last assassination attempt, others were also set up to be victims, with Vice President Andrew Johnson not ultimately faced with an assassination attempt because of cowardice by the person assigned to kill him, while another target, Secretary of State William Seward, miraculously survived an assassination attempt, and contributed to the future expansion of the nation, the gaining of Alaska by purchase from Czarist Russia in 1867 under Johnson's presidency.

Before examining these three assassination attempts, one should first examine just how controversial Abraham Lincoln was, even as he became our sixteenth president in March 1861. He was never an abolitionist, but rather a Free Soil advocate. Originally a Whig Party member, he then switched to the Republican Party when the Whig Party dissolved in the midst of the turmoil surrounding the Kansas-Nebraska Act of 1854. This law allowed the expansion of slavery into territories north of the southern border of Missouri, which had previously been banned as part of the Missouri Compromise of 1820.

Lincoln believed that the ability of whites and African Americans to coexist in America was unlikely long term, and therefore advocated voluntary migration of freed slaves to the West African nation of Liberia, which he pledged to colonize further than it was at the time. Lincoln, nevertheless, was greatly troubled by the horrors and evils of slavery itself, and tormented by the Fugitive Slave Law of 1850, which mandated Northern assistance in the capture of runaway slaves.

Lincoln frequently clashed with Chief Justice Roger Taney, a Southerner, until Taney's death in 1864. Lincoln condemned the Supreme Court's 1857 Dred Scott ruling, which declared that blacks were property, allowing Southerners to bring their "property" with them into the North, thereby extending slavery throughout the United States. This unfortunate ruling helped to inspire the Civil War.

In his campaign for the presidency, Lincoln made clear that his goal was to preserve the Union, not to abolish slavery. He made it clear, however, that if the only way to preserve the Union was to free the slaves, then he would move in that direction. This is why he gave the South the chance to return to the Union during the fall of 1862, after a year and a half of war, by his issuance of the Preliminary Emancipation Proclamation, hoping to avoid the ultimate announcement of the Emancipation Proclamation on January 1, 1863.

Lincoln was not only controversial on the issue of the Emancipation Proclamation but also on the charges that he provoked the outbreak of the Civil War by his refusal to allow Fort Sumter to be surrendered, informing the government of South Carolina of his intentions to provide necessary provisions to the fort in early April 1861. When South Carolina opened up an assault on Fort Sumter on April 12, 1861, the U.S. ships nearing the fort simply withdrew, holding back fire, so the charges that Lincoln provoked the war have been seen by most historians as illegitimate, although those who still contest it continue to assert that charge against Lincoln. That Lincoln refused to allow the South to secede peacefully after the assault on Fort Sumter has continued to make him controversial, but others have defended his actions as the responsibilities of any American president—to preserve the Union at all costs.

Lincoln also caused controversy and division in the North over his handling of the military side of the Civil War, having problems finding generals who could match the leadership capabilities of Robert E. Lee and other Southern generals. Pessimism subsequently grew within the Union about whether it could prevail over the Confederacy on the battlefield. As the body count increased dramatically, Lincoln faced constant criticism from critics within his own Republican Party; from Democrats in the North (Copperheads) who argued that the war was pointless, and that Lincoln should simply allow peaceful separation; and from newspapers and periodicals that ridiculed him viciously, and even published military movement information, which might help the enemy forces on future battlefields.

When Lincoln determined that violations of the Bill of Rights were justified in a time of a war that threatened the survival of the nation as one entity, the reaction was overly condemnatory, and this still remains the most controversial aspect of Lincoln's presidency. The shutting down of opposition newspapers for weeks and months at a time; suspending of the writ of habeas corpus in widespread cases; and imprisoning of some opponents, most famously Copperhead Democratic Congressman Clement Vallandigham of Ohio, all aroused accusations of a Lincoln dictatorship as he stretched the powers of the presidency. These violations of civil liberties increased animosity among Lincoln's critics.

No president had ever been so bitterly attacked by forces both on his side politically, as well as those against him. When Lincoln came up with a plan of Reconstruction (the Ten Percent Plan), which proposed a lenient plan of restoring the rebel states back into the Union as equals with the other states, the Radical Republicans in the party reacted in anger. This group within the party, led by Congressman Thaddeus Stevens of Pennsylvania and Senators Charles Sumner of Massachusetts and Benjamin Wade of Ohio, insisted on promoting a fifty percent plan, requiring a majority of white male citizens, not ten percent, within each rebel state to take an oath of loyalty to the United States before the state could be fully restored to the Union as an equal with other states.

When Lincoln pocket vetoed this proposal (the Wade-Davis Bill) in the summer of 1864, while Congress was out of session, it infuriated the Radical Republicans, setting up a potential confrontation between Lincoln and this wing of the party. This became obvious when the Wade-Davis Manifesto was issued by the Radicals and other Republicans in Congress who sided with them on the issue of Reconstruction policy, a statement which bluntly told the president that Reconstruction policy was their prerogative, not the president's right to decide. So a collision course seemed likely as Lincoln took his second oath of office at the U.S. Capitol on March 4, 1865.

With this tumultuous background and controversy that revolved around Abraham Lincoln, no wonder he was the subject of assassination attempts throughout his presidency, and even before taking the presidential oath.

After Lincoln was elected in 1860, and as Southern states seceded from the Union, there was growing fear from his private security force that the president-elect would be murdered by conspirators on his various train stops on the way from Springfield, Illinois, to Washington, D.C. Traditionally, the president-elect would appear before supportive crowds at every train station along the route and deliver a speech. But private security, headed by Allan Pinkerton, whose name would be famous for security nationally and internationally over time, was concerned for an assassination attempt against Lincoln, trying to prevent his inauguration. There were constant threats to murder the president-elect, whether by bullets, knives, poisoned ink, or even spider-filled dumpling.

This fear particularly centered on Baltimore, Maryland, a city known for its thugs and rowdies at that time. This state was a slave state, with large elements within the state planning to secede from the Union. There was an absolute need, as seen by Lincoln and members of his Republican Party, to prevent that from occurring, as it represented a fundamental threat to the survival of the capital city of the United States, with the likelihood of war imminent. There was concern that Maryland might secede from the Union before Lincoln arrived in Washington, and that his life was in danger while traveling through that city about forty miles outside Washington, D.C.

Allan Pinkerton, and five others working with him, including the first woman detective, Kate Warne, became aware of a supposed plot headed by a Captain Cipriano Ferrandini, an immigrant from Corsica, who was seen as a radical willing to do what was necessary to prevent Lincoln from ever reaching Washington, D.C. Ferrandini was a firebrand, with a group of followers as resolved as he was to eliminate Lincoln before he could become president. Ferrandini and his followers were avid secessionists who were conspiring to kill Lincoln, and this convinced Pinkerton and his assistants that they had to whisk Lincoln through Baltimore before the scheduled time on February 23.

The problem was that Lincoln himself believed he could convince the secessionists of his desire for conciliation and had total confidence in the support of the population as he traveled through each city on his route to the nation's capital. The plan was, as everywhere, to leave the train at each stop on the route, travel through the streets in an open carriage to a local hotel, greet citizens, and speak at each location. But this would endanger Lincoln's safety and security, and this was constantly on the mind of Allan Pinkerton.

So the plan was made to slip Lincoln through Baltimore before the scheduled time and before crowds, who expected him, had shown up at the train terminal. This, of course, would greatly disappoint supporters, who would lose the opportunity to greet him and cheer him on his way to the inauguration. But this change was essential and it was handled efficiently and without any major complications.

This plan would require Lincoln to switch trains in a manner that might draw attention, and also to cover almost two hundred miles in a single night from Harrisburg, Pennsylvania, through Baltimore, to Washington, D.C., and take a different rail line and stop briefly at a different rail station, where the crowds would not be present, and be ushered quickly onto the final train to the nation's capital.

So the long trip from Harrisburg to Philadelphia to Baltimore to Washington, D.C., had lots of intrigue, stealth, decoys, and tense moments worthy of a full-length feature film. Allan Pinkerton and his five assistants, which includ Lincoln's personal bodyguard, Ward Lamon, became the true heroes, accomplishing the goal of escorting Abraham Lincoln safely to the Willard Hotel in D.C. on February 23, where he remained under security watch until his inauguration on March 4.

It has been questioned whether there really was a "Baltimore Plot," but it was a smart move by Pinkerton to assume that the threat was real. There has never been proof whether such threats actually existed. But it is not as important as the fact that folks thought they existed and acted on those thoughts. Cipriano Ferrandini was never arrested or indicted for such a plot, but it seems likely that there were those who wished Lincoln ill.

Sadly, Lincoln was lampooned, ridiculed, and condemned as a coward for failing to show up in public in the Baltimore railroad station as scheduled. Both secessionists and supporters felt it made him look weak, scared, unwilling to show himself in public, lacking courage, being the only president in American history to hide from the American people on the route to the inauguration. This was nothing unusual for Lincoln, who became the most regularly criticized president in American history, probably not matched by Richard Nixon or Barack Obama or any other president. This scenario was unavoidable, as he became president at a time when the nation was falling apart in the worst political crisis ever to occur in the nation's history.[1]

Under constant assassination threats, nearing ten thousand during his presidency, Abraham Lincoln went about the business of being president. He was constantly aware of the death threats, but refused to allow them to interfere with the serious business of conducting a war. He dealt with foreign governments which might support the Confederacy and cause international crisis by so doing, and he also tried to move the nation ahead on economic changes reflecting the westward expansion of the nation. He also understood the need for rapid industrialization and the need to promote education as the way to advance the nation's long-term future.

In August 1864, Lincoln was subjected to an apparent sniper attack as he rode his horse at around 11 p.m. to the Lincoln Cottage at the Old Soldiers Home, about three miles from the White House. The Lincolns often spent summers there during his administration to get away from the oppressive heat in the White House, which could not be cooled off in any acceptable manner. He was close to the Old Soldiers Home when, suddenly, a shot was fired, which went through his tall hat and knocked it off his head.

The horse, startled by the rifle shot, started off at breakneck speed to the home, nearly throwing the president off his saddle in the process.

Lincoln told the story of this event in a humorous manner, wanting to believe that it was simply a case of someone firing an errant shot, with no intention of harming the president. It could be that he said this to reassure the public and his wife that they need not worry, but many wonder whether this was an assassination attempt.

Looking back at the event, it is startling that Lincoln would ride a horse, with only a couple of soldiers on the voyage with him, from the White House to the Old Soldiers Home, indicating a lack of understanding of the dangers to his life, although he was well aware of thousands of death threats against him. From this point on, Lincoln traveled to the home by carriage with an increased number of soldiers escorting his coach, which he finally realized was necessary.

When one looks back at the Lincoln presidency, it is unbelieveable, in the midst of the Civil War, and with ten thousand plus death threats against the president and two perceived attempts against the president's life very much in evidence, that Lincoln went about the business of being president without a formal security detail. Such a detail originated only after President William McKinley's assassination in 1901. Lincoln rejected the efforts to protect him and evaded many attempts to protect him from the public. When he accepted personal protection, he insisted that the security detail remain as inconspicuous as possible wherever he mixed with the population which came to see him speak or to shake his hand in greeting.

As the war came to an end in April 1865, the Confederacy neared final defeat, plots against Lincoln multiplied, with plans to kidnap him or assassinate him, with the hope that it would change the ultimate outcome of the war.

The Confederate government of Jefferson Davis wanted very much to see the demise of not only Lincoln but also the new vice president, Andrew Johnson, and Secretary of State William Seward. And Davis's chief collaborator in this regard was Judah P. Benjamin, who served under Davis immediately after secession as attorney general and secretary of war, and finally became secretary of state for the Confederacy in late 1862, and for the duration of the war.

The failed assassination attempt in August 1864 near the Old Soldiers Home was fortunate, as now Lincoln had protection and rode in a carriage instead of by horse. A plot to kidnap him, engineered by the Confederate government and spies, therefore, had to be abandoned. But a plan to bomb the White House, devised by Benjamin, to be accomplished by an explosives agent, Sergeant Thomas F. Harney, in cooperation with Colonel John Mosby, who was engaged in the original kidnapping plan, was only prevented when Harney was captured. He was later freed, and his mission was unknown for more than a century, only discovered in recent research. Mosby's involvement in plans for the Lincoln assassination adds intrigue and fascination to Lincoln's ultimate death on the part of both scholars and Lincoln specialists.

Judah P. Benjamin fled to Great Britain, never to return, with Secretary of State Seward firmly believing that Benjamin had been the major motivator of the Lincoln assassination plot carried out by John Wilkes Booth. Benjamin had done everything possible to disrupt the presidential election of 1864, hoping for Lincoln's defeat. He had also planned to provoke Britain to enter the war and to provoke riots in Northern cities.

The ultimate threat against the life of Abraham Lincoln took place just as the Union had defeated the Confederacy, after four long years, with approximately 620,000 soldiers killed on both sides of the tragic events, as General Robert E. Lee surrendered to General Ulysses S. Grant at Appomattox Court House in Virginia on April 9, 1865. Lincoln would not survive six days after this moment.

But a stage actor, John Wilkes Booth, known to those who followed American theater, and the brother of an even better known actor, Edwin Booth, would become the only well-known individual who would set out to assassinate a president or presidential candidate in American history. Booth not only had to compete with his brother, but also with the reputation of his father, Junius Brutus Booth.

Booth became involved in a complex plot with nine other conspirators, whose goal was the assassination of Abraham Lincoln, the newly inaugurated Vice President Andrew Johnson, and the second-term Secretary of State William Seward—with the purpose being to eliminate the top three people in the Union government, just as the war ended, and to inspire a continuation of the war, despite Lee having surrendered to Grant. The U.S. government would be paralyzed, discouraged, and demoralized. It could no longer try to pacify the South, and everyday functions of the government would be disrupted right at a crucial moment at the supposed end of hostilities.

The others involved in the conspiracy included: Lewis Powell (also known as Lewis Paine), David Herold, George Atzerodt, Samuel Arnold,

Michael O'Laughlen, John Surratt, his mother Mary Surratt, Edmund Spengler, and Dr. Samuel Mudd.

Lewis Powell was the only other conspirator to try to murder a government official, as he reached the home of Secretary of State Seward on the evening of April 14, 1865, accompanied by David Herold. Seward was recovering from a carriage accident that took place on April 5, which led to him suffering a concussion, broken jaw, broken right arm, and numerous bruises. Powell used the ruse that he had medicine for Seward to enter his home.

Powell commenced to stab Seward several times, but since Seward had a jaw splint from his injuries, Powell failed to stab him in the jugular vein. Also, two of Seward's sons and two other individuals in the home fought with Powell and were injured, but fortunately, Seward avoided death in the confrontation. Powell escaped but was later apprehended when he showed up at the home of Mary Surratt as she was being arrested. With her arrest unfolding, she denied knowing Powell.

Powell was tried under his pseudonym of "Paine," denied an insanity defense strategy, tried by a military tribunal, and found guilty of conspiracy to commit murder and treason. Powell was executed with three others—Mary Surratt, David Herold, and George Atzerodt—although Powell spoke up for Surratt, denying her guilt and involvement in the conspiracy against U.S. government officials.

Herold had accompanied Powell to Seward's home, and also accompanied Booth in his escape, finally leaving the barn where soldiers found them in Maryland, and although not directly involved in an assault on Lincoln or Seward, he faced hanging with George Atzerodt and Mary Surratt.

Atzerodt was supposed to kill Vice President Johnson. He took a room in the Kirkwood House in Washington, the place where Johnson was staying, but was unable to follow through and instead became drunk. He spent the night of the attacks on Lincoln and Seward wandering the streets of the capital in a drunken stupor. This did not save him from the gallows as he died alongside the three conspirators most involved in the plot, as the government perceived it at the time.

The lesser conspirators were Samuel Arnold (who had been involved in plots to kidnap Abraham Lincoln); Michael O'Laughlen (also involved in the same plots, and also thought to be stalking Union war hero Ulysses S. Grant); Edmund Spengler (who worked at Ford's Theatre, knew

Booth, but claimed no knowledge of any plot against President Lincoln); and Dr. Samuel Mudd (who set Booth's broken leg, which was injured at the time of the assassination; Mudd claimed not to know who Booth was or what he had done, although evidence shows that he did indeed know Booth from earlier meetings). All were sentenced to prison at Fort Jefferson in the Dry Tortugas off Key West, Florida, and were later freed by pardon of President Andrew Johnson, except for O'Laughlen, who had died in prison in 1867.

The Surratts, mother and son, are the most interesting story of the Lincoln conspirators, with possibly the exception of Dr. Mudd. Mary Surratt was implicated for owning the boardinghouse at which Booth and the other conspirators stayed at times, and plotted to overthrow the U.S. government. She became the first woman ever executed by the U.S. government, despite much doubt as to her role in the plot and her guilt in the events that transpired. It seems certain, however, that Surratt knew of her son John's involvement with Booth, and knew all of the conspirators, and had met with Confederate agents in the last few months of the Civil War. She was acknowledged as a Confederate sympathizer, and it is known that Booth and David Herold visited her boardinghouse after the assassination to pick up some rifles and binoculars as they fled Washington, D.C. Attempts to avoid the death penalty failed. Her son had fled to Canada, was later arrested and extradited, but found not guilty of involvement in the assassination conspiracy, although he admitted being part of the plot to kidnap Lincoln in the last days of the war.

All of the co-conspirators are part of the story of the plan to assassinate Abraham Lincoln, but ultimately, it is John Wilkes Booth who is the center of attention. The only famous assassin of a president or presidential candidate in American history, he remains fascinating to those who study presidential assassinations and attempts, because he was well known to the educated public who paid attention to theater. His father, Junius Brutus Booth, was a notable British Shakespearean actor. His two brothers were also notable actors, with Edwin Booth being a renowned actor, considered more significant than John Wilkes Booth ever was in his short life. Jealousy of his brother and their different politics divided them, with Edwin being a Unionist and John being a longtime Confederate sympathizer they often fought over issues of the Civil War throughout the conflict.

Young John Wilkes Booth began his career in the theater in 1855, at the age of seventeen, and had become well known over the ten years of his career. Booth came from an aristocratic background, but had an unstable, erratic father who had threatened Andrew Jackson three years before John was born. John was an athletic, popular young man, regarded as handsome, and he demonstrated great passion in his acting career, earning the equivalent of a half million dollars a year income in modern terms. He performed in Shakespearean dramas and many other plays as well, gaining renown in Baltimore, Philadelphia, Richmond, and other locations, and liked the role of Brutus the most, as Brutus was the slayer of Julius Caesar. Was this a portent of his future infamy?

Booth's career soared during the Civil War, although he had critics who were disturbed by his open statement of his political views, supporting the Confederate cause. He would be hailed by many theater critics for his performances and would be pursued by women, who were attracted to his good looks and charismatic presence. He was acting on a national level, including in New York City, Boston, Chicago, Cleveland, St. Louis, New Orleans, and Atlanta, among other locations.

When Ford's Theatre opened in Washington, D.C., in November 1863, Booth was one of the first leading men to perform there, and President Lincoln was in the audience, with Booth reportedly shaking his finger in the direction of the president, who noticed what seemed to be an unfriendly gesture. Booth gave a flower to young Tad Lincoln at another performance when Tad praised his performance, but refused to greet the president in between acts of the play.

Booth's last performance before the assassination was at Ford's Theatre, where staff of the theater knew him well and would not think twice about his entering and exiting the theater through any door of the building. It is also believed some of the staff at the theater were Confederate sympathizers, not uncommon for people living in Washington, D.C. This would assist Booth in his plan to assassinate Lincoln.

Ironically, while acting in St. Louis in 1863, Booth's strong Confederate beliefs, his support of slavery, and his denunciation of Abraham Lincoln led to his arrest as a traitor, but he was released by paying a fine and taking an oath of allegiance to the Union cause. He could have been stopped in his plans against Lincoln if he had been jailed for his outspoken statements at a delicate time, and that would be recalled later as a time that sealed the fate of the sixteenth president.

Booth's obsessive hatred of Lincoln caused older brother Edwin to order him out of his home, as jealousy and politics divided the brothers. He started laying plans to kidnap Lincoln from the Old Soldiers Home. One has to wonder if the sniper shot that went through Lincoln's hat in the late summer of 1864 might have been from Booth, rather than an error by someone else with his firearm. There is evidence that Booth might have been a Confederate agent, and maybe even a spy for the South, and he often consorted with pro-Confederate individuals and groups. He also met with co-conspirators at the boardinghouse of Mary Surratt.

When Inauguration Day came in Washington, D.C., on March 4, 1865, Booth was in the crowd as Lincoln delivered his historic Second Inaugural Address, regarded by many as the greatest delivered until then, and still one of the best Inaugural Addresses of all time. When photographs of this scene were magnified years later, they revealed that Booth was in the crowd. Many people attending the inauguration recalled later that they had seen him there, and had seen him moving toward the inaugural stand, making one speculate whether Booth had plans to kill the president at the actual moment of the inaugural events.

A plot to kidnap the president near the Old Soldiers Home on March 17 fell through as Lincoln did not pass through that area, and instead was appearing at a hotel where Booth was actually staying at the time. The opportunities for the two men to cross paths were clearly coming closer to the fateful events of April 14. Once Lee had surrendered to Grant at Appomattox Court House in Virginia, any plans for a kidnapping were discarded and the plan now was for Booth to take down a man he considered a tyrant.

Booth was also in the crowd outside the White House on April 11, when Lincoln gave an impromptu speech in favor of suffrage for the former slaves, an action which Booth saw as outrageous. Booth commented to someone that this was the last speech Lincoln would ever make.

Ironically, Lincoln had a nightmare about two weeks before the assassination, imagining himself on a catafalque, his corpse in funeral vestments, in the East Room of the White House, and told a friend about this dream three days before the assassination, the same day that Booth pledged to kill him after hearing him speak outside the White House. This revelation that came out over time added to the whole tragedy of his death.

The plot was now in full play, as Booth learned that Lincoln would be attending the play *Our American Cousin* at Ford's Theatre on Good Friday, April 14, 1865, with his wife, Mary Todd Lincoln, and triumphant Union General Ulysses S. Grant and his wife. However, plans were changed and Grant and his wife ended up traveling to New Jersey instead, and Lincoln's guests for the performance were Major Henry Rathbone and his fiancée, Clara Harris.

At around 10:15 p.m., Booth entered the presidential box upstairs at Ford's Theatre as the audience was laughing at a funny line in the play, shot Lincoln once in the back of the head with a .44 caliber Philadelphia Derringer pistol, was challenged by Major Rathbone—who was stabbed with a dagger when he lunged at Booth—and then leapt approximately twelve feet to the stage from the second-floor box, shocking the audience with the shot and the sight of someone leaping through the air in the midst of the play.

Booth utilized a .44 caliber Derringer with a muzzle velocity of 400 feet per second, far less than Civil War muskets, which had a velocity of 1,400 feet per second. The bullet fired into Lincoln's brain did not blow through to the front of his face and was flattened as it penetrated the back of his skull.

Booth suffered a broken leg either in the leap to the stage, or later when his horse tripped and fell on him as he was pursuing his escape. As he leapt to the stage, he declared, "Sic Semper Tyrannis" (Thus Always to Tyrants), the statement of Brutus at the Julius Caesar assassination, which he had often enacted on the stage. Others who were present at the tragic events claimed he also said: "I have done it, the South is avenged!"

President Lincoln was carried across the street from Ford's Theatre to a private home, the Petersen House, where he expired at 7:22 a.m. on Saturday, April 15, 1865, at the age of fifty-six. Secretary of War Edwin M. Stanton took temporary charge of the government in those early hours, and arranged for a pursuit of all of the accomplices, along with Booth, in the conspiracy. Stanton forced Mrs. Lincoln to leave, because of her hysterical reaction to her husband's impending death, and she never fully recovered from the trauma and was later sent to a mental institution by her son, Robert Todd Lincoln, for a time in the early 1870s.

Booth fled into Southern Maryland, accompanied by David Herold, and then to the home of Dr. Samuel Mudd, where the doctor set his broken leg. Booth eventually escaped into Virginia, where Union soldiers discovered him at the Richard Garrett farm, and they shot him in the neck after the barn that he was hiding in was set on fire by Union troops. He died a few hours later, paralyzed by the bullet fired by a Union soldier, Sergeant Boston Corbett. Booth left behind a diary he had been keeping on his escape; it had pages missing from it, apparently ripped out at some point.[2]

The country mourned Lincoln's death in a massive way, with 1.5 million people viewing his open coffin on the thirteen-day journey from Washington, D.C., to Springfield, Illinois. The long-range implications of Lincoln's assassination have never really been fully appreciated, as it brought to power a vice president, Andrew Johnson, who is regarded as a tragic and disastrous leader, who ushered in a period of Reconstruction that many Southerners thought would have been far less divisive if Lincoln had lived. However, it should be pointed out that the Thirteenth Amendment and the Fourteenth Amendment were added to the Constitution under Johnson's watch, although he opposed the Fourteenth Amendment and vetoed the Civil Rights Act of 1866, causing his reputation to suffer. Johnson would face impeachment, which it is believed that Lincoln would have averted, had he survived and finished the term. At the same time, many experts think Lincoln was in poor health, had aged rapidly in office, and might have died in office before the end of his term in March 1869.

The growing feeling in the South, among educated people at least, helped to stir a movement to support the building of the Lincoln Memorial in the nation's capital, as an appropriate action to commemorate the sacrifices and the commitment of our sixteenth president to preservation of the Union. Of course, for many people in the South, even in 2015, there is still bitterness toward Lincoln and the "Yankees" who forced defeat on the Confederacy. Talk of secession and states' rights still reverberates from politicians.

There remain today many thoughts and ideas, what could best be called conspiracy theories, about the Lincoln assassination. These theories include the belief that the Catholic Church was involved in the plot; that Secretary Stanton, who pursued the Lincoln conspirators and assured that four of them would hang in very short order, was a Radical who, being alienated from Lincoln's Ten Percent Plan, plotted to remove Lincoln from the presidency; and that President Jefferson Davis, Vice President Alexander Stephens, and Secretary of State Judah P. Benjamin of the

Confederacy had arranged the murder, and had plotted against Lincoln constantly. Some think that Stanton might have had pages from the Booth diary ripped out and destroyed, which might have shown his involvement in the Booth conspiracy, but it is hard to prove so many years later. None of these theories can ever be fully proved or repudiated, but all of them have their supporters and critics, as the fascination with the Lincoln assassination remains a subject of debate and constant interest, including documentaries and films, as well as stage plays, and constant reassessment of the event in numerous scholarly and popular treatments of this most profound event in American history, the loss of a president who had a greater effect on our national history than anyone, at least until Franklin D. Roosevelt.

Three final thoughts on the Lincoln assassination must be illuminated. There were those who claimed that the real John Wilkes Booth actually escaped, and that the person killed and buried was not Booth, but rather someone else. Supposedly, Booth escaped to Texas, and eventually Oklahoma, and lived out his life until his death in 1903 by suicide. Conspiracy theories led to books claiming that the government had concealed Booth's escape, and one theory was that he had gone to Japan and eventually returned to America and hid successfully without being apprehended. As always, there are those who will believe such theories, but there has never been any solid evidence that Booth escaped and went into obscurity for the rest of his life. His own family members identified his body at the funeral home before his burial at a cemetery.

A second point of interest is the oddity that Lincoln's one son, who had a long life, Robert Todd Lincoln, was within proximity at three presidential assassinations. On the night of the assassination, Robert Todd Lincoln had turned down an invitation to accompany his parents to the Ford's Theatre play, but was in the nation's capital that evening, not far away. Then, Lincoln's son was named secretary of war by James Garfield in 1881 and was at the train station when Garfield was shot by Charles J. Guiteau. Also, Lincoln's son was invited to the Pan American Exposition in Buffalo, New York, by President William McKinley in 1901, and was there, although not close to the site where McKinley was shot by Leon Czolgosz.

Finally, Lincoln's son was saved from a potential train accident during the Civil War at a Jersey City, New Jersey, train station when actor Edwin Booth, the older brother of John Wilkes Booth, grabbed him and prevented a potential danger to his life. Lincoln recognized Booth and thanked him, but only later did Booth realize that this was the president's son. It is important to recall that Edwin Booth, unlike his younger brother, was a Union supporter and admired Lincoln's father.

The odd coincidences of the Lincoln assassination story continue to fascinate many students of history.

NOTE

The assassination of Abraham Lincoln has been the most studied assassination in American history, only rivaled by that of John F. Kennedy.

The pages of newspapers and periodicals overflowed with the coverage of the event and its aftermath, and the *New York Times*, *Harper's Weekly*, and *Frank Leslie's Illustrated Newspaper* are particularly valuable as primary sources. Additionally, documentaries, including that of PBS, *The Assassination of Abraham Lincoln* (2009), and the History Channel's *The Hunt for John Wilkes Booth* (2008) and *The Lincoln Assassination* (2004), offer well done portrayals of the events.

The official autopsy report on Abraham Lincoln is available from the following website: http://www.medicalmuseum.mil/index.cfm?p= exhibits.lincoln.page_03". The question of whether Lincoln had inadequate security, causing his death, is explored at www.gettysburgbattlefieldtours.com/abraham-lincoln-did-lack-of-security-lead-to-his-death. Selected images from the Collections of the Library of Congress on the Lincoln assassination are found at: http:// www.loc.gov/rr/print/list/599_linc.html. The belief that the Confederate government and its agents were implicated in trying to assassinate Lincoln is covered in: http://www.jerroddmadonna.com/orange index3.html.

Finally, the Abraham Lincoln Papers in the Manuscript Division, Library of Congress, Washington, D.C., and the Abraham Lincoln Presidential Library and Museum in Springfield, Illinois, have primary sources and documents that enrich one's study on the plots against Abraham Lincoln.

3

JAMES A. GARFIELD AT THE D.C. RAILROAD STATION

The assassination of President James A. Garfield (1831–1881), our twentieth president, who served only two hundred days in office after being shot after 121 days as our chief executive, is a truly tragic one.[1] Garfield was the youngest president to have died. He was also the only president to have gone directly from service in the U.S. House of Representatives to the White House. He had the second shortest term of any president, with only William Henry Harrison dying of natural causes in his term in 1841, after only one month, thirty-one days in office.

Garfield served nine terms in the House of Representatives from Cleveland, Ohio, and was a very significant member of the lower chamber, being chairman of the Military Affairs Committee and the Appropriations Committee, as well as a member of the Ways and Means Committee. His military service as a major general in the Union Army during the Civil War, and engagement in three major battles of the conflict (Middle Creek, Shiloh, and Chickamauga), preceded his eighteen years of Congressional service.

His humble origins belied these major accomplishments. He grew up on an Ohio farm, raised by a widowed mother after his father died when he was eighteen months old, and worked his way through Williams College, a prestigious liberal arts college in Massachusetts. He developed an oratorical ability at a young age and became a skilled debater while deeply immersing himself in the study of Greek and Latin.

After graduation from Williams College, he became involved in political causes, becoming a Republican with opposition to slavery and its expansion. Switching from teaching to law, he was recruited by local Republicans to run for the Ohio state legislature and served from 1859 to 1861. After serving heroically in the Union Army and being promoted, he took over the Ohio Congressional seat he was elected to in 1862. He quickly became distinguished for his ability to draw attention when he spoke on the House floor.

Garfield became controversial as a Radical Republican, often critical of President Lincoln's strategy and policies. He advocated a military draft and aggressive pursuit of the Confederate enemy, as later utilized by Union Generals Ulysses S. Grant, Philip Sheridan, and William Tecumseh Sherman in the latter years of the conflict. He was also a major critic of General George McClellan's perceived inferior strategies in fighting the Confederacy.

Garfield became more identified with Radical Republicans, including Thaddeus Stevens, and was lukewarm in his support of Lincoln's reelection in 1864. He supported the Wade-Davis Bill, which Lincoln pocket vetoed in the summer of 1864, calling for a harsh Reconstruction plan for the Confederate South, including slavery's end, confiscation of Southern plantations, and prosecution of Southern leaders of the rebellion against the Union.

As Garfield's prominence grew, he was accused by critics of inappropriate involvement in political scandals during the Grant administration. Scandals became a norm in this time, in what was now becoming the Gilded Age in America. Garfield was also on the Electoral Commission which gave the highly contested presidential election of 1876 to Republican nominee Rutherford B. Hayes in March 1877, despite Hayes being about 250,000 popular votes behind his Democratic opponent Samuel Tilden.

At the 1880 Republican convention, Garfield, chosen to take over an Ohio Senate seat after eighteen memorable years in the House of Representatives, suddenly became the compromise choice of the party, a so-called dark horse nominee for the presidency. He was backed by one corrupt faction known as the Half Breeds, led by Congressman James G. Blaine. He chose as his running mate a former New York customs collector, Chester Alan Arthur, backed by the alternative corrupt faction, the Stalwarts.

In the closest election in history, voters elected Garfield by a slim margin of less than ten thousand votes over his opponent, Civil War General Winfield Scott Hancock, with the electoral vote being 214 to 155. After the election, he was still, technically, a sitting House member, a senator-elect, and a president-elect all at the same time, the only such case in American history.

Garfield was also unique in the fact that he was the first left-handed president. He was a preacher in the Disciples of Christ Church. Garfield also was the only president to campaign in a foreign language, German, which he often used on the campaign trail. He was ambidextrous, able to write an answer to a question in Greek with one hand and Latin in the other hand at the same time, and he had such mathematical skill that he came up with a proof of the Pythagorean Theorem. It is clear that he was a true intellectual, with a brilliant mind and great oratorical ability.

Inaugurated as president on March 4, 1881, Garfield stood out in his short term for advocating civil rights for African Americans in the South; for the promotion of civil service reform, as he believed in the need for competence in government positions; and advocacy of a federal commitment to universal education for all Americans. Therefore, he can be regarded as a creative reformer, who might have been an exceptional president, had he lived, possibly the best between Lincoln and Theodore Roosevelt.

His two leading appointments to the cabinet were Half Breed leader James G. Blaine, as secretary of state, and Abraham Lincoln's son, Robert Todd Lincoln, as secretary of war. Blaine would end up as the Republican nominee for president in the next presidential election in 1884, losing in a close race to Democratic nominee Grover Cleveland. Blaine was present when Garfield was shot on July 2, 1881, grabbing him as he fell from the bullets fired by assassin Charles J. Guiteau. In another oddity, Robert Todd Lincoln was also present at the assassination site.

During the last six weeks before Garfield was shot, he dealt with the severe illness of his wife, Lucretia, who was thought to be suffering from spinal meningitis. She was in a serious condition for weeks, and the Garfields escaped in June 1881 from Washington, D.C., and spent time at a beach resort in New Jersey so that his wife could rest and recuperate from her illness.

During these last weeks before the assassination attempt, Garfield was pursued by an angry, mentally ill office seeker, who was upset at not being offered a government position that he felt was his right to have. There is evidence that Charles Guiteau stalked Garfield in Washington, D.C., at Lafayette Square Park and at the Disciples of Christ Church in Washington, where Garfield often attended services. When Garfield was reported traveling with his wife to the New Jersey seashore resort of Elberon on June 18, Guiteau planned to assault him with a .44 revolver, but changed his mind when he saw Mrs. Garfield still recovering from her bout with illness.

The tragic assassination event occurred at the Baltimore and Potomac Railroad Station in Washington, D.C., on July 2, 1881. Journalists reported that President Garfield was leaving for a summer vacation in New Jersey, where his wife was still recovering from her illness, with the plan to stop off first to make a speech at his alma mater, Williams College. Garfield arrived at the station at about 9:30 a.m., accompanied by his two sons, and Secretary of State Blaine and Robert Todd Lincoln about to greet him.

Lying in wait, with knowledge that Garfield would be at the station at a specific time published in the newspapers, was the man who would take the life of the president. Guiteau had grown up in the Midwest and seemed unstable to many. Unable to gain admission to New York University, he subsequently chose to join a utopian religious sect in Oneida, New York, called the Oneida Community. He remained a member of this sect for five years. But he came and left the community numerous times and was seen as irresponsible and insane by the leader of the Oneida Community, John Humphrey Noyes.

After leaving the sect, Guiteau then tried legal work, but promoted his credentials based on fraudulent recommendations from many prominent people, and then became an itinerant preacher. He wandered from one community to another, rambling on about how he had been given a special role in life by the holy deity.

His next venture was in politics, writing a speech which he claimed later had helped Garfield to win the presidency. It was clear to anyone who observed him that he was delusional and seriously mentally ill. But as we saw with the case of President Jackson's assailant, Richard Lawrence, mental illness had yet to be fully understood. Guiteau came to believe that Garfield owed him an ambassadorship and made clear to Garfield his desire to serve in Vienna or Paris. Guiteau made personal appeals to Garfield at the White House, walking in on him in his office, which had no security detail, but instead two police officers assigned to keep people off the lawns. Guiteau also made appeals to cabinet members, including Blaine, who finally told him to stop coming to his offices, and that of President Garfield.

Guiteau, in his sick, deranged mind decided he must kill Garfield and make Vice President Arthur president, which would make the new president owe his elevation to the deed of Guiteau, and therefore, he would reward him with the ambassadorial position he desired. So he went out and purchased the .442 caliber Webley British Bulldog revolver with an ivory handle, which Guiteau envisioned would become a museum exhibit in the future.

Guiteau fired twice from behind Garfield as the president walked through the rail station, with the second shot hitting the first lumbar vertebra and just missing the spinal cord. The first shot was a superficial wound in Garfield's arm. Guiteau was immediately apprehended and proclaimed while being taken away that now Arthur was president. Several doctors rushed to the train station, arriving on horseback, and immediately offered aid, but failed to wash and sanitize their hands from the contact they had with their horses.

The second bullet entered the right posterior thorax, fractured the eleventh rib, and then traveled left and anteriorly to the first lumbar vertebra. It stopped about two and a half inches from the spine, just below the pancreas. This wound became infected, and the bullet could not be located and removed, as X-rays had not yet been invented, and there was limited understanding of the role of germs and infection.

The sad truth was that Garfield could have survived the bullet wound had he lived in more modern times, but instead died after a long, painful seventy-nine days, often going in and out of a coma, while the medical team tried to restore him to good health. Some experts have said infection and blood poisoning were inevitable due to tissue and organ damage and spinal bone damage as well, and that only if the bullet could have been removed, could he have survived.

This was the longest period of incapacity of any president, except for the later eighteen-month incapacity of Woodrow Wilson from September 1919 to March 1921 from a stroke, although Wilson did manage to recover somewhat as the months passed. Garfield suffered from extreme pain and fevers and had pus-filled abscesses emerge all over his body as the weeks went by. He lost one-third of his body weight and was unable to eat and digest food. Physicians made attempts to find the bullet by using a metal detector created by Alexander Graham Bell, the inventor of the telephone, but the detector failed to work due to Garfield lying on a metal bed.

By the time he died, Garfield had gone from having a three-inch wound to a twenty-inch-long contaminated gash, stretching from his ribs to his groin, and oozing more pus each day, as the president suffered in tremendous pain. Doctors performed surgery without anesthesia, and the doctors basically killed their patient, for whom death was a relief. The immediate cause of death was heart failure, secondary to the internal bleeding from the bullet wound and massive sepsis (blood poisoning from the infected wound), but he also suffered from pneumonia from being in bed for seventy-nine days with poor, incompetent medical treatment, and a ruptured splenic artery aneurysm.

Garfield died on September 19, 1881, exactly two months before his fiftieth birthday, the youngest president at death until John F. Kennedy was killed at forty-six years old and 177 days in 1963. His place of death was Elberon, New Jersey, where he was taken to escape the heat of the nation's capital, and where his wife had recuperated from her illness earlier in the spring and summer. Ironically, despite her serious illness that year, Mrs. Garfield survived her husband by thirty-six plus years, dying at the age of eighty-five in 1918, devoting her remaining years to commemorating the life and contributions of her beloved husband.

Garfield lay in state at the Capitol Building in Washington for two days, with seventy thousand people passing his casket, and the entire Cleveland population (150,000) honoring the president in his native city. In honor of the fallen president, citizens erected a monument in 1887, dedicated to his life's accomplishments, and placed it on the U.S. Capitol grounds. It is one of the most impressive statues in Washington, a nine-foot bronze statue mounted on a sixteen-foot Baroque-style base, and contains three male figures on the base, commemorating the life of Garfield as a scholar, soldier, and statesman.

His body was permanently interred in Lake View Cemetery in Cleveland in a mausoleum, with five panels on the monument portraying important moments of his tragically shortened life, with former President Rutherford B. Hayes, President Benjamin Harrison, and future President William McKinley in attendance at the ceremony.[2]

Guiteau, who had been immediately arrested at the train station, was indicted for murder after Garfield's death, after initially being charged with attempted murder. The trial began in mid-November, with the attorney general under Garfield and Arthur, Wayne MacVeigh, leading the case as the chief prosecutor, a highly unusual circumstance. Guiteau had defense attorneys, but insisted on controlling his own case, claiming insanity in a legal sense, but not in a medical sense, causing a rift with his attorneys.

This murder trial became a mockery, as Guiteau demonstrated bizarre behavior, including cursing and insulting everyone involved in the legal proceedings, including the judge. He smiled and waved at court attendees and the news media. He formulated poetry; wrote his autobiography while in court; and interrupted court proceedings regularly with inappropriate gestures and obscenities and assertions that he had no responsibility for Garfield's death, as it was medical incompetence which had led to the president's demise. He claimed that he had divine inspiration to do what he said he must do. In his crazed mind, he imagined himself going on a lecture tour after his acquittal, and imagined himself running for president in 1884. He yelled at the jury, calling them jackasses, when they convicted him in January 1882. The judges rejected his appeal, and he was hanged on June 30, 1882, two days short of a year since he fired the bullets that led to the death of President Garfield.

Even at his hanging, he acted in a disturbing fashion, smiling, waving at spectators and reporters, glorifying the attention, as he had always done throughout his tortured life. He actually performed dance motions on his way to the gallows and recited a poem he had composed, but was denied an orchestra to play music as he wished to sing his poem. In this manner, the death of Charles Guiteau ended the life of one of the most bizarre assassins in history.

The tragic assassination of Garfield, mostly untested but of great promise, denied him to the nation which had elected him to be their president. He had no chance to prove how much he might have contributed to the advancement of American history and government.[3]

Guiteau had claimed that "important men" in Europe had put him up to the assassination, and his statements that he had benefited Chester Arthur by making him president made some wonder if there was a conspiracy in Garfield's death, but both ideas were quickly dismissed and were never pursued. The concept that maybe, just maybe, there was a need to protect the president, now that two presidents had been assassinated in sixteen years, was not seriously considered, as it was felt it was more of an unusual event that would not be repeated. Only when William McKinley was assassinated twenty years later, would the decision finally be made to have the Secret Service, which had been created earlier to combat counterfeiting, start protection of the president in the future. Theodore Roosevelt became the first chief executive to have full-scale protection on a constant basis.

The only real change brought about by Garfield's death was the push by President Arthur for a civil service reform law. Arthur had benefited from the spoils system that had become rampant in the Gilded Age. But Arthur now advocated a civil service system be started for federal employees, although only about 10 percent of the federal workforce would be initially covered. The Pendleton Act of 1883 was, without any doubt, a major step forward to promote a professional government bureaucracy free of political patronage, which had poisoned the political atmosphere for many years, and led to widespread scandals, particularly during the administration of Ulysses S. Grant from 1869 to 1877.

The Mugwump faction of the Republican Party, led by the famous German immigrant Carl Schurz, hailed the step toward reform. Therefore, they refused to back former Secretary of State James G. Blaine, the Republican presidential nominee who succeeded Arthur in 1884, because of his long career as a "spoilsman," with a highly corrupt political reputation. Blaine was, arguably, the most corrupt nominee for president ever in American history, before and since. Instead, the Mugwumps ironically backed the election of the first and only Democrat since the Civil War, Grover Cleveland.

4

WILLIAM MCKINLEY AT THE BUFFALO PAN-AMERICAN EXPOSITION

President William McKinley (1843–1901) served as our twenty-fifth president from 1897 to 1901. He served one complete term and a little more than six months of his second term. He became the third American president to be assassinated in thirty-six and a half years, necessitating, finally, a decision of the U.S. government to provide permanent, systematic, and continuous protection of the president by the Secret Service.[1] The agency had been part of the U.S. Treasury Department; originally assigned to deal with counterfeit currency, it now would have the added, and ultimately more significant, responsibility of protecting America's chief executives.

McKinley had served as a member of Congress from near Cleveland from 1876 to 1890, notable for his promotion and defense of high protective tariffs, including the McKinley Tariff of 1890. He also advocated that the U.S. currency should remain on the gold standard. He had a courageous and dangerous involvement in the Union Army during the Civil War, including active engagement in the Battle of Antietam in Maryland. He came under heavy fire on many occasions at other battle sites and had his horse shot out from under him on one occasion. He demonstrated skill and bravery in his military endeavors, and reached the level of major before the war ended.

McKinley became closely associated with Rutherford B. Hayes, who became governor of Ohio, and was then elected to the White House in the disputed presidential election of 1876, the same year that McKinley was elected to Congress. He also became very close to Ohio "Political Boss" Mark Hanna, who became his advocate and the most powerful Republican adviser when McKinley became president. McKinley served on the House Ways and Means Committee after James Garfield's election to the presidency. He lost his seat for one two-year term in 1882, and then came back to the House of Representatives, and later sought election as Speaker of the House in 1889, but lost the post to Thomas B. Reed of Maine, who became famous as one of the most powerful Speakers of the House in U.S. history.

After serving for more than a decade in the House of Representatives, McKinley lost his reelection bid in 1890. He then was elected governor of Ohio, serving from 1892 to 1896. While the state constitution of Ohio did not give the governor any great power, Ohio was still seen as a key "swing" state, as three Ohioans had already been elected to the White House (Grant, Hayes, and Garfield), and so McKinley was seen as the Republican Party's leading candidate for president in 1896, after being third in convention delegates in 1892. He won the Republican nomination and faced, the Democratic nominee, former Nebraska Congressman William Jennings Bryan, the youngest major party presidential nominee in history at age thirty-six, in the general election.

This campaign was waged between urban, industrial America and rural and small town America. As the United States became the industrial leader of the world in 1894, urban interests wanted to maintain the gold standard for U.S. currency. Rural America wanted U.S. currency to be tied to the silver standard and to eliminate rampant corruption in U.S. cities.

Bryan traveled across much of the nation in his 1896 campaign, but could not win outside of the South and the Western states, except North Dakota, Oregon, and California, with the Northeast and Midwest being the major battlegrounds. McKinley remained at home in Canton, Ohio, accepting the nomination and deciding, with Hanna's help, on the vice chairman of the Republican National Committee, Garret Hobart of New Jersey, as his running mate for vice president, who tragically died in office in 1899.

McKinley is best remembered in office for America's expansion overseas and the start of the American empire. From April to August 1898, McKinley's war with Spain over Cuba led to the acquisition of Puerto Rico, Guam, and the Philippines, as well as the gaining of a sphere of influence over Cuba. The United States easily won the war, but then it had to deal with the Filipino Insurrection, which dragged on from 1899 to 1902, the rest of the McKinley administration and the early part of the Theodore Roosevelt administration.

In 1900, McKinley ran for his second term, and added Spanish-American War hero Theodore Roosevelt to his ticket, despite the strong doubts of his campaign manager, Mark Hanna, who considered Roosevelt "a cowboy," who should not be placed a heartbeat away from the presidency. Facing William Jennings Bryan for the second time, with the issue of American expansion and imperialism now the major issue, McKinley swept most of the nation, except the traditional Democratic South. He began his second term in office, which was tragically cut short by his assassination at the hands of anarchist Leon Czolgosz on September 6, 1901.

The new century had just begun and would be changed in dramatic ways by the death of McKinley. He decided to attend the Pan-American Exposition in Buffalo, New York, although his personal secretary, George Cortelyou, was worried about the president's personal safety, as a wave of anarchism and terrorism had become a growing threat worldwide as the new century dawned, similar in many ways to what happened at the beginning of the twenty-first century. Czolgosz would become Cortelyou's worst nightmare come true.

Leon Czolgosz, son of Polish Catholic immigrants, started working in factories and took the view that labor was under attack by corporations, and advocated labor violence in strikes, not uncommon at that time. Never having developed a normal social existence with others, he became a recluse and spent much time reading socialist and anarchistic literature, particularly that espoused by Emma Goldman and Alexander Berkman.

Czolgosz came to believe that American society had become one of growing inequality, with the wealthy exploiting the poor, and when he heard that the king of Italy had been assassinated in July 1900, the twenty-eight-year-old had found his purpose in life: to do something for the common man in America. He had met Emma Goldman months before the assassination and became an advocate of her anarchistic views, although she had not advocated violence as a method to promote her cause.

On September 5, 1901, McKinley gave a speech at the fairgrounds of the Pan-American Exposition before a crowd of about fifty thousand people. Czolgosz was close to the front of the crowd and had his .32

caliber Iver Johnson "Safety Automatic" revolver with him, which he had purchased only a few days earlier. Yet he decided not to make a move on the president at that time, instead choosing to wait until the next day, September 6. It was announced that McKinley would be at the Temple of Music and would arrive at this location after returning from Niagara Falls. He would be on a receiving line, where the general public would be welcome to pass by to shake hands with the president and other dignitaries. Czolgosz made up his mind to go after the president at that time.

At about 4:07 p.m., Czolgosz had reached the front of the crowd passing by the dignitaries and concealed his gun in a handkerchief. He shot McKinley as the president extended his hand and had it pushed away by the assassin. Shooting twice at point blank range at McKinley's abdomen, one bullet lodged in the jacket of the president, but the other seriously wounded him. A mob descended on Czolgosz, but McKinley urged them not to harm him. Authorities apprehended and arrested the assassin.

It seemed that McKinley's wound was not life threatening, but the bullet that had entered his abdomen was not found. The wound was then cleaned and closed up. X-rays were not routinely used, but a primitive machine was available. Consequently, the bullet remained in the president's body. Over the next eight days, infection and gangrene spread, poisoning his blood. While the general public had been led to believe that the president would recover, it was shocked when after a week, it was clear that the president was nearing death.

Vice President Roosevelt had gone hunting in the Adirondacks in upstate New York, believing that the president was continuing to recover, but was finally located, and returned to Buffalo hours after the president's death at 2:15 a.m. on September 14, 1901. The casket made its way to Washington, D.C., lying in state in the U.S. Capitol, where one hundred thousand people paid their respects. The body was then transported to Canton, Ohio.

The country was in deep mourning, and the stock market suffered a major decline. McKinley died as a much beloved president, and over time, the highest point in North America, known as Mount McKinley in central Alaska, was named after him. Additionally, many memorials and statues were built in his honor, including many in his home state of Ohio. While he established America's overseas colonies, his presidency was overshadowed by his successor, Theodore Roosevelt, who greatly expanded America's navy and its presence in the world and promoted progressive reforms.

Czolgosz refused to cooperate with his defense attorneys at his quickly arranged indictment and trial, and his court-appointed attorneys argued he was insane in the same fashion as Charles J. Guiteau after his assassination of Garfield twenty years earlier. But as in the Garfield case, the insanity plea was also rejected, although Czolgosz had tried to plead guilty, unlike Guiteau. Totally different than Guiteau, Czolgosz refused to speak at all in court, or testify in his own defense.

The trial lasted just two days, and the jury deliberated for less than an hour, but public opinion was heavily in favor of a quick trial and execution. Czolgosz expressed no emotion at the verdict and was executed by three jolts in the electric chair in Auburn prison on October 29, 1901, only forty-five days after the death of the president.

In modern times, it is thought that while Czolgosz was a political radical, motivated by his anarchistic beliefs, he was probably mentally ill most of his life, and could not have been held accountable and would not have been eligible for the death penalty. But attitudes about mental illness were different a century ago. Although presidential security increased after McKinley's assassination, not until 1906 did Congress pass legislation designating the Secret Service formally as in charge of the security and safety of the president of the United States.[2]

By this time, in 1901, the country had witnessed three presidential assassinations, all Republican presidents (Lincoln, Garfield, and McKinley), while one Democratic president had escaped such a fate (Jackson). Never again would a Republican president face such a horrible fate, although two would be wounded by assassins—Theodore Roosevelt in 1912 and Ronald Reagan in 1981—and two others would face threats that failed to victimize them directly, Richard Nixon in 1974 and Gerald Ford, twice within seventeen days in September 1975.

5

THEODORE ROOSEVELT AT THE MILWAUKEE GILPATRICK HOTEL

Theodore Roosevelt (1858–1919), the twenty-sixth president of the United States (1901–1909), became the first former president to face an assassination attempt out of office, about three and a half years after leaving the White House. The law did not require Secret Service protection at that time for former presidents, as it has since the assassination of John F. Kennedy in 1963. He had also faced a threat while in office in 1903.

Roosevelt was not the typical retired president and never was traditional in any fashion. He was running again for president, as the nominee of the Progressive (Bull Moose) Party in the presidential election of 1912,[1] competing against his own successor, President William Howard Taft, along with Democratic nominee and future president Woodrow Wilson, in what many have described as the most dynamic, exciting race in American history.

Never before and never since had a former president, the incumbent president, and a future president competed against each other in a race whereby all three were running for the role of chief executive. This election was seen then and since as the true peak of the Progressive movement. It had been initiated in a public sense by Roosevelt's own declaration that he was a "progressive," setting the standard for a change in attitude about the role of government. The activist role that Roosevelt established in the White House became a model for future presidents.

Were it not for the assassination of President William McKinley in 1901, Roosevelt likely would never have been president, and the concept of a Progressive era might never have happened, despite the commitment and activities of numerous other reformers in all walks of public life to bring about political, economic, and social reforms. Roosevelt brought about a new beginning in the role of the presidency in national life, and revived the presidency from the doldrums it had been in since the assassination of Lincoln in 1865.

Roosevelt had changed the office of the presidency forever and had antagonized many conservatives with his initiatives in many areas of domestic policy, as well as changing America's role in global affairs. He had used the White House as a "bully pulpit," promoting himself as a leader instead of a follower of Congress. This activism forced newspapers around the country to send a White House correspondent to follow the antics of the president, who was always making news, while earlier presidents had rarely created a need for regular news coverage. He had commented on everything imaginable, even areas not part of government responsibility. He made the White House the center of attention as it had never been before, and it would never return to the earlier image of being a place that rarely required news attention.

Roosevelt took and assumed leadership on issues including the conservation of natural resources and preservation of the environment; an open-minded attitude toward labor unions and strikes; and willingness to pursue corporate monopolies in court, through lawsuits brought by the attorney general. He also asserted leadership on the need for government regulation of food and drugs (and the creation of the Food and Drug Administration), after being galvanized into action by the Upton Sinclair novel, *The Jungle*, in 1906.

In foreign policy, Roosevelt made America a world leader in many ways. He negotiated the peace treaty ending the Russo-Japanese War at Portsmouth, New Hampshire, winning the Nobel Peace Prize for his efforts. He took a stand against Kaiser Wilhelm II of Germany during the crisis over Morocco that could have led to war in Europe in 1906. He also manipulated the conditions which led to the building of the Panama Canal and asserted the Roosevelt Corollary in 1904. His belief was that the United States had the right to intervene in the Western Hemisphere to "maintain law and order," including interventions in Cuba and the Dominican Republic (leading to charges of American imperialism). Roosevelt also continued the U.S. intervention in the Filipino Insurrection, begun under President McKinley in 1899, until its conclusion with the end of the rebellion and American assertion of total authority in 1902. U.S. control of the Philippines continued through World War II and finally led to the granting of independence to the Philippines in 1946.

Roosevelt was an accomplished president who left office at the youngest age of any president (fifty), and regretted his decision not to run for a third term. He chose not to because he respected the long-established two-term tradition created by America's first president, George Washington. After Roosevelt left office, he went on an African safari and European tour, confident that his successor, William Howard Taft, would continue his basic policies, but soon discovered that Taft was not a replica of himself. Taft sided with conservatives in the Republican Party and alienated progressives with his policies on the issues of the higher protective tariff and the environmental controversy between close TR friend and head of the Forestry Service Gifford Pinchot and Taft's interior secretary Richard Ballinger and Taft's backing of the powers of Speaker of the House Joseph Cannon in the heated debate with progressive Republicans led by Congressman George Norris of Nebraska in 1910. Roosevelt returned from his travels overseas with the intention of challenging his own successor for another term in the White House. TR felt a personal vendetta against President Taft for his firing of Pinchot over the public lands controversy with Ballinger, more than any other factor in his decision to run again for president.

Roosevelt was determined to run, but played coy, and as a result, progressive Republican Senator Robert La Follette Sr. of Wisconsin, considered a more "pure" progressive, who had the title "Mr. Progressive" for his reform activities as governor of Wisconsin and more recently as the leader of Senate progressives, announced his candidacy in December 1911, but self destructed to a great extent by February 1912. When La Follette showed a temper and emotion at a press convention on Lincoln's birthday, his candidacy fizzled, and within twelve days, Roosevelt was announcing his candidacy against Taft. Since La Follette did not officially drop out despite his embarrassing performance before the press convention, it would seem that Roosevelt had every intention of running, no matter what La Follette did.

With only a few presidential primaries existing at that point, and with most states selecting delegates through party leadership decisions, Roosevelt entered the Republican Convention of 1912 at a great disadvantage, and the convention nominated Taft for another term. Since Roosevelt persisted in opposing Taft to the bitter end, this led to the formation of a serious third-party movement, the Bull Moose Progressive Party, which held a convention that nominated Roosevelt for president, with California progressive Republican Governor Hiram Johnson accepting Roosevelt's offer to be his vice presidential running mate. The battle lines were drawn, and we would witness the only time when three presidents (past, present, and future) competed against each other for the White House. Additionally, Socialist Party nominee Eugene Debs, running for the fourth time, would perform better than anyone would have expected, receiving over nine hundred thousand votes, nearly 6 percent of the total vote. This election would be seen as the "Triumph of Progressivism," as all four candidates were considered "left" of center, although Taft, with some progressive accomplishments, often overlooked in the heat of the campaign, was certainly the least progressive of the four candidates.

Roosevelt found much popular support among Americans during his presidency (including the greatest landslide victory up to that point of time in his reelection campaign of 1904) and during the years after. It is a clear-cut reality that a president with such charisma and controversy surrounding him would engender anger and resentment among some Americans. This would include opposition Democrats who saw him as someone hard to match in popular support, and conservative Republicans certainly uneasy with his growing progressive agenda, more so than when in the presidency. Mentally unstable individuals added to the threat that always exists for anyone who is a public figure and, most particularly, the occupant of the White House.

It turns out that Roosevelt faced two serious assassination threats, one during his presidency but not well known, and another while running for president in 1912.[2] The first threat came from a distance at his home in Oyster Bay, Long Island, New York, in 1903, while the second more serious threat came as he was about to deliver a campaign speech in Milwaukee, Wisconsin.[3] In that second assassination attempt, he was wounded, but heroically (or stupidly) continued his speech before going to the hospital for medical treatment. Much more is known about the latter incident, but some attention to the event occurring while Roosevelt was president is worthy of focus.

On September 1, 1903, after almost two years in the presidency, Roosevelt was home in Oyster Bay, Long Island, New York, at his estate known as Sagamore Hill, with his wife and children. The Secret Service protection of the president was already in effect. A man named Henry Weilbrenner drove up to Sagamore Hill that evening in a buggy and was questioned by a Secret Service agent patrolling the property. When asked why he was there, Weilbrenner claimed he had an appointment with the president, but he was sent away because the agent thought it odd that an appointment would be scheduled at such a late hour. But Weilbrenner returned, insistent on seeing the president if only briefly, and again was told that could not be arranged, to leave, and not to return again.

But at 11 p.m., when Weilbrenner returned for the third time, he was taken into custody by the agent and sent to a stable, with two stablemen given pistols to guard him, while the agent searched the buggy and discovered a loaded .38 caliber Colt revolver with a .44 frame in it. There was also concern about footprints found near the residence, drawing concern about accomplices. Five Secret Service men, staying a few miles away in Oyster Bay for security, arrived rapidly on horses to Sagamore Hill to protect the president and his family. No intruders or accomplices were discovered, however, during the ensuing detailed search of the premises.

Weilbrenner was arrested, arraigned, examined by doctors, and declared insane, and it was revealed that he had suffered from a nervous breakdown a year or two earlier. The twenty-eight-year-old man was from a middle-class family in Syosset, Long Island, only a few miles from Oyster Bay. His appearance in court had made him seem "crazy," according to the *New York Times* report, and his wildest moment occurred when he expressed his desire to marry the president's daughter, Alice, who was nineteen years old at the time and an obviously beautiful young woman. It was judged that Weilbrenner had the intention, however, to kill President Roosevelt, if he had the chance to do so. In the end, Weilbrenner was committed to the Kings Park Asylum for the rest of his life, and the incident was neglected by historians who studied TR's life and presidency.[4]

The more memorable threat to the president, leading to his suffering a bullet wound, was nine years later, as he sought the presidency as the Progressive Party nominee in 1912. This incident occurred in Milwaukee, Wisconsin, as he arrived on a campaign swing. He was in the process of getting ready to deliver a campaign speech, well covered by the local and national press, thanks to the campaign fireworks that had developed in this exciting four-person race with Roosevelt, Taft, Wilson, and Debs. The reality was that any time Roosevelt appeared in public and uttered any thoughts or ideas, it was a news event of major significance in the eyes of journalists and the general public alike.

On October 14, 1912, Roosevelt was at the Gilpatrick Hotel at a dinner provided by the owner of the hotel, a Roosevelt supporter. The former president was about to enter his car at 8 p.m. to go to the Milwaukee Auditorium to deliver a speech of about fifty pages to an audience estimated to be between nine thousand and twelve thousand people. He had the thick speech folded, along with a steel eyeglass case, in his shirt pocket, which ultimately saved him from a fatal shooting.

There, outside the hotel that evening, was thirty-six-year-old John Flamming Schrank, who had a vision that the ghost of President William McKinley had come to him and told him to avenge his death, blaming it on Roosevelt, the man benefitting from his demise. This vision appeared on the eleventh anniversary of McKinley's death on September 14, 1912, exactly a month before the assassination attempt on Roosevelt. Such an assertion in his own handwriting was found upon him after he was arrested.

Schrank had led a dysfunctional life, inheriting some properties from his aunt and uncle who raised him after his parents died when he was not yet a teenager. Eventually, he sold the properties, lived off the sales, and became a drifter, wandering around professing religion and writing poetry, and coming across to many people as odd and unusual, but never arrested on any charges. It seems clear that he was mentally ill, however, as shown by his delusions about McKinley's ghost. At times, he was employed as a saloon keeper, but seemed mentally disturbed to many who knew and worked with him. Many would later claim that Schrank was a paranoid schizophrenic, although knowledge of mental illness was still very limited in the early twentieth century.

Schrank followed politics and became a critic of the concept of a third term for Roosevelt in the presidency, believing that no one should seek a third term as the leader of the nation. He had followed Roosevelt for three weeks across eight states plotting to kill the former president, from Charleston, South Carolina, to Atlanta, Georgia; to Chattanooga, Tennessee; to Evansville and Indianapolis, Indiana; and finally to Chicago, before tracking the former president to Milwaukee. Schrank carried a Smith and Wesson .38 caliber pistol on him, and had no clothes other than those he was wearing and no money.

As Roosevelt entered his automobile and turned to wave to his supporters, Schrank lunged forward and fired at a distance of four to five feet into the former president's chest, but only after his hand was knocked by a spectator who noticed what was happening. An attempt to get off a second shot was blocked by an aide to the former president.

Schrank was immediately attacked and subdued by the crowd. Roosevelt asked that Schrank be brought before him and asked him why he did it, with no response, a chilling moment of a president speaking briefly to his assassin. Then Roosevelt's car left for the Milwaukee Auditorium, with Roosevelt not aware he had been hit until he arrived at his destination and noticed some blood on his shirt, vest, and coat. His aides urged him to go immediately to a hospital, but he refused, stating he wanted to give his folded fifty-page speech, which had actually saved his life, along with the eyeglass case being in the right position in his shirt pocket to deflect the bullet.

Three doctors examined him backstage before the speech and discovered a dime-size hole in his chest, below the right nipple, and a fist-size stain on his shirt. A clean handkerchief was placed on the bloody spot to hide it, as Roosevelt headed for the stage, and told the audience what had happened, saying: "It takes more than that to kill a Bull Moose," a line typical of him throughout his public life.

In an amazing event, which only Roosevelt could be imagined to have accomplished, the former president told his audience that he had been shot, but was alright and would deliver his speech. He continued for nearly eighty minutes, with Roosevelt displaying his usual vigor, energy, and charisma, although speaking in a lower voice as he neared the end of his fifty-page speech, a typical length for the verbose Roosevelt. He started to slow up as he reached the middle of his speech, but still continued until he had finished.

After the speech, which displayed to everyone his heroic nature, Roosevelt went to the hospital, where an X-ray revealed a bullet in a rib. The decision was made not to remove or probe for it, as Roosevelt was not experiencing any significant symptoms. The wound was cleaned and dressed with a bandage. He was seen as having escaped what could have been a very tragic situation. After two weeks recuperation, Roosevelt resumed his presidential campaign, with both Taft and Wilson suspending their campaigns, in respect for the tragic events, until he resumed it in the last week of October.[5]

Roosevelt went on to a second-place finish in the presidential election of 1912, gaining six states in the Electoral College, a total of eighty-eight electoral votes, and 27.5 percent of the total popular vote. He set records in all areas, including being the only third-party candidate to end up higher than third in the election results, surpassing Republican President Taft, the incumbent president, who ended up being the worst defeated president in U.S. history when running for a second term in office.

There has been speculation that *if* Roosevelt had not been shot and forced to recuperate for more than a week, losing valuable time on the campaign trail, that possibly he could have closed the gap with Wilson and become the first and only third-party candidate to win the presidency. The theory is that he might have taken away more votes from Taft and passed Wilson in electoral votes. But this theory ignores the fact that Taft only won two states in the Electoral College, while Wilson won forty states. It seems highly unlikely that Roosevelt could have surpassed Wilson in enough states in popular votes to win the required number of electoral votes, which was an overwhelming landslide for Wilson. As the popular vote victory ensures all of the electoral votes of a state, there was no realistic way for Roosevelt to have triumphed over Wilson. It is great food for thought, but more as speculation than reality.

Roosevelt went off on a dangerous mission exploring the Amazon River basin after losing the election. He called upon President Woodrow Wilson to go to war against Germany after the Lusitania Affair of 1915. He came to oppose Wilson bitterly for his "weak" war policies before and during World War I. He experienced the death of his youngest son in the last months of the "Great War." He died of poor health and a "broken heart" at age sixty in January 1919, just as he was planning another run for president in 1920, when he would have been nearing only sixty-two years of age. And the thought that possibly he would have been running against a Democratic ticket that included his niece's husband, Franklin D. Roosevelt, as vice president is clearly fascinating.

Schrank was committed to a mental institution in Wisconsin, as he was judged insane and incapable of being put on trial, and he lived there until his death in 1943, having no visitors and no mail correspondence all those thirty-one years. At the time he was taken to the mental institution in 1912, he was asked if he liked to hunt, and said in response: "Only Bull Moose."

6

FRANKLIN D. ROOSEVELT AT MIAMI BAYFRONT PARK

Theodore Roosevelt may have been the first former president to be victim of an assassination attempt, but his distant cousin, Franklin D. Roosevelt (1882–1945), who served as our thirty-second president from 1933 to 1945, was subjected to an assassination attempt after his great victory in 1932, as he was planning to deal with the crisis of the Great Depression.[1] He was still president-elect when he went to Miami, Florida, for a Democratic Party gathering and made appearances with the general public on February 15, 1933, just seventeen days before his inauguration at the most difficult time in American history (a 25 percent unemployment rate), other than when Abraham Lincoln had the four-month hiatus between election and inauguration in 1860–1861.

Not only did Franklin Roosevelt have to deal with this threat in February, but as president, he also had to contend with a plot to overthrow him in 1933–1934 that was encouraged by businessmen and other right-wing forces; luckily this attempt was suppressed. They wanted to force his resignation from the presidency. His critics used Fascist-type rhetoric as they called for his removal. Also, Father Charles Coughlin, the "Radio Priest" along with Gerald L. K. Smith, a right-wing Protestant preacher; Louisiana Senator Huey Long (later assassinated in September 1935); and Dr. Francis Townsend led many to believe there were no limits on the threats to the life of the thirty-second president of the United States.

Additionally, there was often concern that totalitarian dictators Adolf Hitler in Nazi Germany and Joseph Stalin in the Soviet Union were conspiring to murder the man who most stood in their way of conquest and aggression. Even the death of Roosevelt in Warm Springs, Georgia, on April 12, 1945, has been subjected to speculation as to whether he died of natural causes, or was murdered by arrangement of his many enemies, which have been delineated by conspiracy theorists.

Before examining the direct assassination attempt, and the other potential threats, an examination of the impact of Roosevelt on U.S. history and the presidency is warranted. Roosevelt transformed U.S. history and the American presidency more than his distant cousin Theodore Roosevelt had done. He took the progressive ideas of TR and Woodrow Wilson, under whom he had been assistant secretary of the U.S. Navy, and expanded federal power to new heights, using the model of Abraham Lincoln, who in the emergency of the Civil War had expanded federal power in ways not imagined earlier. In so doing, FDR not only saved the capitalist system, but also American democracy, at a time when there was great desperation and a sense of impending doom circulating through the American nation.

When Roosevelt took the oath of office on March 4, 1933, he initiated a series of economic reforms that he coined the New Deal, having the national government deal with the issues of banking, the stock market, big business, labor, agriculture, housing, the unemployed and needy, and numerous other areas of national life. He revolutionized the idea of government intervention and regulation, and created a series of programs designed to ensure that the poorest among us would have certain guarantees. These included an old age pension; aid to women, orphans, and the disabled; unemployment compensation when out of work due to economic conditions outside one's control; insuring of bank deposits; and promotion of the rights of workers. He also saw the need for federal oversight of the financial community; the need for corporate responsibility to the general public, as well as its stockholders; the need to change the tax system to provide adequate income for the national budgetary needs; and the abandonment of laissez-faire economics and the recognition of the guarantor state as part of a modern industrial society.

Roosevelt never claimed to have the solution to the Great Depression, but through his fireside chats on the radio and his optimistic personality, the American people had the belief that the economic situation was improving, and that they had a future of eventual prosperity rather than poverty. FDR helped to turn most Americans against the ideas of demagogues, including Coughlin, Smith, Long, and Townsend. Despite charges from conservatives that he had promoted Socialism and Communism, Roosevelt kept the ship of state steady down the left of center of American politics, but not seen as such by the Socialist Party.

Roosevelt not only had to deal with the greatest economic crisis America had ever faced, but also with the growing threat of Nazi Germany, Imperial Japan, and Fascist Italy, as well as the complex problem of having to contend with the leading totalitarian threat on the other side of the political spectrum, Communism, and the specter of Joseph Stalin in the Soviet Union. Trying to navigate the troubled waters of foreign policy did more to cause him sleepless nights, as his health declined during World War II. He arrived at the conclusion that he could not retire and must seek a third and then a fourth term in the presidency as term limits had not yet been ratified into the Constitution. The battle was not just with these foreign powers, but also dealing with such friendly national leaders as Winston Churchill of Great Britain, Charles De Gaulle of France, and Chiang Kai Shek of China, all with prominent egos, and the need to balance their national interests with what was best for America.

Roosevelt also had to deal with the internal and vehement opposition of the isolationist movement in America, including prominent members of the U.S. House of Representatives and U.S. Senate, as well as other major figures, including, most notably, Charles Lindbergh, the great aviator and national hero. Opposition in Congress to American engagement in international affairs had been rampant since the end of World War I, and reached its peak in the mid-1930s, as the world looked to be closer to war, which alarmed the isolationists. They believed that America could and must stay out of any foreign war, and that America was not threatened by war overseas. Isolationists maintained that America had two great oceans to separate us from Europe and Asia, and that even if Nazi Germany or Imperial Japan were to gain control of Europe or Asia, somehow we could be secure in a such a world with our geographical position and a strong navy to protect our shores. This viewpoint made life difficult for FDR as he tried to make America ready for a war he sensed was coming, as much as he hoped otherwise.

In this environment, which FDR had to deal with for twelve plus years, the threat of assassination or overthrow by opposition forces, domestic or foreign, became part of the reality of being president more than at any point in the previous seventy years. The first threat came sooner, rather than later, in the form of a direct assault attempted on the president-elect just seventeen days before the date of his first inauguration.

FDR was visiting Miami, Florida, on a well-deserved vacation before taking on the burdens and responsibilities of the presidency, in a time when another million people had lost their jobs since the election of Roosevelt over President Herbert Hoover. Democratic Party officials urged Roosevelt to make a speech to a crowd estimated at twenty-five thousand people at Bayfront Park, in an open-air touring car, with Miami Mayor Redmond Gautier seated to his left. The time was about 9:15 p.m., and the event was being broadcast on local radio station WQAM in Miami.

The president-elect, who had paralysis in his lower body after contracting polio in 1921, was propped on the top of the rear seat of the open green Buick convertible and spoke to the gathered crowd with a microphone, a short speech of 145 words. He did not realize how vulnerable a position he had put himself in, and neither did the Secret Service.

In the crowd near the open car was his would-be assassin, Giuseppe Zangara, a thirty-two-year-old Italian immigrant, who had migrated to America after World War I, became a naturalized citizen in 1929, and held jobs as a bricklayer, with uneven income. He had had an appendectomy in 1926, which led to physical ills and mental delusions. On February 15, Zangara, a small person at just five feet tall, possessed a .32 caliber pistol that he had purchased from a pawn shop. As FDR spoke, Zangara stood up on a wobbly folding metal chair about twenty-five feet away to get a clear view of his intended target, believed to be the president-elect, although that was never fully determined.

Zangara emptied his weapon, which was chambered for five bullets, although he stopped when a woman named Lillian Cross and a few others grabbed his arm, and the remaining shots were shot wildly, but with devastating results. Five people were shot, including Chicago Mayor Anton Cermak, who had been standing on the running board of the car next to Roosevelt. At the time, no one realized that Cermak had suffered a mortal wound, and that he would tragically die of peritonitis on March 6, two days after the Roosevelt inauguration ceremonies.

When Cermak was shot, he uttered to FDR the words "I'm glad it was me instead of you," words now inscribed on a plaque in Bayfront Park at the site of the assassination events. As the only well-known victim in history to have died as a result of the unfortunate events of an assassination attempt on a president, conspiracy theorists and scholars have theorized that Cermak was the target of Zangara, not FDR. Cermak had angered organized crime figures in Chicago, and Zangara was rumored to be an agent of the Mafia, based on his Italian heritage and his service in the Italian army in World War I.

Raymond Moley, one of the "Brain Trust" advisers in the early New Deal, interviewed Zangara in prison and came away convinced that indeed Zangara intended to kill FDR and that he was not part of a larger plot. Cermak and the other four victims were simply unfortunate bystanders, collateral damage, who became involved in the tragedy. Zangara claimed after his arrest that he intended to kill FDR because he thought the president-elect and all wealthy people and capitalists were to blame for his health problems, particularly his chronic stomach pains.

There are also those who speculate whether Zangara contemplated shooting President Herbert Hoover, who he also blamed for the depression and the terrible conditions so many Americans faced in the height of the Great Depression. There had been concern for Hoover's safety during his reelection campaign in 1932. Zangara clearly seemed to be a believer in anarchism and would therefore see any government leader as a threat who needed to be eliminated.

FDR's reaction to the whole tragedy added to his reputation as a person who would be calm in a crisis situation, as he had his car stopped twice to pick up victims of the shooting and told the crowd that he was personally alright. He traveled with Mayor Cermak to the Jackson Memorial Hospital in Miami, taking care of him on the way, and spent four hours with him at the hospital, demonstrating his concern for the mayor. He also visited the other victims who had been admitted to the hospital, and returned the next morning to visit the wounded, bringing flowers, cards, and baskets of fruit. He demonstrated self-confidence, coolness under pressure, and a sincere concern about those who had been wounded, while he avoided being injured. This was a great image for a nation in trouble, waiting for a new president to give them hope in the future, that things would be better than they were in early 1933.

Zangara, who spoke very poor English, did not deny what he had done and what he had been arrested for, and he was arraigned in the Dade County Courthouse on February 20. A quick trial took place, and by the end of that day, he was convicted of attempted murder of Cermak and three other victims and sentenced to eighty years of hard labor, the maximum penalty possible under Florida law. Zangara crazily asked the judge in the case to sentence him to one hundred years of hard labor instead.

After Mayor Cermak died on March 6, Zangara was brought back to court and arraigned for murder of the Chicago mayor and was sentenced to death by electrocution on March 10, after a very quick trial. Ten days went by, and on March 20, just thirty-three days after the tragic incident, and two weeks after Cermak's death, Zangara was strapped into the electric chair, prepared for electrocution, and was declared dead at 9:27 a.m. This was, without a doubt, the swiftest legal execution in twentieth-century American history.[2]

It turns out that while the Zangara assassination attempt on FDR was the only direct threat we are aware of against the thirty-second president, there is much evidence of a right-wing plot hatched against him, calling for his overthrow, which might have led to a personal threat on his life. This suspected plot was led by a group of wealthy businessmen who were said to conspire with retired Marine Corps Major General Smedley D. Butler months after FDR took the oath, as testified to by Butler in a 1934 hearing before the House Committee on Un-American Activities (known as the McCormack-Dickstein Committee). This "Business Plot" was discussed and debated not only in Congress, but also by major newspapers, including the *New York Times*, although considered as having no serious veracity.

The wealthy businessmen were said to be fearful of massive government spending to create jobs for the unemployed, regarding such a plan as "Socialism." Some considered FDR a Communist, out to destroy the gold standard and cheapen the money supply to subsidize the poor. The push for the National Industrial Recovery Act the same year also meant that labor costs would rise, which also alarmed these wealthy businessmen and corporate leaders.

The testimonies before the McCormack-Dickstein Committee in the late months of 1933 and early 1934 were alarming in their detail. Apparently, the plan was to have a march on Washington by a half million war veterans, who would stage a coup, claiming poor health of the commander-in-chief and being backed by wealthy businessmen. The plan, as revealed by Butler, would have made FDR a figurehead, with Butler assuming absolute power as "Secretary of General Affairs," but no names were listed, and the committee refused to reveal who might have been involved. However, accusations of Jewish financiers supposedly involved in the plot, along with members of the American Jewish Committee, were alleged by a Communist magazine, *New Masses*, but were not taken seriously and seem highly speculative both then and now, and part of the sad history of anti-Semitism so common in America at the time. The concept that Jews were involved in the possible formation of a fascist organization rings totally preposterous to any intelligent person then and now. But again, this was the mood of the times, with the difficult conditions prevalent during the Great Depression.

In retrospect, FDR scholar Arthur Schlesinger Jr., in his three-volume work on the Roosevelt era, concluded that the threat was greatly exaggerated. But recent studies have raised doubts that the conspiracy was nothing to be concerned about. It leaves the issue open as to whether there was a real conspiracy to push FDR aside, how the Democratic Congress would have reacted to it, negating the vote of the population, which had overwhelmingly elected him to replace Herbert Hoover.

As more details have emerged in recent years, it is clear that the American Liberty League, a group of wealthy businessmen who feared what FDR was doing during the New Deal, might have been involved in a plot, including the DuPont family and leaders of U.S. Steel, General Motors, Standard Oil, Chase National Bank, and Goodyear Tire and Rubber Company. Even more shocking is the accusation in a BBC documentary that banker Prescott Bush, father and grandfather of the forty-first and forty-third presidents, was involved in the plot. Also said to be involved was Alfred E. Smith, former governor of New York and 1928 Democratic presidential nominee, who had known FDR very well and collaborated with him in Democratic Party politics, and yet broke with the New Deal very quickly in 1933–1934. Also, John W. Davis, the 1924 Democratic presidential nominee, was said to be involved in the conspiracy.

All of these people were connected to the American Liberty League, which proceeded to label FDR a dangerous man and opposed every New Deal piece of legislation, including but not limited to Social Security. The reality is that there seems to have been a decision to cover up details of the supposed plot, and we will never know for sure whether such a plan was actually in process. It was certainly odd that the *New York Times* and *Time* magazine downplayed the story constantly and may have been part of a supposed cover-up, but again there is no way to prove conclusively that this potential coup existed.[3]

Verbal threats against FDR and his New Deal were also constant from demagogues who were seen as a potential barrier to FDR continuing in power and pursuing his reform programs, with this list including Coughlin, Smith, Long, and Townsend, along with Earl Browder, the head of the American Communist Party. Their vehemence in rallies, on radio, and in government against everything the New Deal represented was a constant challenge in most difficult times, but had little impact on the New Deal programs. These extremists represented ideas that were the totalitarian left and right, while FDR represented the mainstream of American reform ideas.

Beyond the domestic attacks, including a potential government takeover and the attack made against Roosevelt by demagogues, Roosevelt was under constant theoretical threats from overseas as World War II came along, with recognition that Nazi Germany, Imperial Japan, and Fascist Italy, America's World War II enemies, had agents in America who would have been active in trying to undermine and, possibly, eliminate him. And Soviet agents were also seen as a threat, including at the several summit meetings that FDR attended during World War II, as traveling to distant locations by ship was always a danger with the potential of being attacked on the high seas, and with spies always present. There were likely spies at the Yalta Summit Conference in February 1945, and Roosevelt's deteriorating health could have impacted his performance at his last wartime conference, something believed by many Roosevelt critics on the right.

Considering the stress that FDR lived under in his twelve years and thirty-nine days as president, it certainly makes sense to say that stress contributed to his failing health, including congestive heart failure, which caused his death on April 12, 1945. His paralysis was also a major contributor to his failing health, as his legs continued to atrophy as he lost weight, and his braces no longer fit, likely causing sores and pain.

But there are those who speculate that he might have been compromised in his health at the Yalta Conference in February 1945, either by Soviet involvement ordered by Joseph Stalin, or by British involvement ordered by Winston Churchill, who would have been alarmed at FDR's intentions to see the dismantling of the British Empire in Asia and Africa after World War II ended. But there is no way to prove any of this, and it comes down to whether one wants to believe in conspiracy theories, particularly when one could visually witness the rapid deterioration in appearance of FDR in his last year in office.

In conclusion, FDR faced many real and potential threats to his health and life as he presided over the most difficult years in U.S. history since the Civil War. Just as Lincoln's health had obviously declined before his assassination, so too was FDR's health showing similar signs from the stress he was dealing with on a daily basis.

7

HUEY P. LONG AT THE LOUISIANA STATE CAPITOL

The first presidential aspirant who never was elected president to face direct assault and lose his life was the controversial former governor and sitting senator from Louisiana, Huey Pierce Long Jr. (1893–1935), who was shot at the Louisiana State Capitol in Baton Rouge, on September 8, 1935. He survived two days after the attack, receiving what medical experts considered incompetent and inadequate medical treatment. Before he was shot, he had made it clear that he was going to announce his campaign for the presidency, but he succumbed on September 10.

Long represented what was seen by political experts as a possible major threat to the reelection campaign of President Franklin D. Roosevelt, who was under bitter attack from Long and other critics on what Long believed was the lack of success of FDR's New Deal programs. While Long had not yet formally announced his intentions to run for president, he was seen as a major challenge to the whole political establishment, with his ideas and programs seen as revolutionary and extreme by many Americans. At the same time, he had the support of millions of Americans who were victims of the Great Depression, and who found his ideas compelling.

Long came from a farm-owning family in a small town called Winn Parish in the north-central part of Louisiana. Homeschooled for a few years, and then showing promise in local schools, he became a rebel by protesting the need for a twelfth-grade graduation requirement, which led to him being expelled; therefore he never officially graduated from high school. Despite not graduating, his academic record made him eligible to attend Louisiana State University on a debating scholarship, but lack of funds for textbooks led to his spending five years instead as an auctioneer and traveling salesman. He tried seminary classes, but felt that preaching was not his chosen passion. He then attended two law schools briefly, the University of Oklahoma and Tulane University, and was allowed to take the bar exam before finishing either program.

As a lawyer, Long became known for taking on legal cases for small businessmen and average Louisianans, and was noted as a critic of the Standard Oil Company, which he denounced for interference in state politics. He ran for and became a member of the Louisiana Public Service Commission at the age of twenty-five in 1918, and later became its chairman in 1922, running as a critic of Standard Oil and powerful utility companies, campaigning against what he called monopolies working to increase rates on average citizens and businesses. Even at the young age of twenty-nine, he proved to be a masterful legal debater in a case against the Cumberland Telephone and Telegraph Company, which was argued before the Supreme Court under Chief Justice William Howard Taft in 1922. Taft came to regard Long as a great legal mind, very much impressed by the young attorney's performance before the Court.

Long first ran for governor in 1924, but failed to be elected. However, he used radio addresses and sound trucks. In earlier campaigns, he had used printed circulars and posters extensively and had made personal campaign stops at an exhaustive level, and he continued to do this in his first gubernatorial campaign, in which he came out against the influence of the state's Ku Klux Klan. He also started to use a white linen suit as his distinctive trademark image, which would become his norm in public appearances.

In 1928, Long won the governorship, organizing a coalition of Catholics in southern Louisiana and rural farmers and workers, including those poor whites who were able to overcome the state poll tax requirement. The election was won on class resentment and his plan to raise the literacy rate in his state by expanding public education and free textbooks, increasing public works projects in a state with very few paved roads and bridges, and working against the oil interests, wealthy businessmen, and plantation owners, and the New Orleans political establishment. His campaign slogan was "Every man a king, but no one wears a crown," a quote similar to that of William Jennings Bryan when he ran for president in

1896, when Bryan gave his mesmerizing "Cross of Gold" speech. Long called the wealthy "parasites" and stood out as a spokesman for the poor and underprivileged in one of the poorest, most backward states in America at the time.

Long became known as a heroic governor to Louisiana's rural poor. As governor from 1928 to 1932, he utilized political patronage and installed his supporters in many state positions and purged the state bureaucracy of opponents tied to the old system. He also promoted free school textbooks for children, adult literacy courses in the evenings, and a massive public works program, with such projects as schools, hospitals, roads, and bridges. He used personal appearances on the floor of the legislature to push for his programs and was accused of harassment and bullying tactics, which brought him national attention.

Long so enraged his powerful wealthy opponents that an attempt to impeach him led to a brawl in the state legislature over accusations of corruption, including bribery and misuse of state funds. The impeachment attempt ultimately failed, and led to Long firing opponents' relatives from state positions and active campaigns to unseat his legislative critics from their public offices in upcoming election contests.

Long was accused by his enemies of being dictatorial and ruthless in his tactics, and he engendered death threats, which now led him to employ armed bodyguards to protect him against alleged assassination attempts. He became front page news, not only in Louisiana, but also in national media. He subsequently ran for the Senate, won in 1930, but refused to take his seat until the beginning of 1932, so that he could remain as governor and push through his legislative agenda, a strategy never pursued before. But then Long was always unique in how he handled power and presented himself to the public. It was clear that the majority of people in Louisiana had no problem with his political agenda.

Long proceeded to accomplish tremendous change for Louisiana, while holding both the governorship and the Senate seat, which remained vacant. Much of the modern public works of the state were now under construction, and massive investment in schools and universities, particularly Louisiana State University, were initiated. A new state capitol, governor's mansion, and hospitals were built as a result of his efforts, although his tactics and strategies infuriated many in the powerful, wealthy state establishment groups. Long took on a new image, as the "Kingfish," who was fighting the elite and working for the poor of the state. Long had managed to reach this level of power while opposing the Ku Klux Klan's power.

Long became a "star" in the U.S. Senate immediately, with his radical reputation for appealing to the struggling masses suffering from the Great Depression. His populist appeal made him controversial, as he denounced President Herbert Hoover and called for an attack on the concentration of wealth, promoting a "Share Our Wealth" program. He spoke of the concept of "every man a king." Regarded as a member of the progressive bloc in the U.S. Senate, he gave fiery speeches that drew ever more attention to him. He endorsed Democratic presidential nominee Franklin D. Roosevelt as the only hope for the nation. FDR, however, kept his distance from Long, seeing him as a potential nemesis, terming him privately as a dangerous man and preventing Long from controlling patronage appointments in Louisiana. This prompted Long to attack FDR on most of his New Deal programs, maintaining that they were insufficient and catered to the elite. Long verbally assailed Roosevelt for what Long perceived as Roosevelt's unwillingness to radically redistribute the country's wealth.

The public dispute between FDR and Long grew, with Roosevelt believing that Long was using tactics similar to Adolf Hitler and Benito Mussolini. Besides taking control of patronage in Louisiana away from Long, FDR also had the Internal Revenue Service investigate Long's income tax returns in 1934. Long lost most of his allies in the Senate because of his populist rhetoric and aggressive manner. Long also took an isolationist stand in foreign policy, including denunciation of America's entrance into World War I and, even, the Spanish-American War, and in so doing, marginalized himself as a demagogue.

Long became a vocal critic of the Federal Reserve Bank and of powerful banking interests on Wall Street, including the large banking houses of JP Morgan and John D. Rockefeller. He called for a radical redistribution of wealth by limiting personal fortunes, annual incomes, and individual inheritances. He promoted his ideas of "Share Our Wealth" on nationwide radio broadcasts, stating that the redistribution of wealth would allow every American family a basic household grant of $5,000 and a minimum annual income of $2,000–$3,000. Additionally, he wanted to provide free college education and vocational training; old-age pensions; veterans benefits; public works projects; limiting the workweek to thirty hours; four weeks vacation for all employees; federal assistance for agriculture; and overall greater federal regulation of the economy.

Long was accused of being a Socialist, but Norman Thomas, the Socialist Party leader, debated Long and accused him of being a phony Socialist, and really a demagogue. With no support from the Senate for his ideas, Long formed a national political organization, the Share Our Wealth Society, which had a reported 7.5 million members across America, but with anti-Semitic demagogue Gerald L. K. Smith organizing the movement. This led to accusations that Long was an anti-Semite, seen by many not as a Socialist, but a Fascist in line with Hitler and Mussolini.

The pressure of what Long was promoting might have led to FDR's decision to change direction in mid-1935, advocating and initiating the "Second New Deal," which pushed the passage of such legislation as the Social Security Act, the Works Progress Administration, the Wealth Tax Act, and the National Labor Relations Act. However, many scholars have said that it was attacks from the American Liberty League and other right-wing critics that actually led to a change in direction of the New Deal.

Long continued to control Louisiana politics from his Senate perch, often visiting Baton Rouge. Constantly looking for publicity, he gained many loyalists, while making even more enemies, and was portrayed in news articles as a politician who had national ambitions, while stirring the pot both in Baton Rouge and Washington, D.C. He seemed larger than life and was able to upstage even President Roosevelt at times. A book was published right at the time of his death, forecasting his plans when he became president of the United States.

Long became engaged in financial scandals involving favored interests in the oil industry, and he gained a special force of plainclothes police officers answerable only to him. He was perceived as having abused his power and was constantly involved in controversy. He had gained twenty-five million radio listeners, was receiving sixty thousand letters a week, and started to explore his presidential ambitions early in 1935.

He began a national speaking tour and was interviewed on a regular basis in the early months of that year. Despite what seemed to be a plan to run in 1936, his biographers believe that he intended to defeat FDR in 1936 by splitting the Democratic Party vote with another third-party candidate, helping to elect the Republican nominee. Long hoped that conditions would get worse by 1940, and then he would win the Democratic nomination and the White House in that year.

Local tensions in Louisiana grew over the summer of 1935, as Long and his allies took more steps to gain complete dominance over state affairs. This led to special sessions of the legislature taking extreme action, adding to the danger of violence and confrontation, and the belief that a fascist dictatorship was being established by Long and his allies. In a speech in the Senate a month before his death, Long spoke of an assassination plot against him by his opponents in state government.

One of the actions Long was pursuing by early September 1935 was the removal of a longtime opponent, Judge Benjamin Henry Pavy. He introduced a bill in the legislature that focused on redistricting (gerrymandering), which would cause Pavy to lose his judgeship in 1936.

Pavy's son-in-law was Dr. Carl Austin Weiss, who was trying to meet Long at the state capitol in Baton Rouge on September 8, and had been brushed off several times by the bodyguards surrounding Long, when finally, at about 9:20 p.m., Weiss came close to Long and, according to witnesses, opened fire on Long with a handgun from about four feet away, even though Long was totally surrounded by bodyguards. Long was shot in the abdomen and would live two more days before dying on September 10. The police report mentions the hole in Long's coat was consistent with findings that the muzzle was making contact with the cloth.

The possibility of knowing Dr. Weiss's motive was lost due to the immediate overreaction of Long's bodyguards, who opened fire on Weiss and pumped him full of an estimated sixty-one bullets, certainly an extreme action for anyone protecting any public figure. One question that arises is whether Weiss had a background which would indicate a desire to kill Long. Certainly, he was upset that his father-in-law was being harmed by Long's control of the Louisiana state government.

Weiss was born in 1906 in Baton Rouge, educated in local schools, and then obtained his bachelor's degree at Louisiana State University. He gained his medical degree at Tulane University, and then he proceeded to do graduate work in medicine in Vienna, Austria, and had medical internships in Vienna and New York City at Bellevue Hospital. He entered private practice locally with his father at age twenty-six in 1932, and achieved the status of president of the Louisiana Medical Society the following year. His father, a prominent eye specialist, had previously treated Huey Long. Weiss married the daughter of a prominent local judge, Benjamin Henry Pavy, who was connected to an anti-Long faction in Louisiana politics, and who was forced out of his judgeship due to the redistricting arranged by the pro-Long group.

There has been speculation that Weiss did not shoot Long, but that instead Long's bodyguards killed him, as it is asserted that Weiss owned a Browning Model 1910-32, .32 caliber pistol, but that Long was shot by either a .38 or .45 caliber weapon, which only his bodyguards had at the scene of the crime. Long scholars have rejected this thesis, but this continues to be an area of dispute. It is claimed that Weiss's pistol was found near his body, although others have said it was planted there after his death. Supposedly, the pistol had five live rounds and one empty shell jammed in the ejector mechanism.

Witnesses claimed that Weiss was unarmed and simply struck Long with his hand, and that Long was accidentally shot by his own guards when they opened fire on Weiss. It is said that Weiss would not have attacked Long with such a small gun, knowing that Long's bodyguards were heavily armed, and that Long would be thought to be wearing a bulletproof vest, which it turns out he was not wearing. These rumors are based on Long's bruised lip when he was taken to emergency surgery after the shooting. But Long supporters said that he hit the marble wall at the site of the shooting in the state capitol, explaining his bruised lip.

Conspiracy theorists have claimed that Long was murdered as part of a plot by the Roosevelt administration to eliminate Long as a potential threat to FDR in 1936 or later. But that has been dismissed by Long scholars, who tend to see Long as reckless and irresponsible in his public behavior, while admiring his charisma.

Questions still remain, however, about Weiss, such as if he had a weapon, how did he manage to enter the capitol building without having the weapon confiscated? Also, Weiss had made repeated requests to speak to Long before the moment of the assassination, so why did he hold off even seconds before the shooting when Long's back was turned to him? The fact that Weiss had a gun could be traced simply to the concept of self-protection, for a doctor might carry drugs on his person, although many might wonder why when entering a government building.[1]

Long was taken to the hospital, but was given inadequate medical attention and died after two days of internal bleeding caused by damage to his kidney. It appears that the wound in the kidney was missed or not repaired. Was it missed purposely or by negligence? At any rate, it possibly could have been repaired. If he had been bleeding from the kidney, they should have found blood in his urine, but could they have ignored it? The other issue to question seems to be that the whole surgery and postoperative care was simply ignorance of good surgical methods and protocol because they did not know any better at that time period. Long was only forty-two years old at the time he passed away.

The absence of an autopsy has led to questions that cannot be answered. There seems to have been an anesthesiologist who was a political opponent of Long. The number of people, both in surgical scrubs and street clothes, in the operating suite was extremely high, and the scene was one of total chaos before, during, and after surgery. Medical records are missing, and eyewitnesses and those directly involved in the surgery were unwilling to give testimony about what seemed to be timid medical care. The question arises whether it was purposefully withheld, or simply the errors of the available physicians at the time of the tragic events.[2]

Long's funeral brought two hundred thousand people to Baton Rouge with the funeral service conducted by the Reverend Gerald L. K. Smith, the controversial preacher connected with Long and other extremists who preached anti-Semitism. Long was buried on the grounds of the state capitol, which had been built under Long's regime, and a statue at his grave site commemorates his achievements. A plaque within the building marks the site of the assassination in the hallway. Additionally, a bronze statue of Huey Long is found in Statuary Hall in the U.S. Capitol in Washington, D.C.

Weiss's funeral was attended by more people than any other assassin's funeral, according to contemporary reports. His son, who was a few months old when his father died, spent his life trying to rehabilitate his dad's reputation. It seems clear that Weiss confronted Long over family and political matters, and that he was not mentally ill, but the mystery surrounding Long's death remains a mystery even today, almost eighty years later. Weiss's body was removed from its burial site and examined in 1991, but with no clear-cut conclusions. His body was held by the government and never returned to its original site, and it is unclear where his body now lies. Also, no paper trail or evidence of any kind that Weiss indicated plans to shoot Long was ever found.

Huey Long has stirred scholarly interest by such authors as T. Harry Williams, Alan Brinkley, and Richard White, plus documentary treatment by Ken Burns. Fictional treatment by Robert Penn Warren, author of *All the King's Men*, the 1947 Pulitzer Prize–winning novel, led also to the winning of the Academy Award for Best Film in 1949, and was given a modern treatment in another film interpretation in 2006. Warren had been a professor at Louisiana State University from 1933 to 1942 and saw Long and his actions up close, although he denied that his fictional treatment was directly linked to Long's life and career.

Long remains a center of great interest and controversy, even though it is highly doubtful that he could ever have been elected president in either 1936 or 1940.

Long's brother Earl served as governor three times, and his son Russell served in the Senate and became very powerful due to his long tenure in the upper chamber from 1948 to 1987, serving as chairman of the Senate Finance Committee from 1966 to 1981. The Long influence would be part of Louisiana politics for a half century after his demise.

One final point that should be made is that Long, for all his faults and shortcomings, promoted his Share Our Wealth Program for all people living in poverty, both white and black, making him a revolutionary in that regard, and causing him to be clearly opposed by the Ku Klux Klan. But he took no action to work against racial segregation, and New Orleans remained regarded as the most segregated city in America into the 1960s.

8

HARRY S. TRUMAN AT BLAIR HOUSE

President Harry S. Truman (1884–1972), who served as the thirty-third president of the United States from April 12, 1945, to January 20, 1953, faced two assassination attempts, but took it all in stride.[1]

Truman presided over the most difficult times of any president up to 1945, other than George Washington, Abraham Lincoln, and Franklin D. Roosevelt. Truman was not well regarded during his term of office and was overlooked and minimized as a president in retirement, but his historical reputation improved dramatically within a few years of his death in 1972. In fact, *Time* magazine would declare that "Truman Mania" was in vogue by the end of the 1970s, and his historical reputation would soar, to the point that in a C-Span poll of scholars from 2009, he was ranked "Near Great," as number five on the list of all presidents.

During Truman's presidency, political division returned after the cooperative wartime years of the "Good War." As inflation emerged after the war, Truman, a fiery but likeable populist-type president, received criticism and blame. Political experts believed that he stood no chance of victory in the 1948 presidential election against New York Governor Thomas E. Dewey, his Republican opponent. His victory was the greatest upset victory in U.S. political history, and he would end up being a path-breaking president in so many ways.

Truman never considered running for president before he succeeded to the presidency. Coming from a modest background, he was satisfied that he had achieved a Senate seat only a little more than a decade after having declared bankruptcy in a small business venture. Upon becoming president, he wondered if he could fill the shoes of FDR when, suddenly, after only eighty-two days as vice president in 1945, he learned that the greatest president since Abraham Lincoln had died in Warm Springs, Georgia.

After Roosevelt's death, Truman faced many challenges, including what to do about the continuation of World War II in Asia, with the Japanese seemingly willing to sacrifice their lives, rather than surrender, as part of their national pride to defend their homeland. The war against Adolf Hitler and Nazi Germany ended just about a month after Truman took over the presidency, and the realization of the horrors of the Holocaust and the problems of postwar reconstruction of Europe would be enough to have overwhelmed any ordinary man. The realization that the Soviet Union under Joseph Stalin was breaking the Yalta Agreements, only signed two months before FDR's death, also presented a significant challenge to American security and the future of Europe, as Stalin was denying the independence and democracy of Eastern Europe.

What was needed was a leader with courage, guts, and decisiveness, which Truman proved to be in so many cases and situations as president, particularly in foreign policy, but also in domestic policy decisions. His leadership became a model for future presidents of both parties over the next half century and more. The realization that Truman faced these issues with so much equanimity was even more amazing when one realizes that Lincoln and FDR both had four months after their elections in 1860 and 1932 to plan strategy and tactics to deal with the great crises they faced. Truman had no such lead time, since he had not expected to take over the presidency at such a crucial moment, with the war in Europe not yet over; the war in Asia seemingly to continue for two more years in the minds of military leaders; and the growing Soviet menace replacing Nazism in much of Europe.

Truman had to react to events as they transpired, with no time to plan or strategize, as he was suddenly thrust into international war and power politics. He may have come into office with a sense of modesty, but he quickly attained a sense of confidence, whereby he would say in later years that he could make decisions which affected many thousands, if not millions, of American lives, and still sleep at night without any doubts or second-guessing on his part.

Truman would be much remembered for his decision to use the atomic bomb on Japan, despite having no personal scientific knowledge and receiving conflicting viewpoints on the whole concept of atomic energy;

and the ethics of using such a destructive weapon, presented to him by military leaders and even scientists involved in the Manhattan Project.

Truman would also be judged a man of conviction and principle for deciding to pursue the doctrine of containment against the Soviet Union, a policy aimed at preventing the expansion of communism. His decision to offer economic and military aid to Greece and Turkey, what came to be known as the Truman Doctrine of 1947, allowed both nations to fight off Communist insurgencies that could have led to their being added to the Soviet bloc of nations in Eastern Europe.

In addition to protecting war-torn Greece and Turkey, Truman also advocated sending billions of dollars to rebuild Western Europe and prevent communism from gaining ground in the area, what became known as the Marshall Plan of 1948. This was crucial to the revival of the region and ensured that their governments would be democratic, and supportive of and appreciative toward the United States for the long term.

Truman faced a very tense showdown with Stalin and the Soviet government over the Russian attempt to blockade West Berlin in 1948–1949. Truman demonstrated ultimate courage when he decided to utilize an airlift, along with the governments of Great Britain and France, to ensure the survival of West Berlin, despite it being surrounded by Communist East German territory. Such action, however, risked another major war in Europe, which Truman understood and accepted as a possibility. Truman's strong assertiveness ultimately led to Stalin ending the Berlin blockade after nearly a year of the confrontation. This crisis increased international tensions, a sign of the future reality that would mark the Cold War between the Soviets and the Western democracies. In the aftermath of this crisis, the North Atlantic Treaty Organization was formed in 1949, as a necessary defense alliance in the aftermath of the Berlin Crisis.

Yet Truman, along with the shock of mainland China becoming a Communist regime in 1949, also faced a crisis which would require U.S. troop intervention when Communist North Korea invaded the Republic of South Korea in June 1950. Truman did not hesitate to have U.S. and United Nations intervention in what became the undeclared Korean Conflict, which raged on without a satisfactory ending for three years. This war quickly became unpopular because its objective was to stop the spread of an ideology, instead of taking over a territory, such as Berlin or Tokyo. War weariness from the American public led to Truman's dwindling public opinion ratings, which had never been very high, but reached an all-time low in 1952, his last full year in the presidency.

But even in that crisis, Truman showed tremendous courage and guts when he chose to fire General Douglas MacArthur for public advocacy of expansion of the Korean Conflict into mainland Communist China, and for MacArthur's public disrespect of the commander in chief. This led to opposition Republicans suggesting and advocating the impeachment of the president for doing what any president has the authority to do—to have supreme command over the military and require obedience to the commander in chief.

Truman would be criticized by conservatives for failing to "win" the Korean Conflict, but over time, would be attacked by the New Left historians for having promoted the Cold War itself. Despite these bitter attacks, Truman is seen as having set a policy that, for better or for worse, every president, Democrat and Republican, liberal and conservative, would pursue for the next four decades. America's national security would be paramount in the minds of all of our chief executives, as part of the essential responsibilities of any American president.

Truman gained support from the Jewish community for having recognized the new nation of Israel within minutes of its creation by the United Nations in May 1948. What few knew was that a terrorist group supporting the establishment of the nation of Israel, the Stern Gang, apparently, based upon modern revelations, had tried to kill President Truman because he had been opposed to any kind of terrorism to accomplish the group's goals.

Additionally, Truman was hated for his promotion of civil rights, including the executive order that integrated Washington, D.C., in 1948, which had been segregated by another earlier executive order issued by President Woodrow Wilson in 1913. Truman was also determined to integrate the armed forces, an executive order which riled Southerners and the military bases in that section of the country, and spurred the third-party candidacy of Governor Strom Thurmond of South Carolina on the States' Rights (Dixiecrat) party line established for just the presidential election of 1948. Truman complicated that election by his actions, and Thurmond won four Southern states, which at that point was the second-best third-party race in American history, but still, Truman won an upset victory over Republican Thomas E. Dewey.

Truman's stand for continuation and expansion of Franklin D. Roosevelt's New Deal, and his attempts, mostly unsuccessful, to expand it under the slogan of the Fair Deal, would lead over time to a national commitment to education; the advocacy of the rights of workers and the virtues of labor unions; the belief in the need for a national healthcare plan; and his fight against the Red Scare of McCarthyism. Truman was much criticized by civil libertarians for his promotion of loyalty oaths for government workers, mostly in reaction to the fear of domestic communism. Senator Joseph McCarthy of Wisconsin was increasing his power and influence by exaggerating the threat of communism spreading in the United States, and that reality forced Truman's hand to take action on the perceived threat.

The personification of courage, Truman proved his coolness under threats that he was well aware of and would be the only president to face an attack in his own home at the time, Blair House, as the White House was under renovation. This was the second attempt against Truman's life, with the first attempt made by the Zionist Stern Gang.

An attempt by a Jewish terrorist group, the Zionist Stern Gang, in 1947 to target the president was revealed by his daughter, Margaret Truman, in her 1972 biography of her father. The president's daughter maintained that Truman received a letter bomb intended to kill him. This was substantiated by a mailroom employee who informed the president's daughter of the attempt, with the Secret Service defusing the bombs, and giving no public knowledge of these events before Margaret Truman's book, which might not be considered a reliable source in a court of law due to the family connection. Only the Secret Service would be able to legitimize the threat, but it has not been so reported, publicly.

In 1947, the struggle over the creation of the Jewish State of Israel was in full swing, with the British having plans to leave the Holy Land, and the issue of whether a Jewish homeland would be created in the Middle East, where Arabs dominated in numbers. Palestine had been a British Mandate and had led to much bloodshed against the British control by extremist Jewish terrorist groups, including the Stern Gang. They were known for assassinations, kidnappings, bombings, and even letter bombing attempts against those working for the British, who were handing over responsibility for what was known as Palestine to the United Nations.

President Truman had expressed strong opposition to the terrorist attacks of the Stern Gang, which future Israeli Prime Minister Yitzhak Shamir belonged to, as well as other Jewish terrorist groups, including Irgun, which future Israeli Prime Minister Menachem Begin was associated with. And Truman had, unfortunately, the usual anti-Semitic thoughts common to many Americans in the heartland of America, outside the big cities of the Atlantic and Pacific Coasts of the country, where most Jews lived.

In the summer of 1947, popular opinion was that Truman might not support a Jewish homeland in Palestine. In fact, the State Department under George C. Marshall was lobbying him to avoid recognition. But ultimately he endorsed the Jewish homeland within a few minutes of its declaration by the United Nations on May 14, 1948. As a world leader, one could not have expected Truman to endorse violence and terrorism against our World War II ally Great Britain, but despite his anger at Jewish terrorism, the president became the great champion of the new Jewish state when it was finally declared less than a year later. This began the long friendship and alliance between the United States and the State of Israel.

Due to sensitivity about America's relationship with Israel, and the influence of the Jewish community in American politics, there has been little discussion or revelation about this assassination attempt, with it being a different type of threat than the typical kind with firearms. But when one thinks of similar letter bombings that have occurred over the years and the unfortunate victims killed or seriously maimed by them, it is not something to be ignored. With good Secret Service protection, the Stern Gang never directly affected Truman with such attempts.[2]

A much more direct threat was that by two Puerto Rican nationalists who wished to see Puerto Rico liberated from American control, and to become a nation-state rather than the future Commonwealth, which would be drawn up in 1952. Puerto Rico had been seized by U.S. military forces during the Spanish-American War of 1898, and had been a territory of the United States for the next half century. A Puerto Rican nationalist group was actively attempting to bring about a homeland, not all that different from what was going on in the Middle East in Palestine, and the United States was seen as resisting such a nationalist movement. Puerto Rican nationalists saw their relationship with the United States as an example of colonialism.[3]

This led to uprisings starting in late October 1950, causing much violence at different locations on the island, and leading two Puerto Rican nationalists to devise a plan to assassinate both President Truman and his wife, Bess. This plot was conceived by Oscar Collazo and Griselio Torresola, both of whom realized they were likely on a suicide mission and might not survive such an assassination attempt, but were committed to taking action on their belief in an independent Puerto Rico.

Collazo grew up in Puerto Rico, and he was inspired by the independence movement on the island and angered by what he saw as the abuses of American imperialism. At age twenty-seven in 1941, he moved to New York City, where there was a large Puerto Rican population, and worked in a metal-polishing factory. He met and became friends with Torresola, who moved to New York City from Puerto Rico in 1948 at age twenty-three. Torresola had a more difficult work career, in a stationery and perfume store, lost his job, was married twice, and was living on a small welfare check at the time of the assassination plot. Torresola was much more skilled at using guns and taught the older Collazo how to load and handle a gun. The better trained gunman was much more involved in the gunplay that ensued against President Truman.

In a poorly reported event on October 30, 1950, known as the Jayuya Uprising, Torresola's brother and sister participated in a massive revolt in Puerto Rico, which led to the United States declaring martial law. Infantry troops and the National Guard and all kinds of assault tactics were utilized, including planes, artillery, mortar fire, and grenades, to quell the rebellion, which led to major destruction of the town. The U.S. government suppressed widespread knowledge of the event, but Torresola learned that his sister was wounded and his brother arrested.

This unfortunate tragedy provoked Torresola and his friend Collazo, both committed to the Puerto Rican Nationalist Party, to decide to launch an immediate attack, within days of the events, on President and Mrs. Truman at Blair House. The two men were fanatical in their cause of Puerto Rican independence, having vengeful anger, and ready to be martyrs to promote their cause.

In a very brazen move, the two men approached Blair House from the west and east sides in the early afternoon, at around 2 p.m., on November 1, 1950, possessing a total of sixty-nine rounds of ammunition. Compared to the White House, Blair House was very poorly secured. The two men did not even know for sure that President Truman and his wife were at home in the residence when they began their attack. Truman was scheduled to attend a ceremony at 2:50 p.m. at Arlington National Cemetery for the unveiling of a statue. Had the assassins known that, as advertised in a news story that morning, Truman would have been much more endangered, as he would have been out in public leaving his car and walking in the open areas of the cemetery.

Torresola became more directly engaged than Collazo, as he shot Secret Service Agent Leslie Coffelt in a guard booth outside Blair House a total of four times with a 9 mm German Luger, mortally wounding him. Torresola also shot Joseph Downs, a plainclothes White House police officer, in the hip, back, and neck. A third person, D.C. police officer Donald Birdzell, was also shot in the left knee by Torresola from the south side of Pennsylvania Avenue as the officer aimed his weapon at Collazo, who was having trouble loading his weapon. Collazo then shot Birdzell in the right knee. Secret Service Officer Vincent Mroz also engaged Collazo and shot him in the chest.

As Torresola reloaded his gun, the mortally wounded Coffelt struggled outside the guard booth and shot Torresola in the head, hitting him behind the ear with his .38 caliber service revolver, instantly killing him. In so doing, Coffelt prevented the possibility of Torresola entering the building through the basement door, which would have made it possible for Torresola to reach the president and possibly wound or kill him, and with Bess Truman also at home, it could have been a double tragedy, but for Coffelt's dying act of heroism. Coffelt died of his three bullet wounds several hours later, the only Secret Service officer ever killed in the line of duty in protecting the president. Collazo, less engaged in the brief assassination attempt and shot once in the chest, was arrested.

While this less than three-minute engagement took place, President Truman looked out the second-floor window and noticed what was going on, having heard the gunfire. The president had awakened from a nap, and the two assassins were approximately thirty-one feet from the window where the president was looking out at the events. The president was ordered by a shouting White House guard to get down, and he obeyed the warning. Despite the threat to his life, Truman kept his schedule for the rest of that day, seemingly fatalistic that his responsibilities continued, despite what could have been a tragedy.

The less-than-three-minute incident, involving approximately thirty shots, was later portrayed as the biggest gunfight in Secret Service history. Collazo, after an impassioned statement condemning American imperialism against Puerto Rico, was convicted in federal court on charges of murder, attempted assassination, and assault with intent to kill, and sentenced to death. However, President Truman commuted Collazo to a life sentence at Leavenworth Federal Prison in Kansas. President Jimmy Carter commuted the sentence in 1979, leading to Collazo returning to Puerto Rico. Cuban leader Fidel Castro held an honors and decorating ceremony for his actions against "U.S. Imperialism," shortly after his release and return to Puerto Rico.

The guns used by Torresola and Collazo are on display at the Truman Presidential Library and Museum in Independence, Missouri. At Blair House, a plaque was installed to commemorate Leslie Coffelt for the ultimate sacrifice. The forty-year-old Coffelt was buried in Arlington National Cemetery on November 4, 1950, and his headstone reads: "White House Policeman Who Gave His Life in Defense of the President of the United States during an Assassination Attempt at the Blair House, Washington, D.C."

Finally, in 1952, a plebiscite on the future of Puerto Rico was conducted, with over 80 percent voting for Commonwealth status, although in November 2012 elections, there was a move to change Puerto Rico's status in the future to the idea of becoming the fifty-first state, but no final resolution on that matter has been determined.

9

JOHN F. KENNEDY AT DEALEY PLAZA

Until the 1960s, it was always clear that the assassination of Abraham Lincoln in 1865 was the most significant example of a tragedy which affected the nation in a massive way, right as the Civil War ended.

As a college freshman in the 1960s, this author chose the topic of the Lincoln assassination as his term paper topic in his college English course, not knowing that he would eventually write a book on presidential assassinations over a half century later. More had been written and published on this assassination, and on Lincoln himself, the man and the presidency, than on anyone else in American history.

But a year after writing that term paper on the Lincoln assassination, an event took place which surpassed Lincoln's death in the minds of modern America, because of the personal experience of millions witnessing the assassination of President John F. Kennedy in Dallas on November 22, 1963, on television and radio. The news of the event shocked America and this author, who could not conceive of the assassination of an American president, since it had been sixty-two years since the assassination of William McKinley in 1901. The only political leader of renown who had been murdered since was Senator Huey P. Long of Louisiana in 1935.

The assassination of President Kennedy opened up a period over the following twelve years of assassinations and assassination attempts on presidents, presidential candidates, and other prominent public figures, including Malcolm X in 1965, Reverend Dr. Martin Luther King Jr. in 1968, and Senator Robert F. Kennedy in the same year (all assassinated);

Alabama Governor George Wallace, while seeking the presidency in 1972, President Richard Nixon in 1974, and President Gerald Ford in 1975, all surviving, but Wallace being paralyzed for life. After a brief respite, President Ronald Reagan would face the same danger and be seriously wounded in 1981, but, with modern medicine and surgery, miraculously survived and served in the presidency until 1989.

The issue of John F. Kennedy's assassination has spurred more research and writing than ever had been done on Lincoln, and between that and books on all aspects of his life and presidency, Kennedy would be the most written about president since Lincoln and George Washington. The fascination with how life ended for John F. Kennedy continues to grip the American people and has been particularly accelerating due to the fiftieth anniversary of the Kennedy assassination in 2013. The debate over what happened, who might have been involved in the dastardly deed, and the aftermath of the tragedy continue to spur advocacy of conspiracy theories, and there is no lack of material, more than a thousand works, all on different angles and issues dealing with the assassination. It has become an industry, and since there are so many doubts and questions that still remain about the tragedy, the writing and publishing and speculation on the Kennedy assassination will go on for generations, and, in reality, will never be fully resolved.

John F. Kennedy became our thirty-fifth president by election on November 8, 1960, and served for 1,036 days from January 20, 1961, to November 22, 1963, setting the record for our youngest elected president and the first and, so far, only Catholic president, surrounded by all Protestant presidents before and since. He came into office with a glamorous and third-youngest First Lady in history, Jacqueline Bouvier Kennedy, and had two very young children, Caroline, three years old, and John Jr., who was born a few weeks after the election.

Kennedy appeared a very charismatic leader, on the top of the list with past presidents Theodore Roosevelt and Franklin D. Roosevelt, and future presidents Ronald Reagan and Bill Clinton. He possessed great oratorical mastery, along with Lincoln, TR, Woodrow Wilson, FDR, Reagan, and Clinton. He was also one of a small list regarded as very handsome, along with Franklin Pierce, Warren G. Harding, FDR, Reagan, and Clinton.

Kennedy's impact on his times and since would only be matched historically by presidents including George Washington, Thomas Jefferson, Andrew Jackson, Lincoln, William McKinley, TR, Wilson, FDR, Harry S. Truman, Lyndon B. Johnson, and Reagan. But the fact of his tragic assassination would make him the fascination of the American people long after, only matched by Lincoln, TR, FDR, and Reagan.

When Kennedy came into office, the Cold War with the Soviet Union was at its peak. The new president had a rough first year in office in relation to foreign affairs. This included the Bay of Pigs fiasco involving the attempt to overthrow Cuban leader Fidel Castro, leading to a breach on the part of the president with the top leadership of the Central Intelligence Agency (CIA), the top U.S. spy agency. It also included the disastrous Vienna Summit with Soviet leader Nikita Khrushchev, where the Soviet premier talked down to the president, and also the beginning of the construction of the Berlin Wall by the Soviets to block access to West Berlin by Germans in East Berlin and all of Communist East Germany. These failures pushed Kennedy into a fateful decision to escalate American involvement in Vietnam, in an attempt to prove to the Soviets and the whole Communist world that the United States would do what had to be done to prevent the expansion of communism, based on the belief in the U.S. State Department, since President Harry Truman's time, in the doctrine of containment.

Kennedy faced a great crisis in world history when the Soviets established missile bases in Cuba in 1962 and were shipping and installing nuclear missiles which threatened the security of the United States and the whole free world. Showing great courage and statesmanship, the president enlisted his brother, Attorney General Robert F. Kennedy, in negotiating an agreement with the Soviet ambassador to arrange a deal with Soviet leader Nikita Khrushchev to remove the missiles, with a pledge to remove American missiles in Turkey, and pledging no overt action to overthrow Fidel Castro. Kennedy ignored military and cabinet leaders who had suggested an attack on and invasion of Cuba, and a possible nuclear attack on the Soviet Union, which could have led to a worldwide disaster, a plan known as Operation Northwoods.

This greatest moment of leadership in the Kennedy presidency skyrocketed his rating to the top ten of all presidents in a C-Span poll in 2009, where he was rated number six of all forty-two presidential officeholders up through 2008, despite his comparatively short term in office. The Cuban Missile Crisis would also help to lead to the momentous Nuclear Test Ban Treaty of 1963, signed only two months before Kennedy's untimely death, and brought about Khrushchev's growing respect for Kennedy after the missile crisis was resolved peacefully.

Kennedy also faced a crisis in civil rights during his presidency and would be forced to take action that it is clear he would rather have avoided. He arranged to send federal marshals to protect the Freedom Riders in 1961 and sent in the National Guard to protect James Meredith, the first African American student at the University of Mississippi in the fall of 1962. He also had the National Guard intervene to protect two African American students at the University of Alabama in June 1963 and called for the passage of a civil rights law as a result of the mistreatment of marchers in Birmingham and the bombing of an African American church in that city. Finally, he would, after earlier doubts, endorse and support the March on Washington, which took place on August 28, 1963, with the key moment of that event being the "I Have a Dream" speech of the Reverend Dr. Martin Luther King Jr. That summer, Kennedy promoted a civil rights bill that seemed impossible to pass into law.

As Kennedy neared that fateful November day in Texas, he had recorded a skeletal domestic record. No one doubted his commitment to reform and change, what he called the New Frontier. Yet he faced a hostile Congress of his own party, dominated by Southern conservatives who headed the Congressional committees in both houses, and who wanted no progress on civil rights or any other social or economic reforms. Therefore, his civil rights bill was going nowhere, as well as proposals to expand federal education proposals under the National Defense Education Act; the plan to provide medical care for the elderly, which would become known as Medicare; a proposed cabinet agency for urban affairs, later constituted as the Department of Housing and Urban Development; and unannounced plans to wage a war on poverty in America.

Kennedy envisioned success in his proposals for a competitive space program with the Soviet Union, with his ambitious plans to land a man on the moon before 1970. He also promoted the Peace Corps, originally advocated by Senator Hubert H. Humphrey of Minnesota in 1957. This agency was designed to improve the image of America overseas through the sending of young Americans to serve and work in the third-world nations in Latin America, Asia, and Africa, participating in housing, education, health care, and other services that would demonstrate America's concern with fighting poverty and ignorance. In the process, the image of the United States as only interested in these nations in a military sense, as part of the struggle for influence going on with the Soviet Union in the Cold War, would be overcome. Kennedy believed it was important to demonstrate America's interest in promoting democracy, peace, development, and freedom.

Part of Kennedy's desire to improve America's image also was contained in his policy toward our neighbors in Latin America, the Alliance for Progress, which was intended to prevent another Communist revolution in Latin America, like the one in Cuba under Fidel Castro. There was deep mourning in Latin America when Kennedy was assassinated.

Kennedy offered promise and hope for change, not only to Americans, but to people around the world. But it cannot be said that he overcame hatred and resentment, due to his Catholic faith, in a nation which had never had a Catholic president, and with widespread fear and discontent that a Roman Catholic occupied the White House. Kennedy also was seen by many Southerners as the "enemy," a liberal from New England who was out to promote integration and change their way of life. Right-wing conservatism was vehemently opposed to him and his agenda for reform and change. Propaganda was widespread that Kennedy was dangerous to the traditions of America, that he was too weak in his reaction to the Communist threat, that his youthfulness was a negative, and that he lacked adequate experience to be the leader of the Free World.

There was also lack of support from conservative and Southern elements of the Democratic Party in Congress and the state governments. There was skepticism and suspicion that the Kennedy family was more concerned about creating a dynasty for the future, and that his family represented the threat of royalty and would undermine traditions long held in American history. In retrospect, John F. Kennedy had made many political enemies over the years, including in no special order the following: the Soviet Union; Cuba; anti-Castro Cubans; elements of the CIA; elements of the Federal Bureau of Investigation, including Director J. Edgar Hoover; the Mafia and other elements of organized crime; Southern segregationists; Texas oilmen; the Ku Klux Klan; the John Birch Society; right-wing Christians; and numerous other individuals and groups, too numerous to mention. Whether this opposition, often rising to the level of hate and right-wing extremism of the 1960s, was enough to promote a conspiracy to assassinate our thirty-fifth president, a shocking event no one was willing, publicly, to imagine, is hard to pinpoint.

Before we examine the most infamous assassination in American history, a focus on an earlier threat against president-elect Kennedy serves as a reminder of the direct attack on president-elect Franklin D. Roosevelt in 1933 and the Baltimore Plot on Abraham Lincoln in 1861. There is also evidence that Kennedy could have been subjected to attack just weeks and days before his actual assassination in November 1963.

On December 11, 1960, while the president-elect was vacationing in Palm Beach, Florida, a seventy-three-year-old man, Richard Paul Pavlick, a former postal worker who had been stalking Kennedy, planned on crashing his car, laden with dynamite, into Kennedy's car. However, he changed his mind, according to his own testimony, when he saw Jacqueline Kennedy and three-year-old Caroline and realized that the future First Lady had just given birth two weeks earlier to John Jr. The plan was to blow himself up in the process of killing Kennedy.

Pavlick had expressed anti-Catholic statements in his home state of New Hampshire, had been critical of the Kennedy family's wealth, and had a prior history of pointing firearms at government officials on the local level in New Hampshire. Local authorities warned the Secret Service, and they became aware that Pavlick had investigated the Kennedy property at Hyannisport, Massachusetts, on the issue of its security. When Pavlick was finally arrested, authorities found ten sticks of dynamite in his 1950 Buick. For some unknown reason, it took three days for Pavlick to be arrested by the Secret Service, who found the dynamite-laden car, and if it had not been for a driving violation, Pavlick might have escaped without detection. Pavlick spent the next six years in federal prison and a mental institution and was then released at the age of 79.[1] This was the third time a president-elect faced a death threat, although not as direct as the FDR case in February 1933, but more direct than the Lincoln case in 1861.

Additionally, just twenty days before Kennedy was assassinated, the Secret Service foiled a plot to kill the president on November 2, 1963, in Chicago, on a motorcade from the airport to Soldier Field Stadium. The FBI received a tip about a four-man conspiracy involving rifles with telescopic sights, eerily similar to what eventually happened in Dallas, with these men having a map of the parade route. Two of the four men were arrested, with two others not apprehended, but another person, named Thomas Arthur Vallee, similar in many ways to Lee Harvey Oswald, was detained in the incident. Vallee, like Oswald, had been a Marine, had been employed along the parade route in Chicago as Oswald was in Dallas, and both possessed a large cache of rifles.

With insufficient evidence, the suspects were released, and the visit was canceled with just one hour to go before the event would have taken place. It was revealed later, however, that the two arrested suspects were Hispanic, possibly Cuban; that Vallee was a right-wing extremist, member of the anti-Semitic John Birch Society organization, and in possession of large amounts of firearms and ammunition at his home; and that Wallace had a record of mental issues.[2]

Records of these events were destroyed by the Secret Service in the mid-1990s without explanation, which lends support to conspiracy theorists who have not accepted the Warren Commission's conclusions. No information was provided to that commission in the 1960s as they investigated the Kennedy assassination. Additionally, there was evidence of plots against Kennedy in New Orleans and in Tampa, sites of other appearances by Kennedy as he toured the South in mid-November 1963, as he planned his run for a second term by visiting the South, an area won in 1960, and that he would need again to win a second term in the White House.

John F. Kennedy was on this Southern political tour, trying to shore up support for the 1964 election, which civil rights policies had undermined, particularly in Mississippi and Alabama in 1962 and 1963. He was also trying to heal the rift in Texas Democratic Party politics between the forces of Governor John Connally and those of Senator Ralph Yarborough. With his vice president, Lyndon B. Johnson, being from Texas, that made the healing of political differences even more important in preparation for the 1964 campaign against either New York Governor Nelson Rockefeller or Arizona Senator Barry Goldwater.

Kennedy had focused his Southern campaigning on the crucial states of Florida and Texas, well aware that much of the Deep South was probably lost to him as a result of the hate that had been engendered by his decision to take on promoting civil rights for African Americans. Rare for him, Kennedy brought his wife Jacqueline with him, along with the vice president, who was in a limousine only a few behind the Kennedys, and Governor John Connally and his wife in the Kennedy limousine, in the motorcade that was going through the streets of Dallas early in the afternoon of November 22, 1963. It was traditional for the president and vice president to be in separate locations at any campaign or public appearance outside of the security of government buildings, but yet both of the top leaders were in the same motorcade.

That morning, JFK had the premonition that if someone wanted to kill a president all that would be required was to have a telescopic rifle and shoot from a high floor of a building overlooking a motorcade with the president being in an open car passing by that tall building. Astonishingly, that is exactly what happened about six hours later, and the validity of this statement by JFK was confirmed by a number of the aides with him on the trip. It almost seems as if JFK was fatalistic and sensed his own death. This was similar to statements made in 1865 by Abraham Lincoln, who had dreamt of his body being in a casket in the East Room of the White House, and later in 1968 by the Reverend Dr. Martin Luther King Jr. on the evening before his assassination, stating that he might not make it to the "other side of the mountain," but his followers would reach the "Promised Land" of equality and justice without him.

On that fateful day, right-wing hate posters and newspaper ads from Republicans and Southern Democrats had denounced the president, called him a lawbreaker, condemned his Catholic religion, and called for his impeachment. JFK was well aware of the hatred toward him and was surprised by the pleasant reception he received on his visit. This was noted by everyone in the president's motorcade, including, specifically, Nellie Connally, the Texas governor's wife, who commented on the cheering crowds that Dallas was giving the president.

There had been rain on that morning in Dallas and had it remained that way, the president would have passed the crowds on the way to his speech with a closed limousine, but by the time the presidential party arrived at Love Field in Dallas (an ironic name), the rain had ended and the president ordered that the bubbletop be put down, so that the crowds could see and cheer the president on his motorcade. The change in the weather conditions, thus, doomed the president. Also, back problems necessitated medication to deal with the pain, so the president was wearing a back brace, which supported his back and lessened pain, but also prevented him from making a move to duck after the first bullet was fired from the sixth floor of the Texas School Book Depository by Lee Harvey Oswald.

The route of the motorcade was published in local newspapers several days before the event for all citizenry who wished to view the motorcade, but this gave Lee Harvey Oswald awareness of the situation and ability to plan to bring his firearm to the Texas School Book Depository that morning. The crowds were much larger than expected, estimated at about 150,000 to 200,000 people, and the motorcade was behind schedule as a result of the enthusiastic response by the masses excited to see the president pass by them. The motorcade was an estimated five minutes from their planned destination at the Dallas Trade Mart, where the president was scheduled to give a luncheon speech before civic and business leaders.

At approximately 12:29 p.m. local time, Governor Connally's wife, Nellie, turned around to Kennedy and his wife and said "Mr. President, you can't say Dallas doesn't love you," with Kennedy saying something such as "You sure can't," and at that moment shots rang out in Dealey Plaza as the motorcade passed the Texas School Book Depository. A gunman on the sixth floor was seen by bystanders with his telescopic rifle sticking out a window and shooting at the car, second in the motorcade. Kennedy was waving and smiling, and many at the time thought the sound was that of a firecracker, but soon it was recognized that it was gunshots, not firecrackers, and bystanders in the stunned crowd, which had thinned out, began to panic, run, or drop to the ground.

But one person, Abraham Zapruder, was filming at the time with his movie camera and continued to do so. This became the clearest video of this horrible incident, as it showed Kennedy's head seeming to explode as one shot hit him in the throat, and another bullet, the fatal one, shot off half of his head, with brain matter spraying all over the back seat of the limousine and onto Jacqueline Kennedy's dress. Mrs. Kennedy lunged backward trying to grab some of the skull and brain matter that flew onto the back of the limousine, along with blood, as Secret Service Agent Clint Hill lunged forward. Mrs. Kennedy declared: "They have killed my husband!" and "I have his brains in my hand!" She expressed her love for her husband, while trying to keep the pieces of his head together in desperation. The president's blood and fragments of his scalp, brain, and skull landed all over the limousine, the follow-up Secret Service car, and the driver of that car, along with motorcycle officers on both sides of the Kennedy limousine, riding alongside, but a little behind the Kennedy limousine.

At the same time, Lyndon Johnson, further back in another car in the motorcade, was knocked down and covered in his limousine by another agent, anxious to protect him from harm. When Kennedy was shot, one bullet also hit Governor Connally, who shouted "Oh, no, no, no. My God! They're going to kill us all!" Connally suffered a critical injury, but survived surgery and fully recovered.

As the limousine picked up speed on the way to Parkland Memorial Hospital, police officers and spectators ran up to a grassy knoll with a five-foot-high stockade fence atop the knoll, believing a sniper might have fired from there at the same time as Oswald did from the sixth floor of the Texas School Book Depository. But no sniper was found, and the people who witnessed what was going on could not sense any untoward activity in the area, although there were several people there, but not acting suspiciously, and no firearms were noted.

The president was rushed to the hospital, but within less than a half hour, he was declared dead. Lyndon Johnson was notified that he was now the president of the United States. The nation was informed of the death of the thirty-fifth president by Walter Cronkite of CBS News and other television newsmen, a development which totally shocked most Americans. It was later reported that some schoolchildren in Dallas and elsewhere in the South cheered upon the news of his death. But that reaction was rare, as most Americans found it impossible to conceive of the death of a glamorous, charismatic, extremely handsome, and youthful president in the prime of his life. Kennedy died at the young age of forty-six and remains the president who died at a younger age than any other American president.

The search for Kennedy's assassin led to the arrest of Lee Harvey Oswald, who fled his job at the Texas School Book Depository, went home, changed his clothes, then left home with a firearm and, when confronted by police officer J. D. Tippett, shot and killed him. Oswald then fled to a movie theater, where Dallas police apprehended him. His fellow employees reported he had left early without notice, and with other information, Dallas police realized that he was definitely a suspect in the Kennedy assassination.

Oswald was a discontented Marine, who became a dedicated Marxist and defected to the Soviet Union. He met and married a Russian woman and had two children with her. He then returned to the United States with her and settled in Dallas, Texas, and needing a job, obtained one at the Texas School Book Depository just days before the assassination.

Oswald had been born in New Orleans to a widowed mother, with his father dying before he was born. At age five, the family, including an older brother and an older half-brother, moved to Dallas. Growing up, Oswald was described as withdrawn and temperamental by school psychologists. When he was twelve, the family moved briefly to New York City, but soon returned to Dallas after Oswald struck his mother and threatened his half-brother's wife with a pocketknife. While in New York City, Oswald was evaluated by a psychiatrist at a juvenile reform institution after he went truant from a Bronx middle school. He was judged as troubled, said to be living in a fantasy world, having elements of schizophrenic behavior and positive-aggressive tendencies, with a desire for power and omnipotence to overcome his personal frustrations with his life.

Oswald's mother next moved back to New Orleans, and Oswald completed eighth and ninth grade, but dropped out of school one month into tenth grade. He worked for a short time as an office clerk and messenger in New Orleans, until his mother moved to Fort Worth, Texas, where Oswald reenrolled in school in the tenth grade. But then after a few weeks, Oswald quit school finally at age seventeen and enlisted in the U.S. Marines, therefore never receiving a high school diploma. His unstable life included twenty-two different locations and twelve different schools, not something that would promote stability. It seems apparent that Oswald joined the Marines to try to create some discipline in his life and escape an overbearing mother, who had not created any sense of stability in his life.

At the time he joined the Marines, Oswald was about 5 feet 7 inches in height and weighed about 135 pounds—and he was not seen as physically imposing. His experience in the Marines was not a happy one, but he was granted final authority for classified material and given the necessary security clearance to deal with aircraft surveillance and the use of radar. He was sent to Japan for his service in the Marines. His training in shooting firearms led to his designation as a sharpshooter in December 1956.

Oswald's rating was decreased to a marksman, however, in May 1959, when he was court martialed for possessing an unauthorized .22 handgun that he accidentally shot into his elbow; he blamed his demotion on a personal vendetta by a sergeant he had fought against. He was also demoted from private first class to private, and briefly put in the brig. Later, he was punished for a third incident, the firing of his rifle into the jungle in the Philippines while on nighttime sentry duty. Shortly after this incident, he received a hardship discharge from active service and was put on reserve, after claiming his mother needed care, which was not the case.

Oswald had demonstrated interest in Marxist theory and socialism and had studied Russian, although not showing proficiency in spoken and written Russian in a Marine exam on the language. After spending two days with his mother in New Orleans, he left by ship to France and then Great Britain, and then flew to Finland where he obtained a Soviet visa and arrived in Moscow. After a brief few days, and despite his stated desire to become a Soviet citizen, he was informed he had to leave. After a self-inflicted wound to his left wrist in his hotel room bathtub, he was detained and admitted to a Moscow hospital for a few days to undergo a psychiatric examination. He told Soviet officials again that he wanted to become a Soviet citizen and went to the U.S. Embassy in Moscow to renounce his U.S. citizenship, which led to news coverage in American newspapers.

When he stated to the embassy personnel his plans to give secret information to the Russians, it led to his hardship/honorable discharge from the Marines to be changed to "undesirable" discharge, but he seemed unfazed by that decision. The Russians decided to allow Oswald to stay, sending him to Minsk to work in an electronics factory and be taught Russian. The government provided him a fully subsidized and furnished studio apartment in a good building and extra pay beyond his factory income, but they remained suspicious of him and kept surveillance on him. Oswald was unhappy in Minsk, until he met his wife, Marina Prusakova, at a trade union dance, marrying less than six weeks later in April 1961. He then applied to the U.S. Embassy to request return of his passport, which had been held at the embassy, but never revoked. He also asked for documents to allow his wife and their newborn daughter to emigrate to the United States, and, upon arrival in the United States, settled in the Dallas/Fort Worth area, where his mother and brother lived.

Holding several jobs short term, Oswald was rude and confrontational with fellow employees. He found it difficult to support his wife and baby daughter, and their relationship started to deteriorate rapidly, as he professed to others his interest in Russian affairs and Communist theory and practice, even though he had left the Soviet Union by choice. Around the time he lost his job in early 1963, he purchased a 6.6 mm caliber Carcano rifle by mail order, using the alias "A. Hidell." He also bought a .38 Smith and Wesson Model 10 revolver by mail order.

Shortly after, Oswald tried to kill right-wing retired U.S. Major General Edwin Walker, who had denounced President Kennedy for intervening with the National Guard at the University of Mississippi in the fall of 1962. Walker was a member of the John Birch Society and had been removed from his military command in West Germany for distributing right-wing propaganda to his troops, and for his stated belief in racial segregation. On April 10, 1963, Oswald shot at Walker through one of his windows from less than 100 feet, as Walker sat at a desk in his home, with his only injuries being bullet fragments to his forearm, as the bullet struck the window frame. It was not until after the Kennedy assassination that any link to the Walker shooting was made.

Shortly after the Walker shooting, Oswald returned to New Orleans, started working again, but was soon fired, as he spent time at work reading rifle and hunting magazines. He formed a personal organization, of which he was the only member in the city, termed the Fair Play for Cuba Committee, a pro–Fidel Castro group, which was created seven months after the Cuban Missile Crisis; although there was a New York City group of that name already in operation. He used the name "A. Hidell," as he had used in purchasing his firearms through mail order months earlier in Texas. Oswald was the subject of the local media's attention when he engaged in a brawl, was arrested, and was interviewed by a local TV station in New Orleans, and engaged in a radio debate on his political activities in August 1963. He was recorded handing out leaflets and being a vehement advocate of his organization and its viewpoint.

Oswald's controversial political activities in New Orleans led to the investigation of the Kennedy assassination by New Orleans District Attorney Jim Garrison between 1967 and 1969, and the prosecution of Clay Shaw for conspiracy in the assassination, an action which led to a not-guilty verdict. The investigation made Garrison appear to be a demagogue seeking publicity, without having any real facts about the assassination scenario, but helping further to promote the conspiracy theory ideas that would continue to multiply.

A mysterious element was Oswald's decision to leave New Orleans, and instead of going right back to Dallas, where his wife and daughter had gone, he took a bus to Mexico City, applying for a transit visa at the Cuban Embassy there, claiming a desire to visit Cuba and return to the Soviet Union. Facing difficulties in this quest, including arguments and pleas at the Cuban Embassy and with KGB Russian agents there, and gaining some notice from the CIA, he finally gave up on his plans and returned to the United States, although professing a continued desire to return to the Soviet Union in correspondence with the Soviet Embassy in Washington, D.C. Some investigators wondered if someone other than Oswald, but using his name, actually spent time in Mexico, and it is still not clear a half century later whether Oswald really spent time in Mexico.

Returning to Dallas, Oswald got a job at the Texas School Book Depository in mid-October, and his second daughter was born a few days later, although he and his wife had separated months before. Apparently, the FBI interviewed Oswald's wife at the home she was staying at, infuriating Oswald, who gave a note to the Dallas FBI office, threatening to blow them up along with the Dallas Police Department if they did not stop "harassing" his wife. The note apparently was destroyed after the Kennedy assassination by order of someone in the agency, adding a note of suspicion to the whole scenario surrounding Oswald and the Kennedy assassination.

On the day of the assassination, Oswald hitched a ride to work with a fellow employee, carrying a bag he said had curtain rods, but was later determined to hold the rifle used by Oswald that day in the assassination. After firing three shots from the sixth-floor southeast corner window of the Texas School Book Depository, Oswald hid the rifle with boxes and calmly descended the stairs, as described by those who encountered him. He exited the building through the front entrance within about ninety seconds and before the entrance was sealed off, but was soon recognized as the only employee who was missing from the building when police arrived to check out the people in the depository.

Oswald was reported to have returned to the rooming house where he was staying within a half hour after the assassination. He quickly left after changing some of what he was wearing and apparently walked less than a mile when he was stopped by officer J. D. Tippett, who started to ask him questions from the window of his patrol car. Tippett exited the patrol car, walking toward Oswald, who then fired his .38 caliber revolver and shot

Tippitt at point-blank range a total of three times. After Tippett fell, Oswald shot him in the temple, which proved to be the fatal bullet. Witnesses testified later that Oswald had been the person who shot and killed officer Tippett, subsequently fleeing the scene.

Oswald escaped to a nearby theater and police were called, who confronted him in the theater, as he had not paid admission, and they disarmed him as he attempted to pull the trigger on the police officer who was at the scene. Punches were exchanged, but Oswald was successfully arrested and yelled that he was a victim of police brutality as he was taken to the Dallas Police Department building. By 7:10 p.m., Oswald was arraigned for the murder of Tippett, and early in the morning of November 23, after extensive questioning, and confirmation that he was the only employee who had left the Texas School Book Depository right after the Kennedy assassination, he was arraigned for the murder of President Kennedy as well.

In brief contact with reporters, Oswald displayed a black eye, which he blamed on police assault, and denied shooting anyone and said the government was victimizing him for having lived in the Soviet Union for two and a half years between 1959 and 1962, and that he was a "patsy." He continued to deny just about everything about his movements and activities on the day of the assassination and denied that the photos of him holding a rifle, which he had asked his wife to take when he received them via mail order, were real, claiming they were fakes. He said he was not a Communist, but rather a Marxist, and refused legal counsel other than from a counsel with the American Communist Party, or lawyers connected to the American Civil Liberties Union. None had been provided by two days after the assassination, Sunday, November 24, when the unbelievable and unexpected occurred, the murder of Oswald by nightclub owner Jack Ruby who was close to the Dallas police force.

Ruby had a shady background, starting with a troubled childhood and adolescence, including juvenile delinquency and time spent in foster homes. He was a truant from school and spent time involved in horse race gambling activities in Chicago, and eventually moved to Dallas and went on to manage various nightclubs, strip clubs, and dance halls. He developed close ties with the Dallas police officers who frequented his nightclubs and was believed, at the same time, to have connections with Mafia leaders and other elements of organized crime.

After the Kennedy assassination, Ruby lurked in the halls of the Dallas Police Headquarters on several occasions following the arrest of Oswald. He faked being a news reporter at a press conference that evening and had his loaded snub-nosed Colt Cobra .38 revolver in his right-hand pocket during the press conference. It is odd that anyone in a police station would not have been frisked for weapons before entering the headquarters, but Ruby was a friend of the police department and was well known.

On Sunday morning, November 24, 1963, at 11:21 a.m., Central Standard Time, Ruby was in the crowd of reporters as Oswald was escorted through the police basement to an armored car that was to take him to the nearby county jail. As people across the nation, including the author of this book, watched on television, Ruby stepped out from the crowd of reporters and fired his .38 revolver into Oswald's abdomen, fatally wounding him. It was an amazing example of irresponsible security of such an important person's safety, a suspect in the sniper killing of the president of the United States, and reflected badly on the Dallas Police Department. Ruby was immediately arrested, as television viewers covered their faces in disbelief at what they had just witnessed live, an event that still stuns people even a half century later.

Ruby said he had killed Oswald to "redeem" Dallas's reputation, and to save First Lady Jacqueline Kennedy from the need to testify in a trial about the death of her husband. This seemed to be a ploy to gain public sympathy for what Ruby had done, but it was believed that there was likely a Mafia connection to Ruby, and that the Mafia had links to several Dallas police officers who wanted to eliminate Oswald. This would lead to accusations of conspiracy within days, which has continued for a half century.

Ruby was convicted of murder with malice on March 14, 1964, and given a death sentence, despite having renowned defense attorney Melvin Belli as his counsel. Later, the conviction and death sentence were overturned, and a new trial was planned. But Ruby was admitted to the hospital with pneumonia, and then was discovered to have cancer of the liver, lungs, and brain, and died before the new trial on January 3, 1967, at the age of fifty-five. A pulmonary embolism due to lung cancer was said to have been the cause of death.

Accusations of his connections to organized crime, and that he had done its bidding to cover up their involvement in the Kennedy assassination, multiplied, and it was claimed that he was injected with cancer cells so that he could not further discuss the "truth" of the Oswald assassination, as well as the Kennedy assassination. Ruby himself was contradictory in the years after the conviction, sometimes claiming he did the criminal act against Oswald totally on his own, and other times hinting at a more complex conspiracy, including the Mafia and elements of the American government.

Those who believe Ruby was *not* part of a conspiracy point out how upset he was at the death of President Kennedy; how he decided to close his nightclubs for three days through the funeral of the president; that he cried a lot over the events in the less than two days after the events until the shooting death of Oswald; and that Ruby was too talkative and interested in attention to be part of a massive conspiracy. Many believed that he used the time his nightclubs were shut down to plot to kill Oswald in revenge for the death of Officer J. D. Tippett, along with Kennedy.

After President Kennedy died at Parkland Memorial Hospital, a half hour following the sniper shooting, there was a brief confrontation between the Dallas County medical examiner and federal authorities regarding preparation of the body for removal from the hospital to Air Force One. The new president, Lyndon Johnson, insisted that the casket had to be loaded on the plane for return to Washington with the new president; the new First Lady, Lady Bird Johnson; and Jacqueline Kennedy, the former First Lady and widow of the fallen president. Hard to believe, but this conflict resulted from the fact that at the time, it was not a federal offense to kill the president, although it was a federal crime to conspire to injure a federal officer acting in the line of duty.

By 2 p.m. local time, the casket was placed on the presidential plane at Love Field, and at 2:38 p.m. local time, Lyndon Johnson took the oath of office, administered by Federal District Court Judge Sarah Hughes, on Air Force One, with Jacqueline Kennedy on one side and Lady Bird Johnson on the other side, as he held up his hand and swore the presidential oath. The autopsy on President Kennedy's body was completed at Bethesda Naval Hospital in Maryland the evening of November 22, from about 8 p.m. to midnight, at the request of his widow, who selected the site based on the president's service as a naval officer in World War II.

The state funeral for President Kennedy was held on Monday, November 25, 1963, after the body lay in state in the East Room of the White House on Saturday, November 23. It then was taken on a horse-drawn caisson to the U.S. Capitol to lie in state on Sunday, November 24, as hundreds of thousands of Americans, traveling from all over the country, lined up to view the casket and pay their respects to the fallen president. Representatives from over ninety nations were present at the funeral on Monday. This was an amazing number considering the short time span between the assassination on Friday and the funeral on Monday. A Requiem Mass was held at St. Matthew's Cathedral, and the late president was laid to rest at Arlington National Cemetery in Virginia. One of the most memorable moments was John Jr., just three years old on the day of the funeral, saluting his father's casket at the urging of the president's widow, Jacqueline Kennedy.[3]

With his death and funeral, and with the death of assassin Lee Harvey Oswald, the conspiracy theory industry began its quest to prove that the death of the president could not be as simple as one discontented man, with a mail rifle, killing the president by himself and having no participation by or collusion with others. The belief in conspiracy would grow and convince a large majority of the American people that Oswald could not have done the dastardly deed alone. The idea developed that Oswald was a "patsy," as Oswald claimed himself, and might not have been involved in the assassination, but instead had been framed.

President Lyndon Johnson convinced Chief Justice Earl Warren to head a commission to investigate the Kennedy assassination, which included future president and then Congressman Gerald Ford of Michigan. The Warren Commission, consisting of seven members and support staff, spent ten months on the investigation and submitted a report to the president in September 1964, concluding that Lee Harvey Oswald had acted alone in the killing of Kennedy and the wounding of John Connally, and that Jack Ruby acted alone in the killing of Oswald. The commission's conclusions have been both challenged and supported by researchers and authors and continues to be a subject of controversy a half century later, and it is clear the issues and facts of what happened will continue to be hotly debated for the long-term future and will never be fully resolved.

Several investigations were ordered after the Warren Commission report. The Rockefeller Commission, headed by Vice President Nelson Rockefeller during the presidency of Gerald Ford who had been on the Warren Commission, examined evidence including the Zapruder film from the assassination and was the first conducted. The Church Commission, named after Democratic Senator Frank Church of Idaho, which investigated the FBI and CIA in relation to the assassination, as well as the Watergate scandal under President Richard Nixon, was the second investigation. Finally, the U.S. House Select Committee on Assassinations investigated not only the Kennedy assassination, but also that of Martin Luther King Jr. and the attempted assassination of Alabama Governor George Wallace.

The last commission arrived at a different view of the Kennedy assassination, believing it to be a conspiracy, but the conclusion divided the committee members, and four of the twelve members of the committee wrote dissenting opinions. What was clear, however, was that the Secret Service, the FBI, the CIA, the Department of Justice, and the Warren Commission were shown to have multiple deficiencies, including organizational failures, miscommunication, and a desire to keep parts of their operations and activities secret from investigators.

A seventy-five-year rule for access to the files of the Warren Commission in the National Archives was established at the time, but due to later legislation, more records were open sooner than planned, and the remaining Kennedy assassination–related documents are supposed to be open to the public by the year 2017, twenty-five years after the passage of the JFK Records Act by Congress in 1992. Autopsy photographs and X-rays are located in the National Archives under restricted conditions, and there have been accusations that relevant pieces of evidence and documentation have been lost, destroyed, or are missing, thus stoking conspiracy theories. It has been claimed that the brain of President Kennedy was removed from the National Archives by order of his brother, Robert Kennedy, but that cannot be confirmed, as the whispers of conspiracy continue to fuel at least a thousand works that claim a conspiracy against the thirty-fifth president of the United States.

Early accusations of a conspiracy and interest in further investigation included author Mark Lane and his book *Rush to Judgment* in 1966; the investigation and prosecution of Clay Shaw in New Orleans by District Attorney Jim Garrison from 1967 to 1969; the investigations by the Rockefeller and Church commissions in the mid-1970s; and the activities of the House Select Committee on Assassinations in the late 1970s. Numerous other books as well as articles and television shows throughout the 1970s and 1980s added to the controversy, including the controversial film *JFK*, produced by Oliver Stone in 1991. The beginning of attacks on conspiracy theorists began with authors Gerald Posner in his work *Case Closed: Lee Harvey Oswald and the Assassination of JFK* (1993) and the later massive work of 1,600-plus pages of Vincent Bugliosi's *Reclaiming History: The Assassination of President John F. Kennedy* (2007), which also includes an additional 1,200 pages of endnotes and source notes available on a CD-ROM.

Among the theories that have been promoted are the following, not a comprehensive list, but a list of major theories:

There are allegations of witness tampering, intimidation, and foul play against some witnesses of the events, including some of them dying within a year after the tragedy. Also, accusations of evidence suppression, tampering, and fabrication of evidence have been claimed. There are also those who assert there were multiple gunmen, and the issue of number of shots fired and location of bullets (the "Grassy Knoll" theory) has also been advanced. Additionally, there is the "Magic Bullet" theory, dealing with the bullet that hit both President Kennedy and Governor Connally. Supposedly, there are also claims of other conspirators, including later Watergate burglar E. Howard Hunt, said to be in Dealey Plaza at the time of the assassination, based on supposed photographic evidence.

Additionally, groups or individuals accused of involvement in the conspiracy to assassinate President Kennedy include in no special order the following:

- New Orleans elements, as claimed by District Attorney Jim Garrison, including Clay Shaw, who was prosecuted and found not guilty by a jury.
- Elements of the CIA unhappy with Kennedy's limiting influence of the agency after the failed Bay of Pigs invasion of Cuba in April 1961.
- "Shadow Government" elements, including wealthy industrialists and right-wing politicians who were unhappy with the policies of Kennedy in both foreign and domestic affairs, a theory often believed to have a massive effect on American policy in the long-term future of America in the next fifty years.
- The "Military-Industrial Complex," warned about by President Dwight D. Eisenhower in his Farewell Address in January 1961. Supposedly, according to Eisenhower, they wanted sustained military conflicts, with this complex including the Pentagon and defense contractors, which have often been blamed for American

foreign policy blunders under many presidents in the next half century.

- A Secret Service conspiracy by rogue elements within the agency, plus the belief of some that a Secret Service agent riding on the back of the limousine, might have accidentally shot President Kennedy in reaction to the shots fired on the motorcade.
- Elements of the FBI, even including Director J. Edgar Hoover, who was not happy with the president and his brother, the attorney general, and their handling of issues involving the agency, and also disturbed by the alleged scandalous love life of the president, with women, including one connected to the Mafia.
- An organized crime conspiracy by elements of the Mafia, known to have connections to the president's father, Joseph Kennedy, who supposedly arranged for fixed voting in Chicago with the mobsters and Chicago Mayor Richard J. Daley in the 1960 election. Also supposedly the Mafia was angered by Attorney General Robert Kennedy's pursuit of organized crime during the 1950s and early 1960s, and his aggressive tactics against Teamster Union President Jimmy Hoffa, known to be affiliated with the Mafia. Additionally, the sharing of a girlfriend, Judith Campbell Exner, between the president and Chicago mobster Sam Giancana was supposedly a source of irritation, and a conflict of interest for President Kennedy, related to the issue of national security.
- The accusation that Cuban exiles, infuriated by the failure to overthrow Cuban President Fidel Castro at the Bay of Pigs in 1961, and unhappy with the agreement to avoid a direct invasion of Cuba as part of the deal ending the Cuban Missile Crisis in 1962, plotted to kill the president. This discontent led to the vast majority of Cuban Americans becoming conservatives and active in the Republican Party for the next half century.
- The belief that the Cuban government orchestrated the Kennedy assassination in retribution for the attempts to overthrow Fidel Castro.
- The assertion that the Soviet government under Nikita Khrushchev had been involved in plans to assassinate the leader of the free world as part of the Cold War with the West.

- Theories that right-wing extremist groups engaged in a conspiracy, including Southern segregationists, Texas oilmen, the Ku Klux Klan, the John Birch Society, and right-wing Christian elements.

Theories that future presidents of the United States were involved in some form in the Kennedy assassination include:

- Lyndon Johnson, who became president because of Kennedy's death, and supposedly was bitter at his being made irrelevant as vice president, and having the personality and drive to do what had to be done to gain the power of the presidency at all costs.
- Richard Nixon, who was in Dallas on business, and left the Dallas airport just hours before the arrival of President Kennedy, and supposedly was tied to conspiratorial elements who wanted the president murdered, with Nixon being a willing conspirator because of bitterness over his defeat for the presidency in 1960 and his ambition to become president in the future.
- Gerald Ford, who served on the Warren Commission and supposedly cooperated in covering up evidence, and, as the last survivor of the seven members of the Warren Commission, contended to the end that the Warren Commission report was totally accurate and complete.
- George H. W. Bush, whose father had supposedly engaged in an unproven conspiracy to remove President Franklin D. Roosevelt in 1933–1934, as mentioned in chapter 6. Allegedly, Bush, who would later be head of the CIA under President Ford in 1976, might have been a CIA agent who might have conspired against Kennedy, and there is supposedly a photo showing him in Dealey Plaza, said to be at the time of the assassination, as there is also, supposedly, of Watergate burglar E. Howard Hunt, who had been associated with the CIA at the time. The photos make one wonder about whether either Bush or Hunt were really at that site, as they are unclear, as is the time when the photos were taken, and they could have been manipulated.

As author Vincent Bugliosi has pointed out, if one counts all of the conspiracy theorists, and the number of groups and participants, it totals: 42 groups, 82 assassins, and 214 people supposedly involved in conspiracies against President Kennedy. Bugliosi terms it "paranoia."

This does not include the idea that Oswald did what he is accused of, but that his purpose was to kill Governor Connally, not President Kennedy, a new twist on the Kennedy assassination "industry" of multiple books that try to explain the horrible events of November 22, 1963. There is even speculation that one of the mistresses of President Kennedy might have wished to eliminate First Lady Jacqueline Kennedy![4]

Today, the Sixth Floor Museum in Dallas, in the Texas School Book Depository, commemorates the Kennedy tragedy and has attracted a large number of tourists who want to try to understand why it happened and who caused it to happen. The John F. Kennedy Library in Boston, Massachusetts, also commemorates the tragedy in a permanent exhibit. The reality is that we will never for certain know the entire truth of the moment more Americans remember than any other, except for the more recent September 11 terrorist attacks. We will have to be satisfied with that uncertainty, as something that simply cannot be solved in a permanent manner. The Kennedy assassination will remain an eternal mystery.

NOTE

The assassination of John F. Kennedy has caused more investigation, controversy, and theories than any other assassination, other than Abraham Lincoln, and has certainly caused more potential explanations. The nation has never recovered from that tragic event, and the fiftieth anniversary caused a new emphasis on the events of that day.

The *New York Times*, *Washington Post*, and *Los Angeles Times* provide the best coverage of the assassination and its aftermath. The John F. Kennedy Presidential Library and Museum in Boston, Massachusetts, provides documents and other materials and exhibits dealing with the assassination, and the National Archives also has many materials, some not open to research at this point.

An excellent study of the long-term legacy of John F. Kennedy and discussion of the assassination is that of Larry Sabato, *The Kennedy Half Century: The Presidency, Assassination, and the Lasting Legacy of John F. Kennedy* (New York: Bloomsbury, USA, 2013). Also exceptional in coverage about the assassination is James Swanson, *End of Days: The Assassination of John F. Kennedy* (New York: William Morrow, 2013); and Thurston Clarke, *JFK's Last Hundred Days: The Transformation of a*

Man and the Emergence of a Great President (New York: Penguin Press, 2013).

The major investigations of the Kennedy assassination are *The President's Commission on the Assassination of President Kennedy* (Warren Commission, 1964); the *Rockefeller Commission* (1975); the *United States House Select Committee on Assassinations* (1979); and the *Assassination Records Review Board* (1992–1998). The Warren Commission and the House Select Committee on Assassinations' different conclusions about the Kennedy assassination are covered in: "JFK: 2 Official Investigations Reached Opposite Conclusions on Conspiracy," http://www/washingtonpost.com/national/.

With the fiftieth anniversary in 2013, television covered the historical event in numerous documentaries, described online as follows: "9 TV Shows Looking at JFK's Death, 50 Years Later," http://seattletimes.com/html/thearts/2022206120_jfkassassinationtvxml; and "Exhibits, Talks and Films Will Mark the 50th Anniversary of JFK's Assassination," http://articles.washingtonpost.com/2013-10-04/entertainment/426980. The textbook reassessment of JFK's presidency is covered in: "Textbooks Reassess Kennedy, Putting Camelot under Siege," http://www.nytimes.com/2013/11/11/us/.

An art print of the January 30, 1835, assassination attempt of Richard Lawrence against President Andrew Jackson outside the U.S. Capitol in Washington, D.C. The two guns that Lawrence had on him misfired, and Jackson was not hurt. The president helped to subdue his own assassin. Courtesy of the Library of Congress, LC-USZ62-2342.

An art print of the April 14, 1865, assassination of President Abraham Lincoln by well-known actor John Wilkes Booth, a Confederate sympathizer, at Ford's Theatre in Washington, D.C. Booth had conspired with nine other people to kill the president as the Civil War ended and also hoped to eliminate Vice President Andrew Johnson and Secretary of State William Seward, but only Seward was attacked, and he survived and remained in the cabinet. Courtesy of the Library of Congress, LC-USZC2-1947.

An art print of the July 2, 1881, assassination attempt of Charles J. Guiteau against President James A. Garfield at the Washington, D.C., railroad station, which led to a long, torturous 79 days of suffering and decline, leading to the president's death on September 19, 1881. Courtesy of the Library of Congress, LC-USZ62-12825.

An art print of the September 6, 1901, assassination attempt of anarchist Leon Czolgosz against President William McKinley in Buffalo, New York, at the Pan American Exposition, mortally wounding him, leading to McKinley's death after eight days, on September 14, 1901. Courtesy of the Library of Congress, LC-USZ62-5377.

A John Falter painting of the October 14, 1912, assassination attempt by John Flammang Schrank against former President Theodore Roosevelt in Milwaukee, Wisconsin, who was wounded but gave an 80-minute speech before going to a hospital and ultimately recovered from his wounds. Courtesy of the Shapell Manuscript Foundation, Los Angeles, California (www.shapell.org).

A photo of President-elect Franklin D. Roosevelt just minutes before an attempted assassination on February 15, 1933, at Bayfront Park in Miami, Florida, by Giuseppe Zangara, who instead mortally wounded Chicago Mayor Anton Cermak. Had FDR been killed, it is likely that the New Deal would not have occurred. Courtesy of the Franklin D. Roosevelt Presidential Library and Museum, Hyde Park, New York.

A photo of Senator Huey P. Long of Louisiana, in an open casket at his funeral, who had planned to pursue a presidential campaign for 1936, but was mortally wounded in the Louisiana State Capitol in Baton Rouge on September 8, 1935. Dr. Carl Weiss, his alleged assassin, was massacred with sixty-one bullets by Long's bodyguards. Long only survived two days, dying on September 10, 1935. Courtesy of the Leon Trice Collection, #950, Box 1, Folder 36; Louisiana State Archives, Office of Secretary of State Tom Schedler, Baton Rouge, Louisiana.

A photo of the motorcade in Dallas, Texas, on November 22, 1963, with President John F. Kennedy, First Lady Jacqueline Kennedy, and Texas Governor John Connally and his wife, just a moment before the shots were fired by Lee Harvey Oswald, which led to the death of President Kennedy. Courtesy of the Library of Congress, LC-USZ62-134844

A photo of Senator Robert F. Kennedy on June 5, 1968, shown giving his victory speech in the California Democratic primary shortly before being shot by Sirhan Sirhan in the Los Angeles Ambassador Hotel kitchen. It looked like he might become the Democratic presidential nominee, but sadly, he died the next day, June 6, 1968. SWPC-RFK-C020-010. Courtesy of the John F. Kennedy Presidential Library and Museum, Boston, Massachusetts.

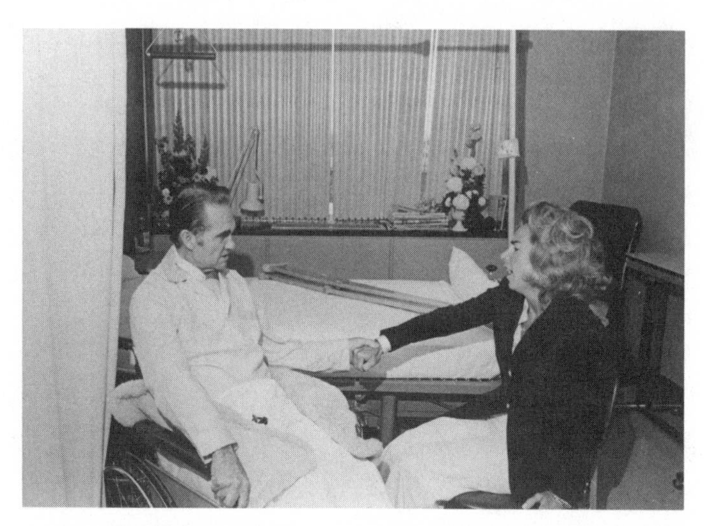

A photo of Alabama Governor George C. Wallace after he was shot by assassin Arthur Bremer in Laurel, Maryland, on May 15, 1972, during his presidential campaign. Wallace was paralyzed for life, and is pictured receiving a visit from Ethel Kennedy, Robert F. Kennedy's widow. Q0000036948. Courtesy of the Alabama Department of Archives and History, Montgomery, Alabama.

A photo of President Gerald R. Ford just as former mental patient Sara Jane Moore fired shots at him as he was about to enter his limousine on September 22, 1975, in San Francisco, California. This was the second assassination attempt in seventeen days, with Ford having also survived unhurt an earlier assassination attempt in Sacramento, California, on September 5, 1975, by Lynette "Squeaky" Fromme, a follower of Charles Manson. Sara Jane Moore firing at Ford failed to harm the president, as her aim was diverted by a former soldier. A6521, 22a. Courtesy of the Gerald R. Ford Presidential Library and Museum, Ann Arbor and Grand Rapids, Michigan.

A photo of President Ronald Reagan waving at a crowd outside the Hilton Hotel in Washington, D.C., on March 30, 1981, just seconds before being shot by assassin John Hinckley, leading to the serious wounding of the president and serious brain damage to Press Secretary James Brady, pictured to the right of President Reagan, and the wounding of a Secret Service agent. C1426-16. Courtesy of the Ronald Reagan Presidential Library and Museum, Simi Valley, California.

10

ROBERT F. KENNEDY AT THE LOS ANGELES AMBASSADOR HOTEL

Despite obvious nepotism, President John F. Kennedy nominated his brother, Robert F. Kennedy (1925–1968), to be attorney general of the United States. RFK held the position for his brother, and for his successor, Lyndon B. Johnson, for another ten months, until he resigned to run for the U.S. Senate in New York in September 1964. He served as junior senator from New York for three years and five months until his tragic assassination, just a short time after winning the California Democratic presidential primary on June 5, 1968. A national television audience watched the tragedy and the image of him lying on the floor bleeding after being shot, causing shock and disbelief. He survived for about twenty-six hours and passed away from three bullet wounds, received at the hands of a Palestinian Christian immigrant, Sirhan Sirhan.[1]

If there was ever a presidential candidate who many thought was a likely winner of the presidency, even before being nominated, it was Robert Francis Kennedy, who was eight and a half years younger than his brother, John, and gained a reputation early in life of being tough, scrappy, ambitious, and vindictive, but also kind, passionate, committed, and loyal to the extreme to the advancement of his brothers, John and Ted.

Americans first noticed RFK when he served as the chief counsel of the Senate Labor Rackets Committee from 1957 to 1959, where he challenged Teamsters President Jimmy Hoffa in an open hearing, accusing him of presiding over corrupt practices of the union and being allied with organized crime, which Hoffa vehemently denied. Earlier, RFK had also served as an aide to Senator Joseph McCarthy, who had become infamous as a demagogue, accusing scores of people of either being Communists or associating with Communists, a factor which would hurt RFK's reputation when he sought political office himself after his brother's tragic assassination.

RFK was the campaign manager for his brother and made many political enemies as a result. Senator Hubert Humphrey learned just how ruthless RFK could be when he challenged John F. Kennedy in the Wisconsin and West Virginia primaries during the presidential campaign of 1960. Lyndon B. Johnson learned to hate and despise RFK as well, when the future president's brother tried to convince him to turn down the offer of the vice presidency which had been offered by JFK.

Their mutual animosity continued during the Kennedy administration, as RFK convinced his brother to avoid giving Johnson any significant role in the administration. The competition between RFK and Johnson escalated as Kennedy stayed on for ten months, hoping to be Johnson's running mate for vice president in 1964, but Johnson selected Humphrey over him. This led to his decision to run for the U.S. Senate seat in New York.

As the sixty-fourth attorney general of the United States, RFK was a trailblazer in many ways, and his record merited his name being placed on the Justice Department Building, honoring his contributions. Kennedy became intimately involved in the promotion of civil rights. The "Freedom Riders" on interstate transportation in the South in 1961 saw the Justice Department intervene with federal marshals after violence ensued against the courageous young people who risked their lives to promote integration. Also, RFK supported the U.S. Marshals and armed troops intervening at the University of Mississippi in 1962 and the University of Alabama in 1963. James Meredith and George C. Wallace became nationally known figures in this integration struggle, with Meredith the first African American student at the University of Mississippi, and George C. Wallace the Alabama governor who became a controversial figure by trying to prevent the integration of the University of Alabama.

RFK also pursued organized crime on a massive scale, causing great opposition in the Mafia, with anger growing, as the Kennedys' father, Joseph, had been closely involved with the Mafia over the years; that information, however, was not public knowledge at the time, although there had been whispers of Mafia involvement in President Kennedy's

1960 victory in Illinois, which helped him gain the presidency. These rumors have since been accepted as reality, and made elements of organized crime resentful and desirous of revenge, in the assessment of many scholars of the JFK assassination.

But RFK was also engaged in foreign policy decision making as a member of the cabinet, trusted by and leaned on by his brother, the president, particularly after the failure of the CIA-encouraged Bay of Pigs invasion of Fidel Castro's Cuba. In the aftermath of this military blunder, RFK played a major role in the Berlin Crisis of 1961 and, particularly, behind the scenes, in the Cuban Missile Crisis of 1962. This confrontation could have plunged the world into World War III. The president expressed his appreciation of his brother's role in the resolution of the crisis in a peaceful manner.

But despite all of the plaudits for RFK as attorney general, it is also known that he accepted FBI Director J. Edgar Hoover's decision to bug and wiretap Martin Luther King Jr. He was also engaged in Operation Mongoose for his brother, the secret plan to attempt to oust Fidel Castro, through raids and encouragement of revolution after the failure at the Bay of Pigs. This was a plan which continued even after the Cuban Missile Crisis had been resolved. The Kennedy administration saw this plan as a continuation of the containment policies of President Harry Truman and his successors in the White House; the Big Stick Policy of Theodore Roosevelt; and the Monroe Doctrine formulated by President James Monroe and Secretary of State John Quincy Adams.

Consequently, many people would argue that RFK can be viewed both positively and negatively as attorney general of the United States, seen by many as secretive, ruthless, and rude, but willing to put himself in the way of anyone harming his brother, the president, and ready to sacrifice himself for the advancement of JFK's goals.

When RFK ran for the Senate in 1964, he was accused of being a "carpetbagger," an outsider who had not lived in New York but now wanted to be its senator, by the incumbent Republican Senator, Kenneth Keating, who had exposed the danger of nuclear missiles in Cuba months before the president made it a national security issue. The Kennedy administration denied Keating's claims two months before the missile crisis in 1962, before deciding to take action in Cuba. For this embarrassment, RFK wanted to retire Keating from the U.S. Senate, from what many called vindictiveness.

RFK would go on to win the Senate race, but be elected on the coattails of Lyndon B. Johnson's massive victory in New York in the presidential landslide of 1964. RFK was not appreciative of Johnson outdoing his performance in the election, and their rivalry and hatred for each other would manifest itself in the following three and a half years as RFK became a nationally followed figure in the Senate and, ultimately, chose to challenge Johnson for the presidential nomination in 1968.

As senator, RFK became involved in many causes. He visited South Africa, the first white American politician to do so, and openly opposed the continuation of apartheid, making him a trailblazer on that topic. He became engaged in the struggle against poverty, which was being pursued by Johnson's War on Poverty. He helped to start and encourage a redevelopment project in poverty stricken Bedford Stuyvesant in Brooklyn, New York, and he visited the Mississippi River Delta to witness the horrific poverty in the South, calling for action to better the lives of its children and adults.

African Americans, Native Americans, and Hispanic immigrant groups hailed him as a hero, as he spoke up openly, and with great emotional feeling, for what he called the "disaffected," the "impoverished," and the "excluded" groups in America. He became aligned with those promoting civil rights and social justice, advocating integration of all public places, the Voting Rights Act of 1965, and antipoverty social programs to deal with health care, education, housing, and employment opportunities.

In foreign policy, he condemned violations of human rights worldwide, and became highly critical of President Johnson's escalation of the Vietnam War, creating the debate on whether his brother would have pursued the same policy of sending hundreds of thousands of troops to fight a war that was unsuccessfully propping up South Vietnam's military dictatorship. Yet while being highly critical, he refused to become the poster child of the antiwar movement and turned down an opportunity to mount a challenge to Johnson when asked to do so in the fall of 1967. This led Minnesota Senator Eugene McCarthy to declare his candidacy for president and to campaign in the New Hampshire primary, the first test of political support.

Kennedy changed his mind the following year after the February 1968 North Vietnamese Tet Offensive, which saw the attack of North Vietnam and Viet Cong troops on the cities of South Vietnam, which caused a massive loss of life. While the U.S. and South Vietnamese forces ultimately overcame the onslaught, public opinion more vigorously turned against the war and against President Johnson. On March 12, 1968, to the surprise of many, McCarthy scored 42 percent in the New Hampshire primary, not a victory, as Johnson won 50 percent, but still a major blow to the president's reelection campaign.

It made RFK rethink the situation, and four days later, he announced his own challenge to Johnson, embittering McCarthy and many antiwar supporters as an example of self-centeredness and personal ambition, ready to enter the race after McCarthy had done the groundwork. It also meant that the antiwar opposition to Johnson was now divided, which would make the struggle against the president all the more difficult to accomplish.

To the shock of most Americans, however, Johnson announced he was withdrawing from the race on March 31, 1968, to promote Vietnam peace negotiations in Paris, and hopefully, but unsuccessfully, pursue an end to the war. Within days, Martin Luther King Jr. was assassinated, and soon, Vice President Hubert Humphrey entered the presidential race and became the front-runner. He faced the major dilemma of having publicly supported the unpopular Vietnam War, even though he was privately against it, because he would otherwise have lost his clout within the Johnson administration. Humphrey had a burden to carry that would undermine his candidacy and chance to become president of the United States, something he had wanted since running against JFK in the 1960 primaries.

Now the race was one of Humphrey, McCarthy, and RFK, but with Humphrey counting on those states that did not have primaries, as well as most members of Congress, mayors, governors, and labor unions. He had entered the race too late to meet the deadlines to enter many of the primaries between April and June. But the number of delegates from states that did not have primaries was enough that, with some endorsements, it might allow Humphrey to have a good chance to compete on an even keel with McCarthy and RFK, even if to many, it seemed unfair that a candidate who had not been in many primaries should have the possibility of being the nominee of the Democratic Party.

RFK represented minorities, the young, and the idealistic, who were disgusted with the trend of American foreign policy under Johnson and Humphrey. He spoke for racial and economic justice and social commitment to those left behind in American society, despite the Johnson administration's War on Poverty. McCarthy had the backing of many intellectuals, who admired his detached and principle-dominated views, but the Minnesota senator had trouble relating to the average person.

While a critic of Johnson's Vietnam War policies, RFK wanted to expand on the liberal activism of John F. Kennedy's New Frontier and Lyndon B. Johnson's Great Society. This antagonized many Southerners and conservatives across the nation. He was perceived as radical by conservatives, a threat to the established order, and much more liberal than his brother had ever shown evidence of being. RFK drew large crowds in troubled inner-city neighborhoods and in rural parts of Appalachia and participated in long motorcades in which he stood up in open automobiles, a reminder and in defiance of his brother's sitting in an open motorcade in Dallas when he was assassinated. Many observers wondered privately if he was endangering his own security, safety, and life in so doing, and also in making stump speeches at street corners, surrounded by thousands, and without any Secret Service protection. Candidates campaigning for presidential nominations had never been protected and only would be after the tragic death of RFK.

It impressed many how Kennedy addressed a mixed race audience in Indianapolis on the night of the Martin Luther King Jr. assassination, and kept them calm and prevented race riots and racial violence, at a time when more than sixty cities experienced such widespread turmoil. RFK showed an innate ability to bridge the gap between the races, and many thought he was the ideal person to unite the working-class whites and minorities in the crusade for social justice against the establishment, even though many would consider the wealthy Kennedy family to be part of the establishment themselves.

After victories by RFK in the Indiana and Nebraska primaries and a McCarthy win in Oregon, California became the ultimate test of which of the two antiwar candidates was stronger as the challenger to Humphrey. After RFK's victory on June 4, 1968, it was thought that he had the advantage and might stop Humphrey at the Democratic National Convention in Chicago in late August, although he was behind Humphrey in total delegates.

But that was not to be, as RFK gave his victory speech at the Ambassador Hotel in Los Angeles, brushed his hair back, which usually hung over his forehead, waved a victory sign at the crowd, and then with his wife Ethel proceeded to exit. He chose to go through the kitchen pantry behind the hotel ballroom, as the cameras continued to show the crowd gathered for the victory speech. Within a minute, shots were heard, panic ensued, and soon, the vision of Kennedy lying on the floor, bleeding from gunshot wounds, became part of the memory of all who were watching on television, including this author.

RFK's bodyguard had recommended that the senator exit the ballroom at a different location, but the senator took what he thought was a shortcut through the kitchen pantry. In a crowded kitchen passageway stood a kitchen employee, Sirhan Sirhan, a twenty-four-year-old Palestinian Christian immigrant, who proceeded to open fire on RFK with a .22 caliber Iver Johnson Cadet revolver, hitting the senator three times. Five other people were also wounded by his gunfire, as all eight bullets were fired despite attempts by bodyguards of RFK to stop Sirhan in the process of firing his weapon.

RFK was hit in the head and twice in the back, with a fourth bullet passing through his jacket. One bullet entered behind his right ear, from a distance of about one inch, and fragments were dispersed throughout his brain. The other two entered at the rear of his right armpit, with one exiting from his chest, and the other lodged in the back of his neck. Lying on the floor, RFK's head was cradled by busboy Juan Romero, who gave him a rosary in his hand, and RFK responded with a query if everyone was alright.

At that moment, the photo of RFK lying on the floor, bleeding, was taken—an image that haunts those who still remember that fateful moment. He underwent surgery lasting three hours and forty minutes, but the surgery did not improve his condition, and he was in a coma until he passed away after a period of about twenty-six hours, at 1:44 a.m. on June 6. The other five victims all recovered from their wounds.

Three supporters of RFK, including author and journalist George Plimpton, former decathlon athlete Rafer Johnson, and former professional football player Roosevelt Grier, wrestled Sirhan to the ground after the shooting. There was total chaos and panic at the scene, with television showing it live.

The assassin of Robert F. Kennedy was a twenty-four-year-old Palestinian Christian immigrant to America with Jordanian citizenship. He was born in Jerusalem in the Palestinian Mandate controlled by Great Britain on March 19, 1944, migrating with his family to the United States at age twelve. After a brief time in New York, the family settled in California, where he graduated from John Muir High School. He briefly attended Pasadena City College, but dropped out. From there, he worked various odd jobs, but had no real direction in his life, and would become emotionally involved in the politics of the Middle East, his former homeland. A strong critic of Israel, he was infuriated by Robert Kennedy's support of Israel in the Six Day War of June 5–10, 1967, and Kennedy's support of sending fifty Phantom fighter jets to Israel as a campaign pledge he had made during his run for president.

Ironically, Sirhan shot RFK precisely on the one-year anniversary of the beginning of that war. He had written in a diary of his determination to kill RFK because of his support of Israel. He had also examined the layout of the Ambassador Hotel two days before the assassination and visited a gun range the day before the tragedy. Someone testified during the trial that Sirhan had told him of his intentions to kill RFK a month before the assassination. At times during the trial, Sirhan's behavior seemed bizarre, and he became furious when testimony about his childhood was given, including his father's abuse toward him. Sirhan claimed that his hatred of RFK was solely based on the Middle East conflict. Many observers have said that the assassination of RFK was the first example of violence or terrorism emanating from the war between Palestinians and the State of Israel.

Years later in prison, Sirhan claimed that his anger was fueled by liquor, and by the sight of a victory parade in Los Angeles celebrating the one-year anniversary of the Six Day War, in which Israel gained East Jerusalem, the West Bank, the Gaza Strip, and the Golan Heights. Jordan, Egypt, and Syria had lost territory to Israel, and the war and occupation led to the formation of the Palestine Liberation Organization by Yasser Arafat and others, who would be termed "terrorists" by the Israeli government, starting a long and tense confrontation that has not ended over almost a half century since that war.

Sirhan was believed to have psychological problems beyond his hatred of RFK on the Israeli-Palestinian issue, as he had been severely disciplined as a child by his stern father. His lawyers claimed that he was not fully aware of what he had done, and as a result, he had "diminished responsibility" for the crime. Sirhan first pleaded not guilty, and then wanted to confess the crime and plead guilty during the trial. The judge refused to accept the confession, and the trial went forward, with Sirhan being convicted on April 17, 1969, and sentenced to death six days later, with the death penalty commuted to life in prison in 1972, after the California Supreme Court invalidated all death sentences.

Sirhan has applied for parole fourteen times over the years, most recently in 2011, but has been denied it and remains in prison after forty-seven years, claiming he has no memory of the crime or his involvement in it. He is presently confined in the Richard J. Donovan Correctional Facility in San Diego County.

RFK's body was returned to New York City and was placed in St. Patrick's Cathedral, and a high requiem mass took place on June 8, with Senator Ted Kennedy giving a very memorable eulogy and singer Andy Williams singing "The Battle Hymn of the Republic" to conclude the service. Then, RFK's body was taken by train to Washington, D.C., with thousands of mourners lining the tracks all along the train route.

Kennedy was buried near his brother in Arlington National Cemetery in Arlington, Virginia, with the funeral motorcade and ceremony occurring late at night due to delays stemming from the large crowds along the 225-mile train route to the nation's capital.

As a result of this assassination, the Secret Service assumed responsibility for the security of all major presidential candidates in the future, and President Johnson declared a national day of mourning. With the reality of this changed situation, it would still not be enough to prevent Alabama Governor George Wallace from becoming the victim of an assassination attempt four years later, during the presidential campaign of 1972, the subject of the next chapter.

Robert F. Kennedy remains the most prominent and most popular politician to have run for president and not live to let us know whether he would have succeeded. The tragedy of his death makes many imagine that he would have been president, as Hubert Humphrey came very close to defeating Richard Nixon in the 1968 presidential election, making one theorize that RFK would have defeated Nixon and become our thirty-seventh president.

The belief of many that he would have been a great president is belied by the reality that he had many enemies, and that no person becoming president can ever end up being as ideal and perfect as people imagine about someone who has not faced the burden of the presidency. So RFK remains the best example of "What might have been," with no conceivable way to estimate his success.

At the time of Sirhan Sirhan's conviction and imprisonment for a life sentence, it was concluded that the sequence of events, and the large number of people present at the time of the shooting of RFK, made it absolutely certain that Sirhan was the gunman who had killed RFK and wounded five others, and that there was no other complexity to this tragic event. But as the years have passed, conspiracy theories have arisen, and the doubts developed about whether Sirhan was the lone gunman. So it is necessary to examine the various theories that have arisen in the past forty-seven years since RFK's death.

The most prominent conspiracy theory is that there was a second gunman, similar to the belief of conspiracy theorists that the same scenario existed in the JFK assassination. The issue has gained some support, due to acoustic experts claiming that a total of thirteen shots were fired, although the weapon Sirhan used only had eight bullets. But not all acoustic experts agree on this issue. It has been said that the location of RFK's wounds make it likely that there had to be another gunman in the kitchen pantry. Sirhan's defense attorneys in 2011 claimed that the bullet taken from Kennedy's neck did not match the gun that Sirhan supposedly used.

A security guard who was working for RFK withdrew his gun at the time of the assassination but claimed it was a different caliber weapon and that he had been knocked down after Sirhan's first shot and never had the opportunity to fire his gun. This man, Thomas Eugene Cesar, was interviewed by the Los Angeles Police Department, cleared, and passed a lie detector test conducted by the American Polygraph Association years later. But there were said to be inconsistencies in his ownership of the gun and the time frame of when he said he sold it to someone else.

Another theory is called the "Manchurian Candidate" Syndrome, based on the film, which was a major success in 1962. Under this theory, Sirhan was psychologically programmed to kill RFK, but that he was not aware of his actions at the time, and that his memory of the events was wiped away in such fashion that he had no recollections of the events, or of the people who programmed him to do the deed. A psychologist, who interviewed Sirhan at San Quentin Prison the year after the assassination, said that Sirhan had no memory of the event and its aftermath.

Another theory is related to the report by a campaign worker of a woman in a polka dot dress, supposedly seen with Sirhan in the kitchen before the assassination, and then yelling "We shot him!" as she ran with a man from the scene. There have been denials that this ever happened, although the campaign worker claimed she was telling the truth and that she was bullied into withdrawing her account about the woman in the polka dot dress. Another campaign worker maintained that he had also seen this incident with the woman fleeing the scene.

There is also the theory that CIA agents were present at the scene and that the agency may have been involved and was angry over President Kennedy's moves to limit CIA influence after the Bay of Pigs affair in 1961. Part of this is the argument that Cubans who had fled Fidel Castro's Cuba were bitter over the failure to eliminate Castro, blamed the Kennedys, and wanted revenge. And also suggested by some is that FBI head J. Edgar Hoover, no admirer of RFK, could have been involved in a plot, and that organized crime, which also hated RFK for his pursuit of Teamsters Union President Jimmy Hoffa, could also have been part of a plot.

Additionally, the argument exists that defense and intelligence interests were concerned that RFK might end the Cold War and revolutionize American foreign policy in dangerous ways were he elected president. Also, Ku Klux Klan and other racist groups were alarmed at Kennedy's support of civil rights and saw his potential presidency as a threat to the South, which was very much angered by the actions of the Kennedy and Johnson administrations on that matter.

Additionally, speculation promotes that Lyndon Johnson, who hated RFK, could somehow have been involved, because of their fierce rivalry stemming from the attorney general's desire not to have him as vice president, and RFK's decision to challenge Johnson's Vietnam War policies and run against him before Johnson decided not to run again in 1968. Under this theory, Johnson also did not want to be seen as the "failure" between the two Kennedys in the White House.

Finally, and not surprisingly, some might think former Vice President Richard Nixon, on his way to the Republican presidential nomination in 1968, and paranoid about another Kennedy possibly being his opponent, somehow was involved in a plot against RFK, just as much as those who think he was somehow involved in the plot against President Kennedy.

Despite these conspiracy theories, there is no solid evidence that anyone, other than Sirhan Sirhan, acting single-handedly due to Kennedy's support of Israel in the Six Day War, pulled the trigger that fatally wounded RFK and the hopes of his followers. RFK's early death at age forty-two left a void that it has been argued no politician ever filled over the next decades. He was a man who was attempting to bridge the gap between the power groups at the top and the disenfranchised and ignored in the middle class, and among the poor. Here was a man appealing to working-class whites, but also African Americans, Hispanics, and Native Americans as well. That gap, it is contended, has never been filled or satisfied by any other American politician from 1968 to the present.[2]

RFK has become a hero to many, and many sites and honors have been named after him since his death. This includes RFK Stadium in Washington, D.C.; the Justice Department Building in the capital; the Triborough Bridge in New York City (renamed in 2008); a Gold Medal of Honor awarded him posthumously in 1978; and finally, a special U.S. dollar coin issued by the U.S. Mint in 1998. One would think he was indeed president of the United States at some point, considering the honors paid to him, and his image and influence are still part of the story of American history.

11

GEORGE C. WALLACE AT LAUREL, MARYLAND, SHOPPING CENTER

George Corley Wallace Jr. (1919–1998) was the fourth-longest serving governor in American history, serving as Democratic governor of Alabama for a total of sixteen years: 1963–1967, 1971–1979, and 1983–1987. He also ran for president four times as a third-party candidate and is considered one of the most influential presidential "losers" in American history, having won five states and forty-six electoral votes in the presidential election of 1968, the second-best total in both areas for a third-party candidate. Only former President Theodore Roosevelt, in the presidential election of 1912, running on the third party known as the Progressive Party, won six states and eighty-eight electoral votes, surpassing him. Wallace also won 13.5 percent of the popular vote in 1968, the fourth-best percentage in American history for a third-party candidate, behind TR with 27.5 percent in 1912; Ross Perot with 19 percent in 1992; and Robert La Follette Sr. with 16.5 percent in 1924.

Wallace proved to be highly controversial, as he pursued a strategy of opposing civil rights and promoting racial segregation.[1] Many journalists and opponents described him as a firebrand, who had no limits in what he would espouse and promote in pursuit of his goal, first of which was to be elected governor of his state. He then went on to regain the office two separate times and to stir up the political scene with his failed attempts to be the Democratic Party nominee for president four times, and ultimately, to run as the candidate of the American Independent Party in 1968.

Wallace would become the victim of an assassination attempt in May 1972, causing him horrific pain, numerous surgeries to relieve his pain, and the reality of having to spend the rest of his life in a wheelchair. Despite that terrible situation, Wallace still managed to remain part of the political scene and to be elected governor of Alabama again in 1982, governing from a wheelchair, like President Franklin D. Roosevelt before him, who had governed for more than twelve years as president, along with FDR's four years as governor of New York before his presidency.

During the twilight of his political career, Wallace mellowed and renounced segregation and even apologized to civil rights leaders for his earlier behavior, seen by many during his years of prominence as "demagogic" in nature, but seen by him and his supporters as wanting to keep a system that they were accustomed to and comfortable with as a norm.

Wallace showed interest in politics from the young age of ten. At age sixteen, he won a contest to serve as a page in the Alabama Senate and boasted that he expected to be governor of the state at some point in the future. He also proved to be a competitive boxer, a symbolism often used when referring to his political career. He graduated from law school at the University of Alabama and served in the Army Air Corps in World War II, flying B-29 combat missions over Japan in the last months of the war in 1945. He served in the Army Air Corps under General Curtis LeMay, who would end up as his vice presidential running mate in his third-party run for president in 1968.

During his war service, he contracted spinal meningitis, which nearly killed him; he was saved by sulfa drugs, but he was left with partial hearing loss and permanent nerve damage, leading to a medical discharge with a disability pension.

Wallace came from a political background, as his grandfather won an election as a probate judge in 1938, when Wallace was nineteen years of age. As a result of his own political interests, he became an appointee as an assistant attorney general of the state after his war service ended in 1945 and ran for and won a seat in the Alabama House of Representatives in 1946, running as a comparative moderate on the issue of race.

When Strom Thurmond ran as a third-party States' Rights (Dixiecrat) presidential candidate against President Harry Truman in 1948, Wallace refused to support him, and backed Truman, something he explained away years later as a political decision that he felt made sense. At the time, however, he was openly critical of Truman's move earlier in 1948 to integrate Washington, D.C., and the U.S. military by executive orders, stating his belief that segregation was a matter of "states' rights."

After years in the legislature, Wallace became a circuit judge of the Third Judicial Circuit in Alabama and had what could be described as a "mixed" record on racial issues. He showed some signs of respect for African American lawyers in court cases and granted probation to some black defendants, but also enforced segregation signs and prevented federal oversight of county voting lists for signs of discrimination against black voter registration. It was clear, in retrospect, that he treaded a fine line, avoiding extremism on race, but unwilling to go too far, in consideration of the racial lines clearly evident in Alabama politics in the 1950s.

But a crossroads was reached in 1958, when Wallace ran for governor in the Democratic state primary, the real race for the governorship, as there was no effective opposition to the party in the state and the general election was a foregone conclusion. Wallace would lose by almost thirty-five thousand votes, having been endorsed by the Alabama branch of the National Association for the Advancement of Colored People, because of his comparatively moderate stands on race. He spoke in the campaign of the need for roads and schools, but his successful opponent, future Governor John Patterson, used the race card, and was backed by the Ku Klux Klan, an organization that Wallace openly repudiated. The racist message won big, and Wallace took a lesson from that election result and would change his tune and be ready to use the "N" word regularly and become a typical Southern demagogue of the period to advance his own career ambitions.

When Wallace ran for the governorship of Alabama again in 1962, he became an entirely different candidate, determined to be the most segregationist candidate in the race, and this time, he succeeded, and became the forty-fifth governor of Alabama on January 14, 1963, making the national news. He declared in his inaugural address: "Segregation now, Segregation tomorrow, Segregation forever!," a line which rang through the minds of those who listened and watched, both those who agreed with him, and those who vehemently opposed his diametrically opposite view since four years earlier. Ironically, he stood on the precise spot where Jefferson Davis, the president of the Confederate States of America, had stood in Montgomery, Alabama, as he was sworn into office 102 years earlier.

It was not long until Wallace became the center of American political discussion, as a controversial, confrontational leader. He "stood in the door" of the University of Alabama in June 1963, trying to block the integration of the university, in a nationally televised event, in which he was threatened with arrest by the federal government if he prevented the registration for classes of two black students. The Alabama National Guard control was taken away from him and given to federal authorities by Attorney General Robert Kennedy after the initial decision to intervene by President John F. Kennedy. He also tried to prevent the registration of elementary school students who were integrating, the first such example of public school enforcement in Alabama, again by federal court order.

Wallace failed to intervene to protect civil rights marchers in Birmingham when the sheriff, Eugene "Bull" Connor, ordered high-pressure water hoses, night sticks, and police dogs to be used on peaceful demonstrators, who had been encouraged by the Reverend Dr. Martin Luther King Jr.; instead, Wallace maintained that King was a "Communist." These images were televised worldwide and caused widespread anger as it symbolized the brutal aspects of resistance to civil rights. The Ku Klux Klansmen's bombing of a black church, the Sixteenth Street Baptist Church, also horrified the nation, but Wallace said and did nothing in reaction, and the tragedy of four black girls being killed in the bombing shocked the nation. Wallace was not interested in national public opinion, was hell-bent on making a name for himself, and seeking a national following, as he now determined to run for the Democratic nomination for president against the new president, Lyndon B. Johnson, who had just succeeded President Kennedy a few months earlier.

Wallace ran against Johnson in primaries in Wisconsin, Indiana, and Maryland, and gained about a third of the popular vote, using the issues of integration and crime as his main points of emphasis. He showed ability to arouse crowds, almost in a dangerous fashion, with his fiery rhetoric, something that worried political observers, as a way to encourage violence against those promoting the civil rights movement, whether white or black. There were rumors that Wallace might join Arizona Senator Barry Goldwater as his vice presidential running mate on the Republican ticket running against President Johnson, but it never came to pass. However, Goldwater broke the "Democratic South," by winning five Southern states in the Electoral College, including Alabama in the 1964 presidential election, marking the beginning of a shift of Southerners toward supporting the Republican Party in future decades.

In 1965, Wallace promoted a hard line policy toward civil rights marchers who were campaigning for the right to vote, via a march from Selma to Montgomery, leading to violence at the Edmund Pettus Bridge, in what became known as "Bloody Sunday," and leading to federal action by President Johnson, promoting a Voting Rights Act. Wallace was not permitted to run for a second consecutive term as governor under Alabama state law in 1966, but his wife Lurleen ran, won, and served as governor (more as a stand in for her husband) for the next sixteen months, until her tragic death at age forty-one of cancer in May 1968. This untimely death occurred as Wallace was running for president, but it did not stop his campaign, and his formation of a third-party movement. The American Independent Party was based on "law and order," and on promotion of opposition to federal intrusion in local affairs, including public schools, voting, and the enforcement of the Civil Rights Act of 1964. He appealed to blue collar whites across the nation with his appeal for less federal government, more local control, and states' rights.

Wallace acted as a "populist," for the "little guy," the man who worked hard every day and wanted the federal government to get out of his life, and yet he stood for increases in Social Security and Medicare, in addition to supporting federal programs begun under Franklin D. Roosevelt and Lyndon B. Johnson. In foreign affairs, he stood for the idea of "winning" the war in Vietnam or getting out within a few months, but then his running mate, retired General Curtis LeMay, suggested that the answer to quickly winning the war was to "nuke" North Vietnam.

No one expected that Wallace, as a third-party candidate, could win the Electoral College, but Wallace hoped to prevent either Democratic nominee Hubert Humphrey or Richard Nixon, the Republican nominee, from gaining the 270 electoral votes needed to win the presidency. Therefore, with Wallace having the balance of power with the electoral votes he would win, he believed that this would enable him to negotiate, as a power broker, with both Humphrey and Nixon for the best "bargain" on his issues, specifically the retraction of civil rights enforcement. It was disturbing to many observers that extremist groups, including the White Citizens' Councils, the Ku Klux Klan, the John Birch Society, and the Liberty Lobby, which promoted pro-Nazi and white supremacist literature, endorsed Wallace, even though Wallace did not openly seek their support, but he also did not reject their backing.

Wallace made very radical statements, saying he would ride over any "anarchist" who lay down in front of his automobile; suggested that when he was president, he would cut the hair and force a shave of any "hippies" who booed and jeered at his campaign appearances; he asserted that the only four-letter words "hippies" did not know were "work" and "soap." There is no question that his candidacy divided America at a very tumultuous time—with the Vietnam War and the civil rights movement dividing the nation—like no time since the Civil War of a century earlier.

In 1968, Wallace won the states of Alabama, Mississippi, Louisiana, Arkansas, and Georgia, and nearly ten million popular votes, and his campaign, while failing to interfere with Nixon's Electoral College victory, taught the Republican Party a strategy to win Southern states by attacking federal intrusion, promoting states' rights, and condemning continued intervention on civil rights matters. The Wallace strategy had also taught Republicans how to appeal to blue collar whites, both middle class and poor, to be fearful of advancements by minorities—all of which helped Nixon to win in 1968 and 1972; Ronald Reagan in 1980 and 1984; George H. W. Bush in 1988; and George W. Bush in 2000 and 2004.

If one thought having lost the election in 1968 would tame Wallace's rhetoric and his ambition, one can come to the conclusion that was the farthest thing from his mind. He now pursued a return to the governorship, claiming he would not run for president a third time, and running an openly racist campaign against Albert Brewer, the lieutenant governor who had succeeded to the governorship when Lurleen Wallace died in office in 1968. Brewer had tried to promote an open attitude on the subject of race, at a time when the Voting Rights Act of 1965 had allowed African Americans to vote for the first time in seventy-five years. Wallace ran a very obvious racist campaign against Brewer in the Democratic primary, accused Brewer of being homosexual and his wife of being an alcoholic, and beat him in a runoff election. He then proceeded to campaign in Wisconsin, starting his third national campaign for the White House. His racist rhetoric was shocking to many, including newly elected "New South" Governor Jimmy Carter of Georgia, who represented the beginning of political change in the South, five years after the Voting Rights Act became law.

Wallace did not officially announce his determination to seek the presidency until January 1972 and entered the campaign as one of a dozen potential candidates, better known nationally than any of them, except for Hubert Humphrey. In this national race, he modified his stand on segregation to acceptance of integration, but strong opposition to desegregating schools by busing students from one area to another. He managed to win six states in the primaries, including Florida (winning 42 percent, including every county), Virginia, Tennessee, Alabama, Michigan, and Maryland the day after he was shot by an assassin, Arthur Bremer. He was third in delegates at the Democratic National Convention with 382 and had been third also in percentage of primary voters with 23.48 percent, not much behind Hubert Humphrey and George McGovern, with a total of 3.75 million votes cast for him. All this meant little, as his campaign was abandoned after his being shot and paralyzed for life, but it showed the appeal that he had, four years after his third-party race in 1968.

After four months of campaigning in 1972, Wallace was campaigning in Maryland on May 15, pleased that his ratings were high in the national opinion polls. He was holding a campaign rally in Laurel, Maryland, at the Laurel shopping center. Stalking him without his awareness was Arthur Bremer, who had been at an earlier campaign rally that day in Wheaton, Maryland; Bremer had also attended a Wallace campaign rally two days earlier in Dearborn, Michigan. Unbeknownst at the time, Bremer had been stalking President Richard Nixon and had written of his plans in his diary as early as March 1, 1972, stating his intention to kill either Nixon or Wallace while at a campaign rally in Wisconsin. He stated in his diary that he wished to do something that would be "bold and dramatic, forceful and dynamic, a statement of my manhood for the world to see." With Wallace's racial attacks, if anyone had imagined that someone wanted to kill Wallace, it would have been a black man, not a blond Caucasian male.

From that point on, Bremer was stalking both Nixon and Wallace at different points. He attended a meeting of Wallace supporters in Milwaukee the following day, as well as a Wallace dinner and rally on March 23, and continued to travel after Wallace by car, plane, ferry, and bus. He also attended a Wallace victory rally in Milwaukee on April 4. But then, he followed Nixon to Ottawa, Canada, on April 13, and was dressed in a business suit and wearing sunglasses, with a revolver in his pocket. He was unable to get close to the Nixon motorcade and realized it would be difficult to get any bullets through the glass of Nixon's limousine. He then went to Maryland for a few days, and then back to Milwaukee, and wrote in his diary: "I'm as important as the start of WWI. I just need the little opening and a second of time."

Who was Arthur Bremer? The third of four sons, he was born and grew up in Milwaukee, having a difficult relationship with both his mother and father, expressing the wish that he had been born to an ideal "television" family, where there was no yelling, and no one hitting him as discipline. He was an average student, had an above average intelligence score, and failed to make friends, and there is evidence that he was bullied by other students, ridiculed for his clothes, his shyness, his awkwardness, and was often stared at and laughed at, making him feel alone in the world and unloved. He caused no problems in school; however, his emotional problems and needs were not addressed in a proper way.

After attending college for one term and dropping out, Bremer worked as a busboy at the Milwaukee Athletic Club, but was demoted to kitchen work when he was heard talking to himself, and sang while cleaning tables, in an inappropriate manner. There was evidence of bottled up anger, withdrawal symptoms, and an assessment of him at the time thought he bordered on paranoia, while being competent at doing his job. He was, obviously, an unhappy and troubled young man.

Bremer had trouble with the law when he was arrested for carrying a concealed weapon and parking in a no-parking zone. A court-appointed psychiatrist examined him, and declared him mentally ill but stable and safe to live in the community. He lived alone in an apartment, after undergoing some psychotherapy. Shortly after, he purchased a snub-nosed Charter Arms Undercover .38 caliber revolver. He proved to be a poor marksman when he practiced at gun ranges, and even shot up his car and almost himself as he readied for his destiny. As he saw it, he was to become famous and, in the process, expected to commit suicide or be killed in the process of trying to assassinate Nixon or Wallace.

He proceeded to date a sixteen-year-old girl, apparently his only relationship, but it ended after a few months, due to his bizarre, unusual behavior, including graphic sex talk, displaying pornographic pictures to her, and acting inappropriately at a concert. He was unhappy that the young woman ended the relationship. He started to stalk her and to shave his head, all evidence that he was a developing problem to society at large. The young woman's mother ordered him to stop bothering her daughter.

He proceeded to take out two books from the library about the assassination of Robert F. Kennedy four years earlier and came to realize that killing Nixon would be much more difficult, so he set his sights on Wallace, although he considered that the Alabama governor was far less prominent than the president and his being a shooting victim would attract much less attention. He stalked Wallace in Michigan, but took no steps toward shooting him when he had the opportunity a few times in different cities, yet he was photographed at one rally in Kalamazoo.

Bremer drove to Maryland and offered to work on the Wallace campaign, appearing at a campaign headquarters in Silver Spring on May 9. Then he returned to Michigan and, after appearances at a few rallies, returned to Maryland, stalking Wallace, without anyone realizing it. On May 15, early in the day, Wallace spoke at Wheaton, Maryland, and Bremer wore a "WALLACE in 1972" button, and vigorously applauded the Alabama governor, while others at the rally booed and jeered, and even threw tomatoes at him, making Wallace decide not to shake hands with the crowd, denying Bremer his opportunity to shoot him.

At about 4 p.m. in Laurel, Maryland, Wallace had a friendlier audience of about one thousand people, and he decided to wade into the crowd to shake hands, despite warnings from his Secret Service agents, so Bremer had his opportunity. Moving forward, the twenty-one-year-old pushed his way forward, yelled "Hey, George, over here!," and aimed his .38 revolver at Wallace's abdomen and opened fire, emptying the weapon of five shots before being subdued and having hit Wallace four times. The assassination attempt was filmed by news photographers at the scene of the rally. Wallace lost a pint of blood, and one bullet lodged in his spinal cord, while the others ended up in his stomach and abdomen. He identified Bremer as the person who had attacked him, and then underwent a five-hour operation the evening of the assassination attempt. Three other people, including a personal bodyguard, a campaign volunteer, and a Secret Service agent, were wounded in the shooting.

Bremer was wrestled to the ground, punched and kicked, and slightly injured before he was seized by police officers. His apartment was searched, and all kinds of strange materials were found, including a Confederate flag, Black Panther literature, pornographic materials, and statements in his personal diary that seemed critical of conservative, middle-class Republicans, mentioned Lee Harvey Oswald, and seemed to condemn racism. A blue steel, 9-mm fourteen-shot Browning Automatic Pistol was also found in his car.

Bremer was tried five weeks after the assassination attempt, in a five-day trial in which the defense argued that he was schizophrenic and legally insane at the time of the shooting, but the prosecution said he was perfectly sane at the time of the shooting, while needing psychiatric treatment, and that Bremer was seeking glory and attention. The jury took just ninety-five minutes to reach the verdict of guilty, and sentenced Bremer to sixty-three years in prison for shooting Wallace and the three other victims. Weeks later, the sentence was cut to fifty-three years. Portions of his diary were published the following year, showing that Bremer hated Richard Nixon, that Wallace was mainly a secondary target, and that he had thought of other scenarios of shooting at random in downtown Milwaukee earlier.

Bremer had a few incidents early in his incarceration at the Maryland Correctional Institution in Hagerstown, but then settled down and had a spotless record and was released from prison on November 9, 2007, after thirty-five years of his original sentence. This was a mandatory early prison release, but with mandatory electronic monitoring and orders to stay away from elected officials and candidates for public office. A mandatory mental health evaluation and mental treatment were part of the agreement for his release. The probation agreement also included a ban on leaving the state of Maryland without written permission from the state agency supervising him until the end of probation in 2025.

Speculation about a conspiracy has never developed very much, but Wallace believed that it was possible that someone wanted him killed, with the key figure hoping for it being President Nixon. The president had ordered prosecution of people around Wallace, including his brother Gerald, for corruption and campaign violations, through charges brought by the Justice Department. These legal actions against Wallace's brother and others mostly ended once Wallace had declared that he was seeking the Democratic Party presidential nomination and not seeking another third-party bid.

Since Bremer had very little income some wonder if others were involved, but it has been shown that Bremer had saved some money, and that at the time of the assassination attempt, he had run down his money, and that motivated him to take action after earlier delays in such planning.

With Wallace being wounded four times, when the firearm used by Bremer only had five bullets, and three other people were also wounded, people wonder if there was another assassin at the location, but no hard evidence has ever been developed. But it remains odd that the Secret Service had no records on Bremer despite earlier evidence of his being at several campaign rallies, and he had his picture taken with Wallace. Apparently, he did not appear suspicious, probably because he offered to volunteer for Wallace and had buttons that showed support for Wallace.

Considering that other people were at the Laurel campaign rally, including police officers and Secret Service personnel, who might have used their firearms and caused the multiple bullet wounds, this was never pursued. It was also odd that Bremer's fingerprints were not found on the firearm retrieved at the scene and that the weapon could not be matched to the victim's bullets. Also, some think that the CIA or FBI could have been involved, and that the "dirty tricks" campaign by Nixon operatives, and in fact the whole Watergate scandal which followed a month after the attempted assassination of Wallace, might be somehow connected. But again, there is no hard evidence, and most of this discussion is based on conspiracy theories hard to prove.

Bremer has been the center of attention in some form in novels, films, a song, and Stephen Sondheim's musical *Assassins*, where he is placed in the audience and asked if he is there by John Wilkes Booth. He has gained the notoriety and attention that he long sought as a young man. The film *Forrest Gump* shows the assassination; the film *Taxi Driver* has a character based on him; the novel *11.22.63* by Stephen King refers to him; and the song "Family Snapshot" by Peter Gabriel describes an assassination attempt which was inspired by Bremer's diary. Ironically, the character similar to Bremer in *Taxi Driver* is said to have inspired the assassination attempt by John Hinckley against Ronald Reagan in 1981. In Bremer's mind, his shooting of Wallace failed to accomplish the level of notoriety that Lee Harvey Oswald and John Wilkes Booth had gained, as he had failed to kill the Alabama governor.[2]

George Wallace's life was transformed forever by the shooting, which paralyzed him from the waist down for the rest of his life. He underwent multiple surgeries to relieve his pain and suffering, but he was never fully relieved from it. But while he abandoned his 1972 campaign, he continued as governor of Alabama and was reelected to a second consecutive term, and his third term altogether, in 1974, due to changes in Alabama election law.

Somewhat surprisingly, Wallace announced for president a fourth time in 1975 and ran third in total popular votes in primaries behind Georgia Governor Jimmy Carter, the eventual nominee and winner of the presidency in 1976, and California Governor Jerry Brown, but only won Mississippi, South Carolina, and his home state of Alabama, and lost several Southern primaries to Carter.

Wallace had a complete change of view, beginning in the late 1970s, after several years of living in a wheelchair, and apologized for his past stands on race and segregation and asked forgiveness from civil rights leaders, including the Reverend Jesse Jackson. He ran for a fourth term as governor and won in 1982, and then announced his retirement in 1986 from public office, after having appointed a record number of African Americans to his cabinet and other state positions.

His record of four terms and sixteen years in office has only been surpassed by New York Governor George Clinton in the eighteenth century and present Iowa Governor Terry Branstad, still in office as of 2015, and South Dakota Governor William Janklow (only three days longer than Wallace).

While Wallace had improved education and highway construction and other public works in his terms in office, he had failed to deal with important issues such as mental health, prison conditions, and the tremendous poverty that still permeated the state, one of the bottom ten states in most economic and social statistics. The state still had a manufacturing sector devoted to low-wage jobs, being anti-union, and special powerful interests were controlling the legislature and preventing tax reform to end a favorable tax code that benefited corporations and large landowners. He had spent more time campaigning for office than actual day-to-day governing of his poor state.

Wallace lost his first wife to cancer and married and divorced twice more, and died at the age of seventy-nine on September 13, 1998, having suffered respiratory problems and complications from his gunshot wounds. He had forgiven Bremer for his misdeeds in a letter in August 1995, a very touching note, but Bremer never answered him. Wallace's willingness to forgive his potential assassin and his apologies to civil rights leaders in his later years redeemed him in many people's eyes, as a man who had exploited a situation for political gain but could admit his failures and shortcomings, and it made most Americans feel more kind and compassionate toward a politician who had so divided America during the 1960s and early 1970s.

12

RICHARD M. NIXON AND THE BALTIMORE AIRPORT INCIDENT

Richard M. Nixon (1913–1994), our thirty-seventh president (January 20, 1969–August 9, 1974), was, without a doubt, our most controversial president, and the only chief executive to resign his office under threat of impeachment by the House of Representatives, and removal by a two-thirds vote of the Senate, caused by the Watergate scandal.

Nixon was born to a family that struggled often in poverty and goes down as having had the second-poorest childhood, as measured by family history, of any president, only being more fortunate in childhood than Andrew Johnson, who also, ironically, faced impeachment, but survived the impeachment trial of 1868 and finished his unelected term in office, following the death of Abraham Lincoln.

Nixon, a very serious student, and trying to make his Quaker parents proud of him, attended Duke Law School in North Carolina, served in the Navy during World War II, and then decided to enter politics in Southern California for the 1946 Congressional midterm elections. Immediately, he showed the willingness to employ innuendos and character assassination to win office, accusing his opponent, Congressman Jerry Voorhis, a New Deal Democrat, of being soft on communism. He won his seat in the House of Representatives the same year as John F. Kennedy.

Nixon proceeded to make a name for himself by exploiting the "communism in government" issue. He became noticed and famous for his attacks on Alger Hiss, a former Franklin D. Roosevelt State Department appointee, who had been with FDR at the Yalta Summit in February

1945. At this conference, FDR met Soviet leader Joseph Stalin and British Prime Minister Winston Churchill for the last time, and according to critics who condemned him, the president "signed away" Eastern Europe to Stalin and the Communists. Accusations that Hiss was a spy for Stalin at Yalta, and a Communist, put freshman Congressman Nixon on the front pages of newspapers. President Truman quickly came to Hiss's defense and called Nixon, who he had not yet met, an "SOB."

Nixon was extremely controversial already, even before Senator Joseph McCarthy became noticed for his accusations of communism in government and elsewhere in America in 1950. That year, Nixon ran for an open U.S. Senate seat in California, and accused his Democratic opponent, Congresswoman Helen Gahagan Douglas, of being soft on communism, and calling her the "pink lady," including having "pink underwear." Despite this name calling, or perhaps as a result of it, Nixon swept to an easy victory, and now became ever more noticed in the Senate.

Within two years, and at the age of forty just before his inauguration as vice president under Dwight D. Eisenhower in 1953, Nixon survived a personal financial scandal as the running mate of Eisenhower. He used a puppy named Checkers that had been given to Nixon for his two young daughters as a distraction from his wrongdoing. As a result, he became regarded by his critics in the opposition Democrats, as well as liberals, as "Tricky Dick," a person willing to do anything, use any dirty tactics, to accomplish his goals of power and influence, and his own advancement.

Despite his bad reputation and controversial record in Congress, Nixon proved to be a very effective and hard-working vice president, and revolutionized the office with Eisenhower allowing him to be more active than earlier vice presidents had been. With the president having three major health setbacks, Nixon was allowed to act unofficially as "acting president," and it gave him stature. He became regarded as very knowledgeable and expert in his judgment of foreign affairs. His meeting with Soviet Premier Nikita Khrushchev in Moscow in 1959 added to his credentials for his obvious plans to seek the presidency in 1960.

After battling with Nelson Rockefeller and Barry Goldwater for the presidential nomination of the Republican Party, Nixon selected Henry Cabot Lodge as his vice presidential running mate. Nixon entered the 1960 presidential campaign in good shape, with a solid team on American foreign policy, and plenty of publicity as vice president. His opponent, John F. Kennedy, had served just as long in Washington, D.C., but did not have the kind of experiences and expertise that Nixon had. But despite these advantages, Nixon lost the presidency in the closest election since 1916. This was in good part due to the televised debates which equalized Kennedy with Nixon, along with the bad, divisive images that Nixon had carried since his Communist "witch hunting" days in Congress.

Nixon believed that Mayor Richard J. Daley of Chicago had fixed the electoral vote in Illinois, and that the election of Kennedy was fraudulent, but chose not to challenge the close results. Instead, he went home to California and ran for governor against incumbent Eugene "Pat" Brown in 1962. When he lost the race, he declared the end of his political career and ambitions, expressed his dislike of the news media, and said "You won't have Nixon to kick around anymore!" He moved to New York City, where he started a lucrative legal career and became personally wealthy for the first time in his life. He campaigned for other Republicans in 1964, convinced correctly that Lyndon B. Johnson was unbeatable, and knew that Republican nominee Barry Goldwater was a "lost cause." He traveled the world and then, in 1967, changed his mind about running for president again, and entered the 1968 presidential race, with many observers skeptical about the chances of a successful comeback.

Nixon ended up overcoming the competing candidacies of Michigan Governor George Romney (who had been the front runner in much of 1967), New York Governor Nelson Rockefeller, and California Governor Ronald Reagan, and chose Maryland Governor Spiro Agnew as his vice presidential running mate. He competed for the White House against sitting Vice President Hubert Humphrey and third-party nominee George Wallace of Alabama. Way ahead in polls at the beginning, Nixon pledged a secret plan to end the war in Vietnam, refused to debate Humphrey or Wallace (as the 1960 debates had helped to defeat him), and won another close race. He became our thirty-seventh president on January 20, 1969, pledging to unite Americans in the most tumultuous decade in a century.

As it turned out, Nixon did not unite Americans who wanted to end U.S. involvement in Vietnam. While he promoted his "Vietnamization" program of helping the South Vietnamese to take over the bulk of the war, he also increased bombing in Laos and Cambodia, followed by a ground invasion of Cambodia in April 1970. He followed a policy of slow withdrawal of U.S. forces (mostly done in the election year of 1972), and continued negotiations with the North Vietnamese and Viet Cong in Paris, earlier begun by President Johnson. This series of policies led to increased American casualties. Nixon's actions led to a growing antiwar movement and a greater division than had occurred under Johnson. The death of students at Kent State University in Ohio, after the Cambodia invasion in 1970 was announced, led to a further division in American society. This was further expanded by strong attacks on the news media, antiwar advocates, and liberals on the part of Vice President Agnew, at President Nixon's request.

Americans were divided over Nixon, but the president made himself look like a statesman by his diplomacy, including traveling to mainland Communist China in February 1972 and negotiating the Strategic Arms Limitation Treaty with Leonid Brezhnev, the leader of the Soviet Union, in May 1972. These two diplomatic steps ensured a landslide electoral and popular vote victory against Democratic presidential nominee Senator George McGovern of South Dakota in November 1972.

This victory was marred, however, by the Watergate scandal, which demonstrated the insecurity and paranoia that existed in the Nixon presidency. This was the cause of his ultimate downfall, as his top lieutenants, including John Mitchell, H. R. Haldeman, and John Ehrlichman, along with numerous others, were linked to the scandal that would lead to his impeachment by the House Judiciary Committee. The Supreme Court subsequently and unanimously voted that the secretly recorded Watergate tapes, created in the Oval Office, be handed over to the special prosecutor investigating the break-in at the headquarters of the Democratic National Committee in the Watergate complex of apartments and offices in Washington, D.C. This was the final doom for Nixon, who resigned within a few days.

Watergate cast a negative shadow over Nixon's presidency, but he also presided over major domestic changes, including the establishment of affirmative action; the creation of the Environmental Protection Agency; and the enactment of the Consumer Product Safety Commission and the Occupational Safety and Health Administration. He also began unpopular wage and price controls in reaction to a comparatively high level of inflation in the American economy. He also tried to devise a national health-care system, though with little progress.

He also supported Israel against Egypt in the Yom Kippur War of October 1973, preventing the introduction of Soviet troops into the Middle East cauldron. But that caused the negative consequence of an oil embargo by Arab nations in the Middle East, led by Saudi Arabia.

Nixon also fought with Congress over executive privilege and his refusal to spend money mandated by the Democratic-controlled Congress in different areas of policy—causing plenty of tension between the president and the Congress on an unending basis.

Nixon made major blunders in some areas of foreign policy, such as his support of dictatorships over democracy in Chile and Greece and support of the dictatorship in Pakistan over democratic India, who was aiding the breakaway independence movement in East Pakistan, which became the independent nation of Bangladesh.

With the growing move to impeach Nixon, he became extremely unpopular in his second term, despite his landslide victory in 1972. Unknown at the time, Nixon also had devised an "enemies list," as he wanted to harm his political enemies through tax audits, and "dirty tricks" against potential opponents and critics before his 1972 election. He also had aides who thought causing the bugging and wiretapping of the opposition Democratic Party headquarters was something he would approve. This was the scenario that existed when the most dangerous threat to Nixon personally took place in February 1974.

Without realizing it at the time, Nixon was a possible threat for assassination by Arthur Bremer, who stalked him at various political appearances in 1972. But as discussed in the previous chapter on George Wallace, Bremer came to realize that it would be much more difficult to get to the president than it would be to the Alabama governor. Nixon was fortunately not the victim of the mental illness of Bremer at the time of the national election of 1972.[1]

Nixon was also under threat, as reported by NBC News on August 20, 1973, while on a trip to New Orleans, Louisiana. The Secret Service had warned of a danger to the president, and the motorcade route was changed and security around the president was tightened. Nixon was to speak at the Veterans of Foreign Wars convention and was well received, but was reported to be quite nervous, as it was claimed a former police officer, Edwin Gaudet, had allegedly threatened his life a week earlier, and he could not be found. The Secret Service hinted at a plot involving three to four men, but nothing developed further and this certainly caused a scare. It was unclear whether the men supposedly involved in the conspiracy ever were arrested.

Gaudet was tracked to New Mexico, fleeing into the mountains for a few days, and then turned himself in, but was released without trial. However, he sued for defamation of character in 1975 claiming his reputation had been ruined by the media reports on television, radio, and newspapers and magazines, and that he lived in fear of his life and being singled out as someone to be denied equality of treatment under the law. He claimed physical, psychological, and emotional harm, after being denied financial relief in a U.S. district court, but apparently lost the case in his appeal to the circuit court, as no further adjudication was found. If one is accused of threatening the president, even if not arrested nor prosecuted, such individual has no prospect of relief through payment of financial damages.[2]

Such resolution was not the case with Samuel Byck, who presented a major threat to Nixon's life and to the White House. Byck was a forty-four-year-old unemployed former tire salesman, born to poor Jewish parents in south Philadelphia, who dropped out of high school in the ninth grade to support his family. He joined the U.S. Army when he was twenty-four, served two uneventful years in the military, and was discharged in 1956, got married, and had four children. He had trouble making a living to support his family, losing a number of jobs and getting divorced, all of which caused severe bouts of depression, and he admitted himself to a psychiatric ward for two months in 1972.

Byck came to the notice of the Secret Service by bizarre actions, including: sending strange tape recordings to public figures, including scientist Jonas Salk, Connecticut Senator Abraham Ribicoff, and composer Leonard Bernstein (all of whom happened to be Jewish, as he was); trying to join the Black Panthers organization; and, most importantly, making a verbal threat against President Nixon after receiving a rejection of a small business loan by the Small Business Administration, in which Nixon had no involvement at all. Byck had the viewpoint that the federal government was out to oppress poor people, of which he was clearly one. While he was investigated by the Secret Service, he was seen as a harmless weird person of no danger to the president.

Byck decided to assassinate Nixon in February 1974, at a time when the president was under severe pressure and being investigated for possible impeachment charges in the Watergate scandal. There was a high level of invective visited against Nixon from many quarters, and he was certainly the most hated modern president up to his time in office since

Abraham Lincoln. This reality incited Byck, who may have been inspired also by news reports on February 17, 1974, of Army PFC Robert K. Preston, who had stolen a helicopter and "buzzed" the White House building, a dangerous action publicized by the news media.[3]

Preston could be considered a threat to Nixon himself, except that the president and Mrs. Nixon were away in Florida and Indianapolis, Indiana, respectively, and were in no danger. Preston stole a U.S. Army Bell UH-1 Iroquois ("Huey") helicopter from Fort Meade, Maryland, flew it to the nation's capital, and hovered over the White House for about six minutes at about 2 a.m. No protective action was taken, and he flew off and was then chased by two Maryland State Police helicopters. Preston forced one of the helicopters down by his maneuvers, returned to the White House, and now, while hovering about the south grounds, was fired upon by the Executive Protective Service with shotguns and submachine guns, which led to his being injured and landing his helicopter.

Preston accepted a plea bargain, pleading guilty to "wrongful appropriation and breach of the peace," and was sentenced to one year in prison and fined $2,400. Preston seemed unstable to many, as the twenty-year-old had hoped to be a helicopter pilot, but when the training was ended at his army base in Panama City, Florida, without completion, he was disappointed, as he wished to show his skill as a pilot. The Preston incident is believed to have had an effect on Samuel Byck, with his plan to crash a passenger airplane into the White House occurring only five days later, with much more tragic circumstances and potential danger.[4]

Byck, being known to the Secret Service by their earlier investigation, decided to steal a firearm, a .22 caliber revolver from a friend, to use in his planned hijacking. Byck recorded his thoughts in audio form, to explain his motives and his plans, which included the making of a bomb out of two gallon jugs of gasoline and an igniter. Byck wanted to be seen as a hero for killing Nixon and to make sure everyone knew why he did what he was about to do.

Byck's assassination attempt, despite its shocking plan to crash into the White House, never was really reported at the time, becoming the most hidden major assassination attempt in American history. Only in later years would it be acknowledged publicly, and become the subject of a 2004 movie, *The Assassination of Richard Nixon*, starring Sean Penn as Samuel Byck. In addition to the Sean Penn reenactment of Byck, the History Channel aired a documentary on the event, *The Plot to Kill Nix-*

on. This happening, occurring twenty-seven years before the similar September 11, 2001, terrorist attack on the Pentagon and the World Trade Center, made many Americans realize what could have happened, but fortunately did not. The idea that Byck might have succeeded in an action similar to what al Qaeda did in 2001 is absolutely stunning when one analyzes it.

On the designated day, February 22, 1974, less than five months before Richard Nixon resigned the presidency, Samuel Byck drove to the Baltimore-Washington International Airport and shot and killed Maryland Aviation Administration police officer George Neal Ramsburg. He then stormed aboard a DC-9, Delta Air Lines Flight 523 to Atlanta, the next flight scheduled to take off at the time of his attack. The pilots of the plane, Reese (Doug) Loftin and Fred Jones, informed Byck that they could not take off until wheel blocks were removed, leading Byck to shoot both, and forcing a nearby passenger to "fly the plane" even though that woman had no training to do so. Loftin survived the shooting, but Jones died, and meanwhile, a flight attendant was ordered to close the door of the plane or the plane would be blown up.

There followed a standoff gun battle between Byck and Anne Arundel County police officers, and one such police officer, Charles Troyer, stormed the plane and fired four shots through the aircraft door with a .357 Magnum revolver taken from the deceased officer George Neal Ramsburg. Two of the shots hit the thick window of the aircraft cabin door and wounded Byck. Upon being shot, Byck abandoned his hijacking plan and shot himself in the head, committing suicide. He was found with a briefcase containing the gasoline bomb under his body. In such a fashion, Samuel Byck's bizarre plot came to an end. Fortunately, the hijacking had not taken place while the plane was aloft, as that could have led to a far greater tragedy, which would have been very public and shocking to the American people.

It was later disclosed that Jack Anderson, the journalist and news columnist, had been sent a tape recording, detailing Byck's plan, but it arrived after the event. It was also disclosed that Byck had been arrested twice for demonstrating in front of the White House without a permit, and had been in a Santa suit for another protest. Clearly, Byck was a case of serious mental illness and had gone over the edge in a dangerous fashion to himself and others. If the Secret Service had determined him as a threat earlier on when he was arrested, perhaps it would have avoided this entire unfortunate situation.

Richard Nixon was, fortunately, not a direct victim of an assassination attempt, but his time in office was limited, and he resigned the presidency on August 9, 1974, and went into "exile" in San Clemente, California. He worked to redeem his reputation, hoping to overcome the Watergate scandal, and wrote ten books and traveled the world, and was pleased to have every president from Gerald Ford to Bill Clinton consult with him on foreign policy matters. He became the subject of many different studies by scholars, and since his death in 1994, while the revelations of the Watergate tapes have undermined his image, the recognition of what he actually accomplished in both domestic and foreign policy has helped to rehabilitate his historical record to a much greater extent than one would have imagined forty years ago.

But the Republican Party of the second decade of the twenty-first century still repudiates him, not only for the Watergate and related scandals, but also because, in retrospect, he promoted a greater expansion of the federal government in domestic policy than any Republican since Theodore Roosevelt. Much of what he promoted has been opposed by the majority of Republicans since Nixon's time, particularly under President Ronald Reagan and the influence of Speaker of the House Newt Gingrich. The Tea Party Movement in the second decade of the new century continued to repudiate everything that Nixon stood for, including the promotion of a national health-care system.

13

GERALD R. FORD AT SACRAMENTO AND SAN FRANCISCO

Gerald R. Ford (1913–2006), our thirty-eighth president, served in the White House from August 9, 1974, to January 20, 1977, making his term of office the fifth-shortest term of all of our presidents, with a total time in office of 895 days. He had the shortest term of any president who survived his term.[1]

Ford became the ninth vice president to succeed to the presidency during a term, but the first to do so for another reason besides the death of a president. He succeeded to the presidency upon the resignation of Richard Nixon, in the face of an impending impeachment by the House of Representatives, as a result of the Watergate scandal. Ford was also the first vice president not elected to that office and then who succeeded to the presidency. The Twenty-fifth Amendment, ratified in 1967, enabled Nixon to appoint a new vice president, after the resignation of Spiro Agnew from his own scandal. Ford became vice president by approval of the House of Representatives and the U.S. Senate, and came to the presidency after only eight months as vice president, knowing the likelihood of succeeding Nixon with the pending investigation of Watergate by the special prosecutor and the Congress.

Ford also was the last surviving member of the Warren Commission, which investigated the assassination of President Kennedy, and always upheld the viewpoint of the commission that Lee Harvey Oswald had accomplished the assassination on his own and was not a part of a conspiracy.

Ford never imagined himself as president, similar to Harry S. Truman, and became the center of attention without having sought the opportunity to be vice president or president. He had no presidential ambitions, and it seemed likely that he would be satisfied simply to unite the nation and finish the remainder of Nixon's term. But once in office, he changed his mind, sought the presidency in 1976, and faced a tough battle for the nomination from former Governor Ronald Reagan and conservatives within the Republican Party who felt that Ford was too moderate and could not represent the growing right-wing trend of the GOP.

Having won a very close battle for the nomination, Ford felt compelled to drop Vice President Nelson Rockefeller, his personal choice to succeed himself under the Twenty-fifth Amendment. He did so to please Reagan and other conservatives. They thought Rockefeller was too liberal, having served as a path-breaking governor of New York for fifteen years and having sought the presidency himself in 1960, 1964, and 1968, but constantly rejected as too liberal for the national party. So Ford chose Kansas Senator Bob Dole, but ended up losing the election to the Democratic nominee, former Georgia Governor Jimmy Carter, by a close margin.

Ford had served in the U.S. House of Representatives from Grand Rapids in western Michigan for thirteen terms, a total of twenty-five years. He imagined himself a future Speaker of the House of Representatives and had turned down opportunities to run for governor or a U.S. Senate seat from Michigan. Instead Ford had served as House Minority Leader under a Democratic-controlled Congress for nine years, from 1965 through most of 1973. He was well liked by the Democratic majority, and had been able to negotiate compromise and work with Democratic colleagues. His confirmation as vice president by both houses of Congress was a simple exercise as a result of his ability to work with the majority.

During his time in the presidency, Ford became best remembered for his nomination of Rockefeller to be his vice president and his controversial pardon of Richard Nixon from any prosecution for his involvement in the Watergate scandal. His rescue of hostages held by the Communist government of Cambodia from the U.S. ship the *Mayaguez*; the severe recession that took place in 1975–1976, the longest and most severe since the Great Depression; and the appointment of Supreme Court Associate

Justice John Paul Stevens, who would serve thirty-five years from 1975 to 2010, also stood out as memorable.

Ford and his wife became personally popular, with First Lady Betty Ford becoming an outstanding activist on women's rights, including support of the Equal Rights Amendment and abortion rights and advocating for breast cancer and alcoholism treatment, both from which she suffered, and made public issues of significance. Her husband came across as a nice, relaxed, easygoing guy, and far more likeable personally than Richard Nixon had ever been. Even when he tripped going up and down the steps of Air Force One, or hit people over the head with golf balls, he was somehow loveable to many, and comedians loved him. The irony was that Ford was probably the most athletic president, having played football at the University of Michigan, and was very talented in other athletic pursuits. Above all, the Fords came across as very human and decent.

By September 1975, Ford had been president for about thirteen months, and he would become a unique president in that month as he would twice be subjected to serious assassination threats, both times in California, both times by women instead of men, and the two attempts only seventeen days apart. These two incidents did not fit the pattern and historical factors in the history of presidential assassination attempts.[2] Ford was spending a lot of time in California, the largest electoral vote state and home of his rival, former California Governor Ronald Reagan. He had decided to declare his intention for a full term in the White House and realized the importance of campaigning in the state that might decide the ultimate result of the presidential nomination battle.

The first attempt, by Charles Manson follower Lynette "Squeaky" Fromme, occurred in the state capital of Sacramento on September 5, 1975. The second attempt, strikingly similar in nature, was by Sara Jane Moore, in San Francisco, on September 22, 1975, and has been considered a copycat attempt, inspired by Fromme's attempt to kill President Ford just two and a half weeks earlier.

Lynette Fromme was twenty-six years old when she tried to kill President Ford. A member of the cult that followed Charles Manson on his murderous rampage in the late 1960s, she was fascinated by the charismatic figure who convinced people around him to commit murders and rapes of innocent victims. She had been born in Santa Monica, California, and had shown talent as a young girl, touring as part of a dance group, which appeared on the Lawrence Welk show, and performed at the White House in 1959, when President Dwight D. Eisenhower was in office.

But she started to rebel as a teenager and began to drink and take drugs and was eventually, after a fight with her father, forced into homelessness. She was suffering from depression, but when she met Manson, she found him fascinating and became one of the followers of this very charismatic man. She became engaged in sexual affairs with many men and women, gaining her nickname of "Squeaky" from her high-pitched voice.

When Manson and some of his followers were arrested for the gruesome murders of Sharon Tate and Rosemary and Leno LaBianca, among others, in 1969, Fromme, while not involved, was arrested for interfering with the prosecutor's case. Her loyalty to the imprisoned Manson and the others involved in the murders made her seem ever more bizarre as the early 1970s passed on. Fromme's association and involvement with Manson's followers continued for many years after Manson's imprisonment. She was questioned by police and held in custody when several murders by his followers continued to occur, but she was never implicated in the criminal activities. However, her behavior continued to be bizarre, fueled by drugs and liquor, and one could consider her actions as signs of mental illness, and she would become a national story in early September 1975.

In the midst of this downward path, Fromme crossed paths with President Ford when he was in Sacramento, California, the state capital, on September 5, 1975. She went to the State Capitol Park with a plan to speak to President Ford about "saving the California redwoods," and was dressed in a nun-like red robe. She was disturbed that Ford was asking for a relaxing of provisions of the Clean Air Act of 1970. The announcement of Ford's visit led a former convict, Thomas Elbert, to phone the Secret Service and threaten the president when he visited Sacramento, leading to his arrest. This made the Secret Service more apprehensive about Ford's visit.

Fromme had on her body a Colt M1911 .45 semi-automatic pistol she had stolen from a friend, and her apartment was a short distance from the hotel that Ford was staying at overnight. Ford was walking toward the State Capitol Park and began shaking hands with people who had gathered in a crowd, waiting to meet the president. Fromme was seen by Ford, who later testified that he thought this woman in a brightly colored dress just wanted to shake his hand.

As Fromme was about two feet away from Ford, behind the first row of the crowd, she reached into her flowing red robe and withdrew the firearm from her leg holster. She raised her right arm and pointed the weapon between Ford's knees and his waist. Although the pistol had four rounds loaded, there was no cartridge in the chamber. She was immediately attacked by Secret Service Agent Larry Buendorf, restrained and handcuffed, as the cameras recording the presidential visit captured what was happening. She claimed five years later that she had intentionally left the chamber of the weapon vacant before she left for the meeting with the president in the park as she had no intention to kill him.

Fromme refused to cooperate in her own defense, and after being convicted and given a life sentence under a new federal law, she threw an apple at the U.S. Attorney arguing the case, hitting him in the face, and knocking off his glasses. She made a crazy comment, asserting that she was campaigning for "clean air, healthy water and respect for creatures and creation."

In 1979, Fromme attacked an inmate with the claw end of a hammer and was then transferred. In 1987, she escaped a prison camp in West Virginia, but was captured two days later and transferred to a federal prison in Texas. She had visions of somehow meeting up with Manson, who was still in prison in California, where he still resides. She was granted parole in August 2009, and reportedly moved to upstate New York, as no longer a threat to others, having served thirty-four years in prison.

The shock over this near assassination reverberated through the nation, with great relief that the very likeable president was safe. Vice President Rockefeller had been informed of what happened, and it probably planted the seeds of conservatives to demand that Rockefeller, far too liberal for their taste, would not be seen as acceptable, were Ford to be the nominee for a full term in the White House.[3]

But before there was much time for relief about the safety of President Ford, again, and unbelievable to most Americans, seventeen days later, on September 22, 1975, while again campaigning in California, in San Francisco, another assassination attempt took place, and again by a woman, to the shock of everyone. This time, it was a forty-five-year-old political radical, who seems to have been motivated by her revolutionary views and probably by the news of Lynette Fromme just two and a half weeks earlier.

Sara Jane Moore, born in West Virginia, had been a nursing school student, a recruit in the Women's Army Corp, and an accountant. She had had five marriages and divorces, four children, and then became extremely radical, having a fascination with the kidnapping of Patricia Hearst, one of the heirs to the Hearst journalism family's fortune, by the radical group known as the Symbionese Liberation Army. Surprisingly, Moore appears to have been an FBI informant, maybe because of her involvement with radical groups, because she is so listed in records of the Secret Service.

In what seems to be a very odd circumstance, Moore had been arrested the day before attempting to shoot President Ford, in possession of an illegal handgun, but with police confiscating her .44 caliber revolver and 113 rounds of ammunition. Earlier, the Secret Service had become aware of her, but saw her as no threat to the president. She was a danger, however, a far greater threat than Fromme. But despite the Secret Service confidence that she was not a concern, in actuality, she was a greater menace as she actually fired one shot. Fortunately, Moore was not two feet away, like Fromme, but was forty feet away, which saved the president. She had a .38 caliber revolver, while standing in a crowd across the street from the St. Francis Hotel. The sight on the gun was off center by six inches, and she narrowly missed hitting the president.

Realizing she had missed, she raised her arm again, and a Marine no longer on active duty, Oliver Sipple, lunged toward her, knocked her arm, and in so doing, almost certainly saved President Ford's life, and the shot went awry. The first shot ricocheted off the entrance to the hotel and slightly injured a bystander. If Moore had not had the firearm confiscated the day before, it is considered certain that she would have killed President Ford with the first shot, and Nelson Rockefeller would have been president, bringing to completion the worst nightmares of conservative Republicans, including presidential candidate Ronald Reagan.

The question that arises is whether Rockefeller would have been better able to defeat Jimmy Carter in the 1976 presidential election, and whether Ford, who came close to defeating Carter, might have won if he had kept Rockefeller on the election ticket, instead of selecting Senator Bob Dole of Kansas. This is all speculation, but many hearts stopped briefly, symbolically, on the news that Ford had been shot at a second time. As it turned out, this attempt was far more serious, and it had to sober President Ford on his extraordinarily good luck. Yet, it did not leave him afraid to appear in public, as he clearly understood that any president faces this kind of danger.

Moore pleaded guilty to attempted assassination in her trial, and was sentenced to life in prison and served thirty-two years, being released under probation at the end of 2007. She escaped from prison once in West Virginia for a few hours in 1979, and then was transferred to a federal women's prison in California, where she served the rest of her sentence. When she was released, she expressed the thought that she was glad she did not succeed in her mission to kill President Ford.

Although there were no more assassination attempts of this kind against Ford, there were a growing number of "White House intruders." This was a growing phenomenon, beginning with the threats of Robert K. Preston and Samuel Byck against President Nixon in February 1974. The number of reported attempts at "White House intrusion" grew to five cases, with one being repeated by the same intruder. The people involved include: Marshall H. Fields on December 25, 1974; Gerald B. Gainous on November 25 and December 6, 1975; Chester Plummer on July 27, 1976; and Steven B. Williams on December 1, 1976.[4]

Fields attempted an intrusion into the grounds of the White House complex on Christmas Day 1974. He surrendered, but only after four hours of negotiation, with White House security personnel being threatened by Fields. He crashed his car into the northwest gate, dressed in Arabic clothing, said he was the Messiah, and that he was laden with explosives, which were later shown to be flares. He got as far as the North Portico, several feet from the front door. The Ford family, fortunately, was not home at the time. The iron gates around the White House grounds, dating from the nineteenth century, were replaced as a result of this nerve-wracking incident.

Gainous was a D.C. resident, who climbed the fence surrounding the White House twice in eleven days in 1975, and apparently again in 1976, although no date is available for the latter year. In the first incident, he was on the grounds unimpeded for about an hour and a half, and actually approached presidential daughter Susan Ford as she was unloading camera equipment from her car. For that incident and the others, he was put on probation, but it unnerved the Secret Service. He claimed he wanted to ask the president for a pardon for his father, who had been convicted of conspiring to import heroin.

The most tragic intrusion under the Ford administration was that of Chester Plummer, an African American, who jumped the White House fence with a piece of pipe and was ordered to stop walking toward the White House by a Secret Service officer. He was shot when he failed to obey the order, dying later at the hospital. Plummer was the first known shooting victim on White House grounds, and an investigation led to the conclusion that he might have been looking for a way to commit suicide, attributed to mental problems from a divorce and an earlier arrest and probation for an indecent exposure charge. This seems to have been similar to "suicide by cop," wishing to draw attention to his unhappy life by being killed on White House grounds. There was no way to know if Plummer intended to attack President Ford, who was in the building at the time of the incident.

Finally, Steven B. Williams attempted to drive his pickup truck at twenty-five miles per hour through the new gates installed in reaction to the intrusion of Marshall Fields two years earlier. The truck was damaged, but the gates held strong and Williams was arrested.

Clearly protection of the president and first family and of the White House grounds became a much bigger security problem beginning with the 1970s, and continues so to this day with threats having multiplied constantly in the four decades since Gerald Ford became president.

14

RONALD REAGAN AT THE WASHINGTON HILTON HOTEL

Ronald Reagan (1911–2004) was the fortieth president of the United States (1981–1989) and had the second-greatest longevity of any American president, only six weeks less than Gerald R. Ford, both dying at the age of ninety-three. Reagan is regarded as a transformative president, who changed the direction of the federal government, which had been growing by leaps and bounds in the previous half century since the accession of Franklin D. Roosevelt and his New Deal programs in the 1930s.[1]

Reagan became the image of the revival and success of American conservatism, and he rejuvenated the Republican Party, which had been in decline after the success of American liberalism and the Democratic Party, and then harmed by the scandals of the Nixon administration in the decade before his election. Reagan also promoted "family values" and patriotism, which came under attack from hippies and protestors during the Vietnam War, but which made conservatives come to love him, his charisma, and his rhetoric.

With acting experience under his belt, Reagan became regarded as the "Great Communicator," who promoted cuts in domestic spending, a rebuilding of America's defenses by a direct challenge to the Soviet Union in the Cold War, and the advocating of social conservatism favored by the Religious Right. A former New Deal Democrat and a union leader (of the Screen Actors Guild in Hollywood), he offered a new direction on economic, social, and foreign policy issues, and became an iconic figure to many. From a Hollywood acting career where he attained moderate success, but never was considered a movie star, he became nationally noticed when he gave what many considered the best speech for the conservative Republican candidacy of Barry Goldwater in the presidential election of 1964. While Goldwater lost in a massive landslide to Lyndon B. Johnson, the political career of Ronald Reagan was born.

With encouragement of Southern California businessmen, Reagan ran for governor in 1966. He was considered an underdog to popular Governor Eugene "Pat" Brown, but won an upset landslide victory, demonstrating how underrated he had been and would continue to be. He would become controversial on his stands on education, law and order, and other issues, very willing to speak his mind and not worrying about being "politically correct." He made many enemies, but also gained many loyal supporters, and after a brief, uninspired run for president in 1968, won a second term as governor and became the national successor to Goldwater as the leading American conservative figure by the early 1970s.

As a result, he decided to challenge President Ford's attempt for a full term as president in 1976, and the struggle for the nomination created great tensions and stresses between the moderate wing of the party, represented by Ford, and the conservative wing, led by Reagan. Ford won the nomination by the tiniest of margins in delegates at the Republican National Convention, but Reagan won in convincing Ford that he should drop Vice President Nelson Rockefeller, who was anathema to conservatives, in favor of Kansas Senator Bob Dole as the vice presidential nominee.

When Ford lost to Jimmy Carter, it seemed to many that Reagan was the heir apparent, but his age seemed to be a negative, as he would reach just near seventy within months of the next national election. Many thought his career was over, but that was not to be. Reagan, challenged by much younger men, including George H. W. Bush, Howard Baker, and Bob Dole, Gerald Ford's vice presidential running mate from 1976, surprised everyone by winning the nomination, and choosing Bush as his running mate.

With a three-party race—Jimmy Carter and independent, but former Republican congressman, John Anderson—Reagan performed well in a debate with Carter, although he did poorly in a separate debate with Anderson, with Carter unwilling to debate Anderson. After what seemed like a close race, Reagan surprised many observers by winning a clear-cut and easy victory by ten points, with 51 percent to 41 percent for Carter and 7 percent for Anderson. The Iran hostage crisis and high inflation were the key issues that assisted Reagan's attack on Carter's term as president.

As Reagan entered the presidency, the Iranian hostage crisis that had gone on for 444 days under President Carter came to an end with the release of the hostages. This was a good beginning, but before Reagan had a real opportunity to pursue his goals of less federal spending on social programs and more on defense spending, social conservatism, and lowering the taxes on income and investments, the nation was jarred by the shock of a serious assassination attempt.[2] A young man fascinated with actress Jodie Foster, and wanting to impress her, decided that a way to do so would be to shoot and kill President Reagan.

This individual was John Hinckley Jr., twenty-five years old at the time of the assassination attempt and one of the children of John Hinckley Sr.—ironically, a financial supporter of the George H. W. Bush presidential campaign in 1980. The assassin's older brother, Scott, had been scheduled to be at the home of Vice President Bush's son Neil; he was a scheduled dinner date of a female friend of Neil Bush's wife the following evening after the assassination attempt.

This would lead to conspiracy theories that somehow the vice president and his family were connected to the attempted assassination of Reagan, as a way for Bush to become president. No one has seriously believed this to be fact, but it has added to the theory that Bush may have been a CIA agent somehow involved in the assassination of President Kennedy eighteen years earlier. Some have also wondered if Bush could have been involved in a conspiracy to bring down President Nixon in the Watergate scandal, with also the reality that Bush was one of the people on the short list to replace Vice President Spiro Agnew when he resigned in 1973 and Gerald Ford getting the nod instead.

John Hinckley Jr. grew up in a prosperous family with his father, John Hinckley Sr., being the president of an oil corporation. Hinckley grew up in the Dallas metropolitan area of Texas, was very athletic in high school, was skilled in playing the piano, and was elected class president twice. His life drifted after high school, dropping in and out of Texas Tech University, and going to Los Angeles in hopes of becoming a songwriter. Unable to fulfill his dream, he returned to his family home, which had been moved to Colorado.

Hinckley's troubles prompted him to take tranquilizers and antidepressants, and he started to buy firearms and practice with them on a regular basis. He also became obsessed with young actress Jodie Foster, who played a child prostitute in the 1976 film *The Taxi Driver*, in which actor Robert De Niro plots to assassinate a senator running for president. Hinckley saw the film at least fifteen times and became fixated on the character that De Niro played, which was based in part on the diaries of Arthur Bremer, the man who shot and wounded Alabama Governor George Wallace in 1972 in Laurel, Maryland.

Hinckley started to stalk Foster first when she entered Yale University and moved to New Haven, Connecticut. He slid poems and messages under her dormitory door and made phone calls to her that she hung up on. She made it clear in their brief conversations that she was not interested in meeting him. But still, he pursued her by enrolling himself in a writing class to be near her on campus, although never directly confronting her in person. After abandoning this fantasy, he now fantasized about hijacking a plane, as Samuel Byck had attempted to do in 1974 while stalking President Nixon and committing suicide, as Byck had done when confronted by police on the Delta airplane.

While laying out his plans to assassinate someone on the presidential level, Hinckley was arrested on a firearms charge in Nashville, Tennessee, where he had been stalking President Jimmy Carter, campaigning for reelection against Reagan and independent candidate Anderson. He was seen in crowds at Carter events in October 1980, but no direct threat was attempted at that time. His arrest on a firearms charge was not reported by the FBI to the Secret Service, even though it clearly should have been seen as a potential threat to Carter. He had three handguns and several rounds of ammunition in his carry-on luggage when he was arrested.

Hinckley's stalking of Carter weeks before the election brings about the scenario of what might have happened had he chosen to shoot and kill Carter. He got as close as one foot to the president without taking any action against him. If Carter had been seriously wounded or killed, it is conceivable that history would have been changed, as it is possible to believe a wounded Carter might have turned the tide in the upcoming election and defeated Reagan. If Carter had died, and Vice President Walter Mondale had become president with only a short time to the election, it is hard to imagine that sympathy and shock over what had happened would not have led to Mondale winning the election for a full term and, therefore, preventing Reagan from ever being president.

Instead of pursuing Carter, Hinckley went home after the arrest on firearms charges and underwent voluntary psychiatric treatment, which he desperately needed, but his mental health did not improve in a noticeable manner. After the inauguration of President Reagan, Hinckley started gathering information on Lee Harvey Oswald, the assassin of John F. Kennedy and the man he came to see as a role model, much like Arthur Bremer. He wrote a few more times to Foster, saying he was determined to "impress" her, leaving notes to her dean at Yale, which were turned over to the Yale police. The college police tried to track him down, but did not go further than that. On the morning of the assassination attempt, he wrote one more letter to Foster, but did not mail it. In the letter, he expressed his hope that she would be impressed with him and his action against the president. He wrote that he would abandon the idea of shooting Reagan if only he could "win your heart and live out the rest of my life with you."

In an ironic moment, on March 21, 1981, President Ronald Reagan visited Ford's Theatre in Washington, D.C., the site of the Lincoln assassination in 1865, and mused that if an assassin really wished to shoot a president in the present, even with lots of Secret Service protection, he probably could get close enough to accomplish his goal. This reminded observers of what John F. Kennedy had said in his hotel room the morning of his assassination in Dallas in 1963. It also reminded people of Lincoln having dreams about his own death and his casket being in the East Room of the White House weeks before his assassination.

Nine days later, on March 30, 1981, the nation was shocked to learn of the attempted assassination of Reagan as he left the Washington Hilton Hotel after a luncheon address to a labor audience of the AFL-CIO. Considered the safest hotel in D.C., with its enclosed passageway built after the Kennedy assassination, Reagan used that passageway to enter and leave the hotel. While generally wearing a bulletproof vest in public appearances, the president did not wear it that day, as his only public appearance would be the thirty feet between the hotel and the limousine he had arrived in. Even the Secret Service agents involved in the event were not wearing bulletproof vests, a major blunder on the part of the agency. Hinckley was in the crowd right near the front, but there was no thought that something horrible was about to happen.

At 2:27 p.m., President Reagan exited the hotel and was walking the short distance to his limousine. The Secret Service had screened those present at the hotel speech, but did not do so with the crowd behind a rope line in the front of the building, and Hinckley stood within fifteen feet of the president. By chance, Reagan passed right in front of Hinckley, and Hinckley fired six times with a Rohm RG-14 .22 long-rifle, blue steel revolver, firing the bullets within 1.7 seconds.

Thankfully, all six shots missed Reagan, miraculously, but the first shot hit White House Press Secretary James Brady in the head. The second shot hit D.C. Police Officer Thomas Delahanty in the back of his neck as he was turning to try and protect the president. The third shot hit the window of a building across the street from the incident. The fourth bullet hit Secret Service Officer Timothy McCarthy in the abdomen, as he tried to spread his body to protect Reagan. The fifth bullet hit the bullet resistant glass on the open side of the limousine.

The sixth bullet ricocheted off the armored side of the limousine and hit President Reagan in his left underarm, grazing his left-sided seventh rib, and entered his left lung, just about an inch from his heart. The lung began bleeding and collapsed. At the outset, Reagan's wound was more life threatening than that of James Garfield or William McKinley, who would have survived had modern surgical care been available to them.

Special Agent in Charge Jerry Parr had pushed the president into the limousine, and by knocking him into the car, had prevented Reagan from being hit in the head, which would have likely killed him, or left him paralyzed, as Press Secretary Brady would be so affected.

The agents at the scene knocked Hinckley down to the ground, but were intent to protect him from the crowd and not to lose him for prosecution, as Lee Harvey Oswald had been in Dallas in 1963. The gun was checked out by the ATF (Alcohol, Tobacco, and Firearms) agency, and it was revealed that the bullets were explosive in nature and would explode on contact. This was the case with the bullet in Brady. It caused massive brain damage, although Brady would survive and do as well as could be expected, thanks to a dedicated wife, Sarah Brady, and medical science. As a result of what happened to Brady, the "Brady Bill" became law in 1993, promoting gun control for ten years until 2004, and being promoted by Reagan as essential action. Sadly, Brady passed away on August 4, 2014, it was said, as a result of the wounds he suffered thirty-three years earlier. Fortunately, the bullet in Delahanty's neck was removed surgically with precautions, and it did not explode. McCarthy also recovered from his wounds.

Reagan had great pain in his rib, thinking his rib had been cracked by Parr pushing him into the limousine, but when he coughed up bright, frothy blood, it was realized that he had been shot, although indirectly by a ricocheting bullet. He was rushed to nearby George Washington University Hospital within four minutes, and First Lady Nancy Reagan left the White House and hurried to the hospital, while Hinckley was taken by Secret Service agents to a District of Columbia jail facility.

Reagan walked under his own power into the hospital emergency room, but then buckled at the knee, complaining of breathing troubles. His blood pressure was abnormal, and Reagan lost over half of his blood in the emergency room and in the surgery he underwent to remove the bullet and clean the wound. Had the bullet exploded and had he not arrived at the hospital within minutes of being shot, the damage could have been life threatening. He recovered without any unusual complications.

When Reagan arrived at the hospital, he remained conscious and joked to his wife: "Honey, I forgot to duck!" In the operating room, he took off his oxygen mask and joked: "I hope you are all Republicans!" The doctors and nurses laughed, and one doctor said all of the people involved in the surgery and medical treatment were Republicans for the day. The surgery went well, and antibiotics routinely were used because of fever complications after surgery.

Reagan's recovery was amazing for a seventy-year-old man. He left the hospital on the thirteenth day after the incident. Vice President George H. W. Bush was there to assist him, but Reagan worked a couple of hours in the residential quarters of the White House and held a cabinet meeting on day twenty-six, and there was no invocation of the Twenty-fifth Amendment, allowing an "acting president" in an emergency. He spoke to Congress on April 28, to thunderous applause. He went on a trip outside D.C. after seven weeks of recovery and held a press conference on day seventy-nine after the event. Reagan came to believe that his survival was thanks to God's intervention, and it motivated him to work to fulfill his mission to pursue his programs. His popularity soared to 73 percent in public opinion polls. There was a sense of unity for a while not common in the nation's capital.

Some have speculated that the shooting undermined Reagan mentally, and that there were signs of dementia and Alzheimer's showing up in the second term after 1985. Reagan's son Ron Reagan Jr. believed this, but it was vehemently denied by Reagan's other son, Michael Reagan, the adopted son of Reagan and his first wife, Jane Wyman, who denounced his stepbrother for his claims about their father.

John Hinckley Jr. was found not guilty by reason of insanity on June 21, 1982, with the defense winning the argument over the prosecution, which declared him sane. He did not testify in the trial. Hinckley was confined at St. Elizabeth's Hospital in Washington, D.C., and is still detained there, although he has been allowed to leave the hospital over the years, first for supervised visits with his parents, and then unsupervised visits, which have led to great criticism, most notably from Nancy Reagan. Some experts have said that Hinckley is no longer a threat to anyone, but others have claimed that he is still a danger to others and has elements of suicide and lawlessness in his personality, after thirty-four years. Some have said that he is perfectly capable of deceiving medical personnel relating to his true mental state.

As of 2015, Hinckley is allowed up to seventeen days a month at home with his aging mother in Williamsburg, Virginia. But he has Secret Service agents trailing him, and he must wear an ankle bracelet GPS tracker that records his movements. He has been known to visit Petsmart stores and Wendy's Restaurants on his travels by foot around his mother's home. There is still great dismay that he can walk around freely, since he had come so close to the assassination of a president. But the triumph is that Reagan became the first sitting president to be shot and survive the assassination attempt fully recovered, with only former President Theodore Roosevelt in 1912 having the same good fortune.[3]

Besides the Hinckley incident, the White House continued the trend of having "invasions," despite the new security measures put into effect during the Ford administration. Two such cases have been documented. The first was David Mahonski, a twenty-five-year-old electrician from Williamsport, Pennsylvania. Mahonski was shot by a White House guard on March 15, 1984, after being under FBI surveillance for making threats against Reagan. He was noticed in front of the south grounds of the White House, and he took out a sawed-off shotgun from underneath his coat, and as a result, he was shot in the arm with a revolver, arrested, and sent for psychiatric evaluation.[4]

Robert Latta, forty-five years old, a water meter reader from Denver, Colorado, passed security on Inauguration Day, January 20, 1985, by following the Marine band and wasn't checked by the Secret Service. He wandered around the White House for fourteen minutes before being stopped, claiming he just wanted to see the White House. He was jailed for five days, sent to a psychiatric examination, and committed to St. Elizabeth's Hospital, where John Hinckley was already residing. He was later released and was not further tracked, but it was clear that he could have been a danger to the president, the First Lady, or others on Inauguration Day, but luckily nothing happened.

Ronald Reagan went on to serve two full terms as president and to be regarded as a path-breaking, significant president, who changed the tone of American government and politics. There has been constant debate and arguments, then and since, about Reagan's record in office. Many critics would point out that Reagan often strayed off conservative dogma. He raised taxes multiple times, while tripling the national debt. The worst unemployment since the 1930s occurred in 1982, reaching a level of 10.8 percent. Reagan showed little concern for the poor and the homeless and ignored the issue of AIDS until his second term, when actor Rock Hudson died from the disease. Reagan also produced the worst environmental record of any president, and this following one of the three best environmental presidents, Jimmy Carter. At the same time, Reagan signed an immigration amnesty bill in 1986, which has been condemned by conservatives in their determination to prevent any further immigration reform bills which allow the possibility of amnesty.

Reagan also vetoed an anti-apartheid bill relating to South Africa, with Congress overriding the veto, a rare occurrence, in 1986. Reagan also fought a proxy war with the Soviets by training, arming, and funding the Islamic Mujahideen, including Osama bin Laden. He also allowed selling of arms to Iran, using the proceeds to help the "contras" in Nicaragua, who were fighting against the Marxist government of Daniel Ortega. This became known as the Iran Contra scandal. However, he signed arms limitation agreements with Soviet Premier Mikhail Gorbachev to lessen the danger of nuclear confrontation, after first terming the Soviet government under Leonid Brezhnev the "evil empire."

He remained highly popular with the American people, based on public opinion polls, and when he left office in 1989, he was a rare case of a president leaving office with a positive image. Even when his low point of popularity had occurred during the Iran Contra scandal in the second term of his presidency, his personality and manner helped him to overcome the temporary decline in his public image.

When he informed the American people of his Alzheimer's diagnosis in 1994, and disappeared from public scrutiny for the last ten years of his life until his death in 2004, his popularity continued to be very high, and the nation mourned his death on June 5, 2004. He was given full honors and respect as any former or sitting chief executive of the nation has upon death.

Reagan would be remembered positively for helping to undermine the Soviet Union with his "Strategic Defense Initiative," and therefore helping to bring the Cold War to an end early in the administration of his successor, George H. W. Bush. He would also be remembered for having rebuilt American defenses and for promoting a restoration of patriotism among the American people. He had proven resolute when he needed to be, and realistic when that was necessary, as well as having an idealism about the American republic and people that was contagious. He has been ranked as number ten or number eleven in most polls of our presidents. On Presidents Day in February of every year, he and John F. Kennedy switch positions as the most popular and respected presidents in American history.

15

LATE TWENTIETH-CENTURY PRESIDENTS AND ASSASSINATION THREATS

The late twentieth-century presidents all have faced assassination threats, but none of them have had a direct confrontation with a would-be assassin.[1] All have been part of a growing spread of death threats and White House grounds intrusion.

Jimmy Carter, our thirty-ninth president, born in 1924, was president for one term from 1977 to 1981, and seen by many as an outstanding former president, with his numerous activities promoting democracy, human rights, advancement of health and education worldwide, and international diplomacy, and he remains active despite his advanced age. Carter has gained more stature in the years after his presidency than during his controversial White House tenure, and he remains the subject of intense debate by scholars and political activists. Regarded by many as a "failed" president, or at least a president who should be ranked low on the list of presidents, others would argue that he will have a renaissance once he passes from the scene, similar to what occurred with President Harry Truman after he died in 1972.

Carter was seen as a dark horse, who no one expected would ever be president, when he announced what seemed like a long shot bid for the presidency after his one term as a reform-oriented governor of Georgia from 1971 to 1975. Seen as a "New South" governor in the era of civil rights advancement, Carter personified the changes coming to the South after the passage of the Civil Rights Act of 1964 and the Voting Rights

Act of 1965, the latter law restoring the right to vote of African Americans, which had been denied for three quarters of a century. Carter represented a new trend in Southern politics, and his brilliant smile and determination to bring change to a state which had elected racial supremacists throughout the years after Reconstruction up to the late 1960s was a refreshing change. He was noticed by many for his reforms of state government.

But the thought that the nation was to have its first elected president from the South since Zachary Taylor in 1848 who had not previously succeeded to the presidency by the death of the incumbent, as with Lyndon B. Johnson, seemed highly theoretical and unlikely to happen. However, Carter surprised everyone when he organized a great campaign team, won the New Hampshire primary, and overcame the opposition of Arizona Congressman Morris Udall, Idaho Senator Frank Church, and California Governor Jerry Brown to win the Democratic nomination for president in 1976. An unknown quantity in the nation's capital, Carter wisely selected Senator Walter Mondale, a close associate of former Vice President Hubert Humphrey (himself the Democratic nominee for president in 1968, and a contender in 1972 and briefly in 1976), to be his running mate. Mondale was seen as an "insider" to D.C., while Carter had never visited the nation's capital in his entire life.

After the Watergate scandal under President Richard Nixon soured the American people on government, Carter ran a campaign promoting "honesty in government." This was an effective campaign, as this unknown quantity would overcome President Gerald Ford in a close race in the Electoral College. Most observers believed that Ford would have won if he had not pardoned former President Nixon from prosecution, and if he had selected Vice President Nelson Rockefeller for his full-term run for the White House—a move that Ford felt unable to do because of conservative Republican opposition led by former Governor Ronald Reagan.

Carter came into office with great optimism that he would transform American politics with his decency and honesty. Carter was certainly fortunate to have Vice President Mondale, a solid and seasoned politician, to whom he gave much authority and responsibility, and their relationship would bring them closer personally than any presidential–vice presidential team in the past. Carter and Mondale would eventually become the longest surviving team after the presidential term—in 2015, thirty-four years and counting.

The optimism that Carter and the nation felt in early 1977 would, however, become tinged with disillusionment, as the president faced many issues and controversies that would undermine his term in office. He would have great success in negotiating the Camp David Accords between Israeli Prime Minister Menachem Begin and Egyptian President Anwar El-Sadat, bringing about the first diplomatic recognition of Israel by any Arab nation. Carter would also negotiate the end of American control of the Panama Canal by the year 2000, with a tough, hard fought struggle on a treaty, which narrowly gained passage in the Senate. He would also promote the concept of human rights in foreign policy and cut off aid to the right-wing dictatorships that violated the rights of their citizenry. This would include such nations as Chile, Nicaragua, Haiti, Taiwan, the Philippines, and Liberia, among others. This promotion of human rights split conservatives and Republicans from him and led to a change in direction and emphasis under his successor, Ronald Reagan.

Domestically, Carter promoted a massive increase in public lands and environmental regulation. Many experts now regard him as the third greatest environmental president, only trailing Theodore Roosevelt and Richard Nixon. He worked to promote alternative sources of energy, including solar and wind sources, as reaction to the Arab oil embargo of 1978–1979. He also made advancements in civil rights and advocated deregulation of many industries. Additionally, three new cabinet agencies were created, including the Education, Health and Human Services, and Energy departments.

But seen in a negative light were the problems of inflation, as a result of the Arab oil embargo, and the oncoming of an economic recession in 1980, as the reelection campaign of the president began. As Reagan would later declare, "Are you better off than you were four years ago?" with higher consumer prices, higher interest rates, and higher mortgage rates, along with higher unemployment, later referred to by him as the "Misery Index," which helped to build opposition to Carter.

At the same time, the Soviet invasion of Afghanistan and the Iranian hostage crisis made Carter look weak and ineffective in late 1979, up to the election of 1980. Carter's inability to stop the Soviet invasion, his decision to begin a grain trade embargo, and the prevention of U.S. participation in the Moscow Olympics made him more unpopular. Also, the inability to gain the release of fifty-two Americans held hostage by radicals backed by Ayatollah Khomeini of Iran for a total of 444 days was a crisis that constantly undermined Carter. His attempt at a rescue mission in 1980 was a total disaster and seemed to seal his fate.

When Fidel Castro initiated the Mariel Boatlift in 1980, allowing about 125,000 Cubans, mostly released from prison or desperately poor citizens, to leave Cuba on rafts and rickety boats for the Florida Keys and the mainland of Florida, Carter was unable to stop the massive influx. This added to the feeling that Carter was weak, ineffective, and lacked international respect as the leader of the Free World.

His inadequate performance in debate with Ronald Reagan assured his defeat, and he sustained the second-worst percentage in defeat in American history (41 percent) up to that point of time, but later the third worst, when George H. W. Bush lost to Bill Clinton in 1992 and received a lower percentage of the total popular vote (37 percent).

While in office Carter came under threat from an unemployed American drifter from Ohio named Raymond Lee Harvey, who was arrested on May 5, 1979, by the Secret Service. The similarity of his name to Lee Harvey Oswald has unnerved many people. He was found in possession of a starter pistol with blank rounds just ten minutes before President Carter was to give a speech in Los Angeles at the Civic Center Mall. He was in the crowd waiting to hear Carter's speech and drew the attention of a Secret Service agent because he seemed overly nervous and had rapidly walked away when being approached.

Harvey talked freely and claimed to be connected to three Latino men who had asked him to create a diversion by shooting the starter pistol into the ground, allowing these men to fire upon Carter from their hotel room or some undisclosed other location. Harvey claimed he had tested the starter pistol the night before the event, firing seven blank rounds on the roof of the Alan Hotel, and then spent the night with a man named Osvaldo Espinoza Ortiz. Ortiz was standing ten feet away when Harvey was apprehended.

It was clear that Harvey had been drinking, and that he had a history of mental illness, but he was found with the pistol, with eight spent rounds in his pocket, and seventy unspent blank rounds for the weapon. Also, a room at the Alan Hotel had been rented to a man with an Hispanic name, Umberto Camacho, one of the three Latino men. Ortiz, also detained, gave the name, and the room had a shotgun case and three unspent rounds of ammunition, so the whole situation appeared to be a serious threat. Harvey and Ortiz were both jailed under suspicion of being involved in a plot, but both were later released, with the case dismissed for a lack of evidence. The two other supposed conspirators were never found, including the person who had rented the hotel room, but left the morning of the Carter speech. Harvey was thirty-five at the time of the incident, and Ortiz was twenty-one years of age.

Had Carter become a victim of this reported threat, Mondale would have become president, and he would, most likely, have conducted himself very well in the office, as he had been well informed about all presidential decisions as one of Carter's closest advisers, and had briefly sought the presidency himself for 1976 before deciding not to run. Of course, he later ran for president in 1984, losing to Reagan, and then went on to be U.S. ambassador to Japan under President Bill Clinton in the mid-1990s.

As discussed earlier in the chapter on Reagan and John Hinckley, Hinckley had stalked Carter in October 1980, and had Carter been harmed or killed, one can speculate that Reagan might not have won the presidency over Carter in light of sympathy of the assassination attempt on Carter. And if Mondale had succeeded Carter with only weeks to go before the election in 1980, it is possible to believe that Mondale might have defeated Reagan and served at least one full term as president, in addition to finishing about three months of the unexpired Carter term in the White House.

There were also two reported White House intruders, or "fence jumpers," during the Carter administration. In October 1978, Anthony Henry, claiming that the words "In God We Trust" on U.S. currency was blasphemy, decided he would speak to President Carter directly on that subject. He was carrying a Bible and wearing a white karate suit as he climbed over the White House fence onto the north grounds. Having walked about fifteen yards, Henry was apprehended by Secret Service agents and Uniformed Division officers. He then proceeded to pull a knife from inside the Bible and slashed one officer's face and another agent's arm. He was subsequently surrounded by officers with long batons, and they poked the knife out of his hand and forced him to the ground and arrested him. No further information is available as to the disposition of the case.

Also, on August 4, 1980, a man named Michael John Strickland jumped the White House fence on the southwest corner, walked on the property, and came within one hundred yards of someone believed to be

President Carter on the South Lawn, before being arrested by Secret Service agents and park police. Eventually, he received a one-year sentence, but it was commuted to one day, and he was given one-year probation.[2]

The Raymond Lee Harvey case was the only reported possible attempt on Carter's life while in office, but the former president claimed in 2013 in an interview that he has been targeted for assassination consistently since he left the presidency. He asserted that he has faced at least three domestic assassination attempts since 1981 and is constantly warned by the Secret Service on potential threats during his consistent overseas travels. He has become the most threatened former president in American history, and yet, he says he does not worry about his safety and is determined to continue his commitment to conduct humanitarian activities as part of his Carter Center's work overseas.

There is one reported assassination threat against former President Carter after he left office, on which we have details, and that involved one of Carter's many trips to the Middle East, trying to resolve the Israeli-Palestinian dispute over the West Bank and the Gaza Strip, and the "two state" solution, long promoted by Carter and many others. Carter had visited Israel, the West Bank, the Gaza Strip, Lebanon, and Syria on his continuous mission for peace and reconciliation in June 2009. On this trip, the radical Palestinian group Hamas had foiled an attempt by terrorists to assassinate the former president. Supposedly, an al Qaeda–linked group had planted two roadside bombs along the road that Carter was traveling on, at a checkpoint between Gaza and Israel. It was also reported that Israeli security officials had passed on the warning of the threat to Carter's security detail.[3]

It is clear that Jimmy Carter, winner of the Nobel Peace Prize in 2002, will not allow threats against his life to deter his commitment to the causes he believes in, all of which add to his stature. In good health at his advanced age, he moves toward life longevity that, with good luck, will allow him the opportunity to challenge the age of presidents Ford and Reagan, both of whom reached ninety-three.

Eight years after Jimmy Carter was forcibly retired from the White House, George H. W. Bush became our forty-first president and successor to Ronald Reagan. He was born in 1924 about four months before Carter. He served one term as president from 1989 to 1993, after having served as Reagan's vice president for two terms. He became the first vice president to succeed directly by election, rather than by succession as a result of death or resignation of the sitting president, since Martin Van Buren followed Andrew Jackson into the presidency in 1837, 152 years earlier.

Bush's father, Prescott Bush, had been a banker and has been accused in retrospect of having had financial dealings with Adolf Hitler in the 1930s and early 1940s, and also of being involved in the reported Business Plot conspiracy that was never completed under FDR in 1933–1934. Prescott Bush later served as a Republican senator from Connecticut.

Prescott Bush's son, George H. W. Bush, has been said by some conspiracy theorists to have been a CIA agent in the early 1960s. As stated earlier in the John F. Kennedy chapter of this book, there is a photograph supposedly of Bush in Dealey Plaza in Dallas on November 22, 1963, making some people believe he is implicated in the JFK assassination, although most of the accusation is simply conspiracy, and it is known photos can be manufactured.

Bush tried for election to the U.S. Senate twice, in 1964 and 1970, but failed to become part of the upper chamber. He had made his own personal wealth by leaving his New England boyhood in Maine and Connecticut and migrating to the oil fields of Texas. While failing to become a U.S. senator, Bush served two terms as a congressman from Houston, Texas, from 1967 to 1971, the only elected office he ever held, other than the vice presidency and presidency.

Despite his lack of electoral successes early in his career, Bush became regarded as a solid person of accomplishment and experience, as a result of having served as ambassador to the United Nations under President Nixon; Republican National chairman under Nixon and President Ford; ambassador to China under Ford; and CIA head under Ford. Few presidents have had the wide variety of experiences and responsibilities that Bush had before serving as vice president and president. He was seen as significant enough that he was on a list of potential vice presidential appointments to replace resigned Vice President Spiro Agnew, but Gerald Ford was chosen.

Bush sought the presidency in 1980 as the major rival of Ronald Reagan, ending second in delegate numbers, and accepted the vice presidential nomination. He was not seen as personally close to Reagan in his views on public issues, but adapted to the president while in office as vice president for the next eight years. Bush was seen as a positive force on foreign policy, and on knowledge of D.C. and how things worked, in that regard playing a similar role to Reagan as Walter Mondale had done for Jimmy Carter. The Reagan-Bush connection, while not quite as close as Carter-Mondale, was still an effective governing duo.

When Bush ran for the presidency, overcoming GOP opponents including Bob Dole, he came into office regarded as the most experienced and qualified president in foreign affairs since Richard Nixon. His time would see the end of the Cold War, including the dismantling of the Berlin Wall; the liberation of Eastern Europe; the downfall of the Soviet Union, with its replacement by the Russian Federation; and the reunification of Germany. In domestic matters, Bush would promote the passage of the Americans with Disabilities Act, an important piece of legislation to add to the Civil Rights Act of 1964.

However, Bush will always be most remembered for his prosecution of the Persian Gulf War of 1991 against Iraq's dictator, Saddam Hussein, in an alliance with the United Nations. Bush launched the war after Iraq's invasion of Kuwait, and because of the growing threat to Saudi Arabia and to the oil supply of the Middle East by the ambitions of Hussein. This short six-week war was a great success and led Bush's public opinion rating to soar to 91 percent in the polls, making him seem invincible in his reelection bid in 1992. For a while, it seemed almost pointless for any opposition Democrat to run for president, but once the nation fell into a recession in 1992, Bush's public opinion ratings dropped dramatically.

Bush would be opposed in the presidential primaries by former Nixon and Reagan adviser Pat Buchanan, although he would easily overcome the challenge. But then he faced the young, charismatic Arkansas Governor Bill Clinton and billionaire independent nominee Ross Perot, and lost the 1992 presidential election, gaining the second-worst popular vote performance in defeat of any incumbent president in history, with only 37 percent of the popular vote. Only William Howard Taft in 1912, with 23 percent of the popular vote, had performed worse than Bush.

While in office, George H. W. Bush certainly had many death threats against him, particularly as a result of the Persian Gulf War against Saddam Hussein, but there are no published reports of such threats, and none were direct. But there was one White House intruder, who went over the fence in 1991, named Gustav Leijohhufved, a Swedish national, who was on the White House grounds undetected until he reached a guard post outside the West Wing. Thankfully, he was not armed.

Based on public records, Bush had fewer threats to contend with than Nixon, Ford, Carter, and Reagan. However, there was one serious threat against Bush which occurred after he left the presidency; this apparent attempt against his life came from Saddam Hussein, who wished revenge on Bush for the Persian Gulf War. Bush, just months after leaving the presidency, had traveled to Kuwait on April 14–16, 1993, and two suspects were arrested for having planted a 175-pound car bomb in Kuwait City. The bomb had a remote control detonator, plastic explosives, and electronic circuitry and wiring, which would have allowed it to cause a massive explosion as Bush traveled in Kuwait City.

The two arrested suspects were Iraqi nationals named Ra'ad Abdel-Amir al-Assadi and Wali Abdelhadi Ghazali, who had plans to park the bomb laden car near the motorcade route. From a distance of 300–500 feet, a remote control would have set off the bomb, and it was later estimated by the FBI that it would have destroyed everyone and everything within a quarter mile of the explosion. If by some chance, the detonation failed, then the plan was for Ghazali to approach Bush, wearing a bomb belt around his waist, and blow up both of them.

The plot was connected to Saddam Hussein and his public declaration after the Persian Gulf War that his aim was to punish Bush for the war defeat of Iraq. Once this information was gathered and confirmed, President Bill Clinton responded by having U.S. Navy ships launch twenty-three Tomahawk missiles against the headquarters of the Iraqi Intelligence Service in Baghdad on June 26, 1993, as the U.S. government's response to the attempt to assassinate President Bush. Clinton gave an Oval Office address to the nation to announce the action, which was hailed by leaders of both political parties in Congress as proper and the best action that could be taken to deter future aggression, as attempts to target an individual, namely, Saddam Hussein, would be much more difficult to accomplish.[4]

Bush has gone on to be respected and honored as an elder statesman in the twenty-plus years since he left the presidency, and he has lived to see two of his sons become governor of their states, Jeb Bush in Florida and George W. Bush in Texas. He survived to see George W. become the forty-third president of the United States, and Jeb to be seriously considered as a presidential candidate, even as we look ahead to the presidential election of 2016.

George H. W. Bush's successor, Bill Clinton, born in 1946, and serving as our forty-second president from 1993 to 2001, became the first Baby Boomer president, and was the first Democratic president to be reelected to a second term in office since Franklin D. Roosevelt. He would become supremely popular among the vast majority of the American people, even when he was impeached on what many thought were flimsy legal grounds by the Republican House of Representatives in 1998. He survived the impeachment trial in early 1999 and left office at an unusually high public opinion rating, very rare for a president who served two terms in office.

Clinton overcame a difficult childhood, with a widowed mother and an abusive stepfather, and yet developed into a confident, outgoing, charismatic young man who attended both Georgetown University and Oxford University, and he graduated from Yale Law School, where he met his future wife. Hillary Rodham Clinton would be an activist First Lady on the level of Eleanor Roosevelt. Then, after her husband's presidency, she would serve as a U.S. senator from New York and as secretary of state under her political rival for the 2008 Democratic presidential nomination, Barack Obama. She is now seen as the leading Democratic candidate for the presidential election of 2016, with many observers thinking she has a lead for becoming the next president of the United States on January 20, 2017.

Bill Clinton would serve as Arkansas attorney general at the young age of thirty, and at age thirty-two, he would be elected governor of Arkansas, the second-youngest governor in American history, with only thirty-one-year-old Harold Stassen of Minnesota in 1941 having been younger in office. Clinton would serve twelve years as Arkansas's chief executive, only losing a two-year term in 1980, but coming back for the next ten years until his election to the presidency in 1992.

As president, Clinton attempted a massive health-care reform, which became known as "Hillary Care," as the First Lady was intimately involved in its unsuccessful promotion. He faced constant investigation on charges stemming from his time as governor of Arkansas, and the connection of his wife to the Rose Law Firm in Little Rock. Clinton also faced defeat in his attempt to end discrimination against gays and lesbians in the military, instead accepting the concept of "Don't Ask, Don't Tell" as the best deal he could get on that matter. Clinton did accomplish the North American Free Trade Agreement to promote international trade without major tariff barriers. He promoted education and health reforms of a more modest nature, in line with his centrist Democratic approach, and the reality of opposition Republicans controlling both houses of Congress in the last six years of his two terms in office.

In foreign policy, he accomplished the end of Serbia's war in the Balkans by utilizing bombing to stop the mass murders in Bosnia in 1995, and similar action in Kosovo in 1999, but he failed to stop genocide in Rwanda in 1994. He also brought a resolution of the conflict in Northern Ireland between Great Britain and the Irish Republican Army in 1998, and attempted, unsuccessfully, to bring about a resolution of the Israeli-Palestinian conflict in his last years in the presidency.

However, terrorism by al Qaeda and Osama bin Laden was difficult to resolve, and there were a number of terrorist incidents, including the first bombing of the World Trade Center in New York City in 1993, and bombings in two American embassies in Kenya and Tanzania in 1998. Clinton spent a lot of time trying to overcome al Qaeda, but was unable to do so, and some have blamed the second attack on the World Trade Center and the Pentagon under his successor, George W. Bush, on Clinton's failures. Clinton also tried to rein in the continued threat of Iraq under Saddam Hussein, including the bombing of the Iraqi Intelligence Service offices after Hussein attempted the assassination of former President George H. W. Bush on a visit to Kuwait in April 1993.

During Clinton's presidency, he received great support from the American people because of the robust economy that he served under, in which Americans enjoyed the greatest economic expansion and prosperity they had seen in many decades. In later years, this was attributed to the technology boom, making Clinton more the recipient of good fortune, rather than the initiator of it. But he remained extremely popular in the second decade of the twenty-first century, nearly fifteen years after leaving the White House. He hoped his popularity would help his wife win the presidency and allow a return of the former president to a major role in another Clinton administration.

Bill Clinton faced a number of threats, none direct, but still disconcerting, while in office. This included White House intruders Frank Eugene Corder on September 12, 1994, and Francisco Martin Duran about seven weeks later on October 29, 1994. But even before these intruders, there was the January 1994 case of Ronald Gene Barbour of Florida, a former military officer, freelance writer, and limousine driver, who made traceable calls to kill the president, planning on attacking him while Clinton was on one of his morning jogging runs on the National Mall. Clinton was in Europe at that particular time, and thirty-nine-year-old Barbour returned to Florida, but he was quickly arrested the following month and charged with threatening to kill the president. A handgun was found, and he was remanded for psychiatric evaluation and eventually served five years in prison, being released in 1998.[5]

Just about the most startling threat toward Clinton was that of thirty-eight-year-old Corder, who crashed a stolen Cessna 150 plane on the South Lawn of the White House in September 1994, with apparent intention to hit the building. He was alone in his plane, and crashed the plane at 1:49 a.m., dying upon impact. There is no indication of Corder having any issues with President Clinton, who was living at Blair House with his family, since the White House was undergoing renovations. Corder had gone through rough times, including an arrest for theft and one for drug dealing. He had served time in a drug rehabilitation center, and then his third wife left him, putting him into a state of deep depression and suicidal tendencies. He had a drinking problem as well and had stolen the plane while intoxicated, and it was believed he just wanted publicity for what was seen as a stunt and not politically motivated. However, it was still seen as dangerous as he had entered restricted air space, and there had been no response by the Secret Service. It seemed as if that agency had flubbed on this potential security risk.[6]

An even more dangerous and real threat was that of twenty-six-year-old Duran, who fired twenty-nine rounds from an SKS rifle at the White House from outside the fence of the North Lawn of the White House in October 1994. The firearm was a 7.62 x 39 mm SKS semi-automatic rifle (Chinese-made copy Type 56), and it was fired at a group of men in dark business suits. Duran, wearing a trench coat, was immediately attacked by three citizens who tackled him and pinned his arms until he was subdued by Secret Service agents running across the lawn toward the fence with their guns drawn. The president was inside the building watching a football game, but was unharmed, and no one was hurt by the incident.

In a two-week trial, Duran was charged with attempted murder of the president and four counts of assaulting a federal officer, referring to Secret Service agents. He was also indicted for illegal possession of a firearm by a convicted felon, since he had been convicted of aggravated assault with a vehicle while in the U.S. Army and had served time in prison. He was also prosecuted for use of an assault weapon, destruction of U.S. property, and interstate transportation of a firearm with intent to commit a felony.

Duran pleaded insanity, including his belief that he was saving the world from aliens in Colorado, but more than sixty witnesses testified of his past statements of hating President Clinton and the U.S. government, and he was convicted by the jury after about five hours of deliberation and sentenced to forty years in prison. He is presently serving his sentence at a prison in Colorado, and he has the possibility of release in 2029 after thirty-five years served.[7]

A fourth threat was presented by Leland William Modjeski, thirty-seven years old, who was shot on the White House grounds by Secret Service agents on May 24, 1995. A Virginia resident, Modjeski had serious psychological problems and was deeply depressed, and seemed to want to be shot and killed by law enforcement authorities. A former doctoral student at George Mason University in psychology, Modjeksi had recently lost his pizza delivery job.

Wearing a business suit, Modjeski scaled the White House fence at 10:45 p.m., in possession of a .38 caliber revolver, but it was unloaded, and he had no ammunition on his person. He moved toward the Jacqueline Kennedy garden near the East Wing, and was then seen by Secret Service agents who tackled him. He was shot by another Secret Service agent when he saw what turned out to be an unloaded weapon, with Modjeski being hit in the left arm, as well as the agent who tackled him being hit by that agent in the left forearm. Both underwent surgery for non-life-threatening injuries.

President Clinton was in a White House meeting with his chief of staff, Leon Panetta, and had only recently returned to the mansion from a Democratic Party fundraiser, making some wonder if Modjeski was stalking Clinton, but it seemed highly unlikely. Hillary Clinton was sleeping, and daughter Chelsea Clinton was finishing her homework at the time of the incident. Modjeski was sent to St. Elizabeth's Mental Hospital in Washington, D.C., upon recommendation of a psychologist, and no further information has been uncovered about this matter. His wife and neighbors said he seemed normal and sensible, but something had gone awry which led him to arrest and mental hospital admission.[8]

This marked the fifth incident in nine months, including one involving undetected and never identified assailants who fired on the White House from the south side of the mansion, eventually leading to a decision to close off Pennsylvania Avenue to cars and trucks in front of the White House as a security measure.

In addition to this series of threats in 1994 and 1995, Clinton was also subjected to a potential attack overseas in Manila, capital of the Philippines, in 1996, when he attended the Asia-Pacific Economic Cooperation summit, and was scheduled to pass over a local road.[9] His route had to be changed after evidence was uncovered that explosives had been planted on a bridge that the Clinton procession would have traveled over. Thankfully, by precautions to protect the president from possible harm, Clinton was safe, as he might have been killed had he overruled his Secret Service detail to save time on his schedule. It was later revealed by government sources that the plot had been hatched by, of all people, Osama bin Laden. Altogether, six threats were made against the life of our forty-second president while in office.

No other reported threats against Bill Clinton are known, but there had been some harrowing moments from 1994 to 1996, and it is certain that there were other threats uncovered by the Secret Service, but not revealed to the public, and that this likely continued in his post-presidential years.

As the twentieth century ended, the number of threats against Bill Clinton were a hint of what was to come, although no one could have known it at the time. We were not yet fully aware of the nature of domestic and foreign terrorism, and lived in a hope and belief that the security of the president of the United States would not become ever more difficult. But the presidency of George W. Bush, and then, even more, of Barack Obama, made clear that there would be constant and growing threats against our national leaders, making essential the need for upgraded security, and the importance of having a supremely qualified vice president that would be able to step in if an emergency arose regarding the president's life and security. The mounting threats made one wonder why anyone would want to take on the challenge of the presidency, as it was clear, no matter what political ideology, race, nationality, or gender a future president might be, there would be constant threats against whoever was president, presenting a massive challenge to the Secret Service.

16

TWENTY-FIRST-CENTURY PRESIDENTS AND ASSASSINATION THREATS

In the twenty-first century, as of 2014, both presidents George W. Bush and Barack Obama have faced growing numbers of assassination threats and dangers, but none directly.[1]

George W. Bush, born in 1946, our forty-third president, the son of the forty-first president, George H. W. Bush, served in the Oval Office from 2001 to 2009. This was only the second case of a father-son presidency, after that of John Adams and John Quincy Adams; both sons had the distinction of losing the national popular vote, but winning the Electoral College and being inaugurated as president. George W. was also the second Baby Boomer president, about six weeks older than his predecessor, Bill Clinton.

Bush served six years as governor of Texas and was seen by many as the front-runner for the presidential nomination of his party in 2000, although he faced a serious challenge from Arizona Senator John McCain. Bush ended up as the nominee, and chose former Defense Secretary Dick Cheney as his vice presidential running mate, with Cheney being the Washington "insider," who had also served in Congress from Wyoming, and had earlier on been chief of staff under President Gerald Ford. Cheney was five and a half years older than Bush, and was seen by many, particularly in the first Bush term, as being very close to a co-president, but his power diminished in Bush's second term.

Bush came into office intending to focus on domestic matters, but as it turned out, the al Qaeda attack on the World Trade Center and the Pentagon on September 11, 2001, transformed his presidency and the future of America for both its future presidents and its citizenry. Congress quickly passed the PATRIOT Act in response to 9/11, which is seen as a violation of the civil liberties of Americans, but justified by the government, both under Bush and President Obama, as essential and necessary to deal with the threat of domestic and foreign terrorism for the long-term future security of the country.

Bush became highly controversial for his decision to promote massive tax cuts for the wealthy, as well as his decision to pursue a war with Iraq and its leader, Saddam Hussein, who had lost the Persian Gulf War under Bush's father, and had tried to kill his father in Kuwait in 1993, when the father had already retired as president. His pursuit of al Qaeda and Taliban terrorists in Afghanistan failed to accomplish its goal, and the war in Afghanistan would end up as the longest continuous war effort in American history, with the Iraq War the second longest in our nation's history. Finally, his mishandling of Hurricane Katrina and the damage to New Orleans, and also Mississippi and Alabama, undermined his popularity.

His attempt to privatize the Social Security system failed to pass, but his push for a prescription drug plan for senior citizens, which had a difficult beginning, has become quite popular as the years have gone by. His popularity suffered when America went into severe recession in 2008–2009, often called the Great Recession, the worst economic downturn since the Great Depression of the 1930s. Many have criticized his economic policies as the causes of the Great Recession, with its aftermath still affecting Americans in the middle of the second decade of the twenty-first century.

Because of the times that he lived through as president, and his controversial decisions and actions in the Oval Office, Bush would be subjected to a number of assassination threats, with a couple of them being quite challenging, but fortunately failing in accomplishing their goal of harming the president.

Just weeks after his first inauguration, on February 7, 2001, a forty-seven-year-old accountant from Evansville, Indiana, named Robert W. Pickett, who was a disgruntled former employee of the Internal Revenue Service, fired a .38 caliber handgun at the perimeter fence of the south lawn of the White House and was shot by Secret Service agents after a standoff lasting about ten minutes. Pickett was involved in litigation with the IRS as a former employee of the agency, and he had a history of mental illness. He had been hospitalized six times and made two suicide attempts, although never having been arrested on any charge.

At about 11:30 a.m., Pickett started firing his weapon in the direction of the White House, and Secret Service agents evacuated tourists from the White House and nearby while a patrol officer started talking with Pickett. Then, in the ten-minute standoff, he was shot in the knee by Secret Service Emergency Response Team officers, after he refused to drop the handgun and instead waved it in various directions, and even put it in his mouth. After a plea agreement, he was sentenced to three years at the Federal Medical Center in Rochester, New York, followed by three years of probation, but was released after two and a half years of incarceration.[2]

The September 11, 2001, attacks on Washington, D.C., and New York followed, and in theory, Bush was in danger as long as he was flying on Air Force One around the nation, avoiding a return to Washington, until later that day, with Vice President Dick Cheney in charge in the Situation Room in the White House. There was great concern at the time for the president's safety, and the recognition that protection of the president, and of all government agencies and buildings, was never to be the same.

The next time that there is public evidence of a threat to the president was on May 10, 2005, when the president was traveling in Europe, and was visiting the Republic of Georgia. He was giving a speech in Freedom Square in Tbilisi, Georgia, and Vladimir Arutyunian, of Armenian nationality, threw a live Soviet-made hand grenade toward the podium. The pin had been pulled on the grenade, but it failed to explode because of a handkerchief tightly wound around it, which delayed the firing pin. The grenade landed near where First Lady Laura Bush was sitting, but about sixty-one feet from the podium, where the president was standing. The assailant escaped, but was apprehended two months later and was sentenced to life in prison. A large cache of explosives was found, indicating that the suspect could have committed several future terrorist acts. This was the most dangerous threat that President Bush faced while in office.[3]

Then, on December 4, 2005, twenty-nine-year-old Shawn Cox, a resident of Arkansas, scaled the White House fence while the president was inside, and was immediately arrested by Secret Service agents. He was unarmed, wearing a sweatshirt and unshaven, when he was apprehended. Cox claimed he was destined to marry Chelsea Clinton, the daughter of former President Clinton, who he seemed to think was still president, although it had been nearly five years since Bush had been sworn into the presidency. Cox claimed his own head was a cell phone implanted by Jesus Christ, and psychologists said he was a danger to himself and should be closely monitored, with the belief expressed that he was psychotic and manic in nature. He was committed to St. Elizabeth's Hospital in Washington, D.C.[4]

Then, on April 8, 2006, a three-time White House "fence jumper," forty-year-old Brian Lee Patterson, made it to the front lawn of the White House while President Bush was home, screaming at the top of his lungs. The New Mexico resident, bearded and wearing blue jeans and a white T-shirt, screamed "God Bless America" and "I am a victim of terrorism!" as he moved toward the White House. He was stopped by barking dogs and drawn guns of Secret Service agents, and he was charged with unlawful entry and contempt of court for violating a judge's orders to stay away from the White House at several other times.[5]

Two months later, on June 4, 2006, a D.C. resident, Roger Witmer, forty-four years old, was arrested trying to scale the fence on the south side of the White House, and faced charges of disorderly conduct and unlawful entry, at a time when President Bush was away from the mansion, bike riding in Maryland. Similar to Patterson, he did not have a firearm on his person when arrested.[6]

Then, on October 13, 2006, twenty-four-year-old Alexis Janicki jumped the White House fence and was charged with trespassing and possession of a controlled substance, cannabis. This occurred while Bush was at Camp David, Maryland. Again, no firearm was found.[7]

On March 16, 2007, a more serious incident took place when a sixty-six-year-old from Miami, Cuban born, and a former convict, Catalino Lucas Diaz, scaled the White House fence with a package he claimed was a bomb, causing a security lockdown for three hours. A water cannon was used to destroy the package, which had no dangerous substances. Diaz had been in prison for twenty-seven years in Fidel Castro's Cuba, and then went to prison for attempted murder in Miami for seven years. With his mental state declining, he was sentenced to further mental treatment.[8]

On December 14, 2008, as Bush was finishing his last weeks in the White House, he visited Iraq, where the United States had been engaged in war for nearly six years. He was conducting a press conference in Baghdad when an Iraqi journalist, Muntadhar al-Zaidi, threw his shoes in the direction of the president, missing him as Bush ducked. In Muslim culture, throwing a shoe is seen as a sign of contempt toward someone. Al-Zaidi was roughed up as he was taken into custody, and it was claimed that he was tortured in detention.

In February 2009, he was given a ninety-minute trial and sentenced to three years in prison for assaulting a foreign head of state during an official visit. He was later released after serving nine months of his sentence. He claimed he had acted from emotions at the destruction of mosques, the loss of a million people due to the U.S. invasion, and the massive displacement caused by the war, but also the president's smile and joking banter at the news conference. Many in the Arab world hailed al-Zaidi for his action, a sign that Bush's war policy had not won friends among civilians in Iraq.[9]

Finally, on January 31, 2014, in the first reported incident involving Bush since his White House years, a New York man was found sitting in a car in midtown Manhattan with a loaded rifle, machete, and container of gasoline. Forty-four-year-old Benjamin Smith of upstate New York threatened Bush, and said he was working on a relationship with Bush's single twin daughter, Barbara. He spoke of hoping to "slay a dragon and then Barbara Bush is mine." It seemed likely that he might not be convicted, but might be sent to a mental hospital, but that was undetermined for the time being.[10]

With this tenth and final incident, the threats to President George W. Bush while he was in office and since had come to a conclusion. No one could possibly imagine that the number of incidents that would occur under his successor, Barack Obama, would be more than triple the number under Bush. With the inauguration of President Barack Obama on January 20, 2009, as our forty-fourth president and the first African American occupant of the White House, he would incur more death threats and plots than any president of the United States since Abraham Lincoln and the onset of the Civil War.

Barack Obama was a true dark horse, with no one realistically imagining that an obscure state senator in Illinois, of mixed race heritage, would become a national figure overnight, once he delivered his famous speech at the Democratic National Convention in 2004, and went on to be elected to the U.S. Senate. Even then, no one would have bet money that he could overcome much better known and more experienced rivals for the Democratic presidential nomination in 2008, including Joe Biden, Bill Richardson, Chris Dodd, and, most notably, Hillary Clinton, but he achieved what seemed a miracle. Then, he chose Joe Biden as his running mate, knowing that Biden had had thirty-six years of Senate experience and was a Washington insider, similar to the judgment of Jimmy Carter toward Walter Mondale, Ronald Reagan toward George H. W. Bush, Bill Clinton toward Al Gore, and George W. Bush toward Dick Cheney.

In the 2008 presidential election, Obama faced off against Republican Arizona Senator John McCain. McCain came into the race with a noted disadvantage, specifically the Great Recession of 2008–2009, that caused great economic hardship for millions of Americans. McCain's campaign did not fare well as, to everyone's surprise, he chose Alaska Governor Sarah Palin as his running mate. McCain hoped that this selection would help him to gain votes from women who were upset when Obama defeated Hillary Clinton for the Democratic presidential nomination. However, that plan did not work, and backfired as Palin's inexperience became evident on the campaign trail. Obama won the election and was inaugurated in the worst economic times since FDR's inauguration in 1933.

Obama immediately pushed for an economic stimulus, but discovered that he was unable to gain support from the Republican Party, which was united against any cooperation with him, except for a few Northeastern senators. Nevertheless, his stimulus plan still passed by a very slim margin in both houses of Congress, where Democrats held the majority, but the stimulus that passed was smaller than had been desired.

Once this was completed, Obama set out to accomplish what Bill and Hillary Clinton had failed to achieve, a national health-care plan based on the Massachusetts health-care law enacted in 2006, known as Romney Care. Ironically, former Governor Mitt Romney distanced himself from this plan when he ran against Obama in 2012, and opposed what had come to be known as ObamaCare. The health-care legislation only became law based on a party-line vote, without any GOP support, with it going into effect in 2014, but some aspects of it went into effect immediately, including coverage of preexisting conditions and allowance for young people to be covered on their parents' plan to age twenty-six.

ObamaCare became the most contentious piece of legislation passed through Congress in many decades, with the Republicans, once gaining control of the House of Representatives in 2010 midterm elections with the rise of the Tea Party Movement, working constantly to undermine and repeal the legislation, but failing to do so. Obama's presidency has been characterized by stalemates and gridlock in Congress, with constant confrontation and an inability of Congressional leaders to keep the government operating in a responsible manner. In 2013, a government shutdown involved disputes over the national debt and about raising the debt ceiling. In fact, this led to a downgraded credit rating for the United States.

In foreign policy, Obama had the major accomplishment of finding and killing Osama bin Laden, the perpetrator of the September 11, 2001, attacks, in his compound in Pakistan. The United States also ended its involvement in the Iraq War, and cut down troop commitment in Afghanistan, with a planned finish to combat missions by the end of 2014. But Obama faced many problems in foreign policy in the Middle East and elsewhere including the newly emerging ISIL (ISIS) or Islamic State of Iraq and Syria and challenges from governments hostile to the United States and its interests, including Iran and North Korea, as well as dealing with traditional rivals, including Russia and China. Even friendly nations started to have problems with the Obama administration upon the revelations of whistle-blower Edward Snowden, relating to the massive spying done on all nations, including American allies, by the National Security Agency (NSA) and other intelligence agencies.

Domestically, the revelation of NSA spying on all Americans and their cell phones, emails, and social media caused great discontent that our civil liberties were being compromised in the name of national security and defense against terrorism. That, plus the use of executive orders by President Obama on many areas of policy, and the controversies over gay rights advancements, abortion restrictions in many states, and the growth of inequality in America raised political temperatures. The restrictions on voting rights after the Supreme Court limited the enforcement of the Voting Rights Act of 1965, and unlimited campaign contributions by corporations allowed by the high court in the Citizens United case in 2010 also added to making the Obama years in office the most contentious seen according to some observers, since the 1960s, and, to some, going further back to the Civil War in the mid-nineteenth century.

In this environment, Obama would face more total death threats than any president since Abraham Lincoln, estimated at thirty per day by the Secret Service, or a total of over ten thousand threats per year, beginning even before he was elected president. He began receiving Secret Service protection in May 2007, earlier than any candidate in the past; this began just after his announcement of candidacy, acknowledging an awareness that he was a target for many, because of his mixed race heritage, and the concept that he might become the first non-white president in American history. Sadly, this brought the old element of racism out of the woodwork. The civil rights movement had promoted much change in race relations, but had not removed the old tradition of racial hatred that is still part of American society and is still taught in many homes to children by their parents and other relatives.[11]

This is a continuing and developing story, with the purpose here to point out the major known examples of threats of harm to our forty-fourth president from his announcement of his candidacy to late 2014.

On July 15, 2008, an accountant from Charlotte, North Carolina, Jerry Blanchard, was indicted for a threat to kill Obama while Blanchard was at breakfast at a Charlotte Waffle House, overheard by two customers who reported it to the Secret Service. Blanchard also made a threat at the hotel he was staying at, the Crowne Plaza Hotel in Charlotte. Blanchard told Secret Service agents that Obama was the antichrist prophesied in the Bible. Blanchard was placed in custody on felony charges of making threats against a presidential candidate, and a psychiatric evaluation was ordered, although there was doubt that his statements were more than just talk.

Two weeks later, in Miami, Florida, Raymond H. Geisel, a student in a bail bonds training class, referred to Obama with a racist epithet, and said he would assassinate him if he was elected. He also made a death threat against President George W. Bush, but said he was joking. However, a search of his hotel room revealed ammunition, body armor, a combat-style hatchet, tear gas, a loaded 9 mm handgun, and four loaded magazines. Geisel was held in custody for a month, then released, but the Secret Service keeps track of him as a possible threat, and as unstable in his behavior.[12]

In late August 2008, Barack Obama was in Denver, Colorado, where the Democratic National Convention was about to nominate him for the presidency. A plan to assassinate him at the convention was hatched by twenty-eight-year-old Tharin Robert Gartrell; his thirty-three-year-old cousin Shawn Robert Adolf; and their thirty-two-year-old friend, Nathan Dwaine Johnson. The plan, revealed by a woman who was present as they plotted, was to hide a gun inside a hollowed-out television video camera, similar to what was used in the 1992 Kevin Costner film, *The Bodyguard*.

All three men had made racist statements in the presence of others, and they were quickly arrested on the morning of August 24. Large amounts of equipment (including rifles with attached hunting scopes, a bulletproof vest, camouflage clothing, wigs, and fake IDs), along with drugs, were found in Gartrell's truck and in the hotel rooms of Adolf and Johnson. The plan was to shoot Obama as he gave his acceptance speech before tens of thousands of people at Invesco Field at Mile High Stadium in Denver, Colorado, on August 28. Discussion of Lee Harvey Oswald was mentioned as part of their motivation to copy the John F. Kennedy assassination.

Although all three were implicated in this plot, Adolf seemed to be the primary motivator, and it seemed clear that much of what they had planned was fueled by a hate for African Americans, and the reality that all three were deeply influenced by the use of methamphetamines and were considered "meth heads." The controversial decision made by the U.S. attorney for the Denver area was to decide not to prosecute the three men, saying that racist statements were not enough to rise to the legal standard that would have allowed the filing of federal charges for threatening a presidential candidate. The belief was that the three suspects did not have the planning or the means to follow through on any plan to assassinate Obama. This was disputed by others, but eventually, the three men were indicted for drug charges and spent some time in prison for that and also for firearms possession, in the case of Adolf and Johnson. The news media covered the story briefly, but dropped it after the decision not to charge the three men with assassination threats.[13]

This threat was followed in October 2008 by an assassination plot in Tennessee, two weeks before the election. The men involved were eighteen-year-old Paul Schlesselman of Arkansas and twenty-year-old Daniel Cowart of Tennessee. The two men were neo-Nazis and were introduced to each other by a mutual friend via the Internet, who shared their white supremacist beliefs. Within a month, they plotted a murdering spree, intending to kill eighty-eight black school children at an unidentified middle school, with the additional plan to behead fourteen of the victims. They planned to rob a gun store to obtain additional weapons and to commit home robberies to fund their plans. After killing the students, they would drive at high speed toward Obama at a public appearance, shooting from the windows. All of this was discussed over the internet, and they bragged about shooting at an African American Baptist church to a friend, who reported it to her mother and notified police. This led to an investigation by the Bureau of Alcohol, Tobacco, Firearms and Explosives, and then by the Secret Service and the FBI.

Once they were arrested, with their car having swastikas on it, a rifle, a sawed-off shotgun, and three pistols were seized, and they were indicted for making a threat against a presidential candidate. Although it seemed highly unlikely that the plot was a very advanced one, both pleaded guilty to several federal charges, and Schlesselman was sentenced to ten years in prison and Cowart to fourteen years in prison.[14]

At rallies for Republican vice presidential nominee Sarah Palin, and for Republican presidential candidate John McCain, as the campaign for president entered its last days, there were people in the crowds who called for Obama to be killed, and some who called him an "Arab." McCain discouraged and spoke up against such statements, while Palin ignored what was said, and was criticized by many for remaining silent.

After the inauguration, on February 10, 2009, a Louisiana man named Alfred Brock drove up to the Capitol Complex in D.C., and told guards he had a delivery for President Obama. He was questioned, and he admitted he had a rifle in his truck, so he was arrested without incident and charged with possession of an unregistered .22 caliber rifle.[15]

In early April 2009, while on his first foreign trip, President Obama was the subject of a serious plot to assassinate him, involving a Syrian man arrested in Turkey, who had planned with three accomplices to stab the president with a knife during the Alliance of Civilizations summit in Istanbul; they gained access by using fake press credentials for the summit. Turkish security officials were said to have resolved the issue, with the assistance of the Secret Service.[16]

On June 9, 2009, another "fence jumper" made news, when Pamela Morgan, a forty-six-year-old white female, vaulted over the fence in the northeast corner of the White House compound, carrying a backpack with her. She was apprehended immediately, and the backpack was examined by explosives experts, at a time when Congressional members were coming out of a closed-door meeting with President Obama on the health-care reform bill. The compound was on lockdown until it was clear that there was no danger. Morgan was transferred into the custody of the D.C. Metropolitan Police Department.[17]

There were even potential threats against First Lady Michelle Obama. A thirty-five-year-old mentally ill woman named Kristy Lee Roshia contacted the Secret Service office in Boston and threatened Michelle Obama while the Obamas were on vacation in Hawaii in December 2009. Seen as a threat due to her unstable behavior, she was arrested two miles from where the Obamas were to stay in Honolulu, and she assaulted the federal officer who was detaining her. She was charged with threatening a family member of the president, assaulting a federal agent while being arrested, and was sent to a mental institution for observation.[18]

In early September 2010, twenty-nine-year-old Robert Anthony Quinones, a former soldier, took hostages at a Georgia army hospital, and later told investigators that he planned to kill President Obama and former President Clinton. Quinones took three hostages in a two-hour standoff at Winn Army Community Hospital at Fort Stewart, forty miles southwest of Savannah, but surrendered without any harm to the hostages. Quinones was discharged from the military a few months earlier, diagnosed as having posttraumatic stress disorder. An Iraq War veteran, Quinones was shown to have at least fifteen firearms, including high-powered rifles with scopes, at his home. But he also had books and DVDs on Secret Service protocols, Israeli sniper techniques, Osama bin Laden, and Oklahoma City bomber Timothy McVeigh. He told FBI and Secret Service agents that on a scale of one to ten about being serious on killing Obama and Clinton, he would say a ten and that he was very serious.[19]

On November 26, 2010, the report of the arrest of a former New York City police officer, Michael Stephen Bowden, on charges that he told a Secret Service officer that he would like to put President Obama up against the wall and shoot him, was revealed when he told a South Carolina Veterans Administration counselor of his plans, even though, as a man in his seventies, he was seen as no realistic threat. He underwent mental evaluation through the federal prison system.[20]

On the night of November 11, 2011, an Idaho man, twenty-one-year-old Oscar Ramiro Ortega-Hernandez, fired a Romanian Cugir semiautomatic rifle from his car parked on Constitution Avenue, with nine rounds being fired, one lodging in a window of the living quarters of the Obamas in the White House. It took five days for him to be found and arrested at a hotel in Pennsylvania. Hernandez said he believed Obama was the antichrist and the devil, and he was committed to a mental facility.[21] New revelations about this attack were revealed on September 29, 2014. The number of shots that hit the White House was more like seven, instead of the originally reported one, with the Secret Service unaware for four days that the White House had been shot that many times.[22]

Another threat came in July 2012 from a twenty-two-year-old Uzbekistan immigrant named Ulugbek Kodirov. He came to America intending to attend the medical school at Columbia University, but he never enrolled because of his poor command of English. Instead, he took a job at a mall kiosk in Alabama, where he was arrested for threats that he made on Islamic jihadist websites. Islamic jihadists actually turned him against the nation which had admitted him for a better life. His contact with a terrorist group on the internet led him to threaten to kill Obama, and he had gathered firearms in the process of his planning. He revealed his plans further when he was in touch with an undercover agent, from whom he purchased a Sendra M115A1 automatic rifle and four hand grenades with the powder removed. He was sentenced to more than fifteen years in prison and had faced up to thirty years.[23]

In August 2012, a plot by an anarchist militia within the U.S. Army was uncovered, with the arrest of Private First Class Michael Burnett, who pleaded guilty to manslaughter in the December 2011 slayings of a former soldier and his girlfriend, both killed because of their knowledge of the militia group's plans. The militia group, including Private Christopher Salmon and Private First Class Isaac Aguigui, had plotted to take over Fort Stewart, Georgia, after buying $87,000 of guns and bomb-making materials. Their plan also included criminal actions in Savannah, Georgia, and in Washington state, and also plans to assassinate President Obama.[24]

In June 2013, six men from upstate New York were arrested after building a radioactive death ray device and planning to use it against Muslims, other perceived enemies of Israel and America, and President Obama, another perceived Muslim and enemy. Two of the men, Glenn Scott Crawford and Eric J. Feight, were arrested by the FBI after a fifteen-month operation, with agents acting as co-conspirators. Crawford was specifically affiliated with the Ku Klux Klan and a Tea Party organization and had supposedly contacted an Albany, New York, synagogue asking for assistance on the technology involved in the death ray. Both men were charged with conspiracy to provide material support to terrorists and faced the possibility of fifteen years in prison.[25]

In the last months of 2013, the number of reported threats grew again, after having had a decline from what had occurred in the election year of 2012. Larry Klayman, a right-wing activist, organized a White House march in October, which became one of a very small crowd, advocating that Obama back away from his belief in the Koran, come out with his hands up, and surrender for trial. Earlier in the year, Klayman had called for the military to overthrow the president and called Obama "an evil tyrant." He had said more recently that violent revolution was in the offing. It became apparent that his funding came from billionaire Sheldon Adelson, who had spent more than a hundred million dollars trying to defeat Obama in the 2012 election, exploiting the ability for wealthy individuals to spend as much as they wish under the Citizens United case of the Supreme Court in 2010.[26]

As the year 2013 ended, a bank robber, who had killed a police officer, was killed after a nationwide manhunt. The Secret Service revealed that forty-year-old Mario Edward Garnett of Oklahoma had been arrested in 2010 for threatening the president, had been sentenced to eight months in federal prison, been ordered to get mental health care when he was released, and informed that he would never be able to own a firearm again. But of course, he had used a firearm to rob banks and kill the police officer in Mississippi, along with robbing banks in Georgia and Arizona, where he was ultimately killed. His death threat in 2010 had consisted of writing on a White House website that he would "blow his brains out on national TV," meaning Obama, if he ordered a strike on Iran.[27]

Even retired Army General Paul E. Vallely, at the end of 2013, called for the forced resignation of Obama because of "crimes" he had committed in office, without delineating them. He called for a citizens' arrest of the president, a march on Washington, and a national recall process. He bemoaned that if Obama were removed, Vice President Joe Biden would be his successor, and therefore, revolution was necessary. In fact, Vallely advocated the removal of the president, vice president, and the Democratic and Republican leaders of both the House of Representatives and the Senate, and the Tea Party Movement coming to power in both the executive and legislative branches.[28]

In the early days of 2014, Georgetown University professor and former CIA official Michael Scheuer became controversial, when he declared justification for the removal of "tyrants" by violence and asserted that Obama deserved the death penalty for his failure to save four diplomats in the Benghazi, Libya, tragedy of September 11, 2012. He stated his belief in assassination while being interviewed by talk show host Lou Dobbs, who had no counter reply to Scheuer's assertions.[29]

It was clear that even more threats of all kinds would be visited upon Barack Obama in his three remaining years in the presidency. Just listing the reported cases in this chapter, the number of threats had reached twenty in number, but there were actually closer to forty cases publicly reported through the beginning of 2014, and new cases were occurring regularly.

As Barack Obama woke up on the morning of September 20, 2014, at the presidential retreat of Camp David, Maryland, he came to realize that he had come close to possible danger on the previous evening of September 19, 2014. Fortunately, he and his daughters had just left by helicopter to Camp David. But suddenly, a "fence jumper" named Omar J. Gonzalez managed to scale the fence on the Pennsylvania Avenue side of the grounds of the White House. It was reported that Gonzalez rushed across the lawn unimpeded and entered the North Portico of the White House, the furthest any "fence jumper" had ever reached, and was only, finally, stopped by the Secret Service as he entered the White House. Later, the report showed new evidence that this "fence jumper" had actually run deep into the White House across the East Room and into the Green Room, not far from the stairs leading to the White House Private Quarters a half floor above the main floor level. This therefore represented an even greater theoretical danger, since it was revealed he had a knife, and could have, in theory, been a suicide bomber. This necessitated a full-scale investigation as to the shortcomings of the Secret Service.[30]

How this could have happened was alarming and indicated a breakdown of the security of the building, and an unexplained failure of the Secret Service. With exactly two years and four months left of his term in the presidency on the morning of September 20, 2014, the multiplication of death threats or possible harm to the forty-fourth president remained in the front of the minds of security experts and the American people, as they wondered if Obama would remain safe until he left office on January 20, 2017.[31]

In January 2015, further realization of the growing threat against American presidents was demonstrated by news of the death threat by a bartender in Ohio against Speaker of the House John Boehner and the incident of shots being fired near the Delaware residence of Vice President Joe Biden. These two men are two heartbeats and one heartbeat away, respectively, from the presidency under the Presidential Succession Act of 1947. So the issue of security and safety of the president and his immediate successors, in case of emergency, remains an issue constantly on the minds of the Secret Service and other government agencies.[32]

Presidential security, safety, and protection remain a serious problem, having reached the grand total of 181 years since the first known threat to Andrew Jackson in 1833, by the end of 2014. No matter how one feels about the personality and policies of any American president, we can all wish that the lives of the presidents stay safe, and that we do not add to the four presidential assassinations and two presidential candidate assassinations that this nation suffered from 1865 to 1968.

17

FIFTEEN "MIGHT HAVE BEEN" PRESIDENTS IN HISTORY

When one examines the history of presidential assassinations and assassination threats, where a president could have been victimized, including indirect threats as well as direct confrontations with a weapon or other threats, it becomes clear that America could have had fifteen individuals who would have succeeded to the presidency, if history's fortunes had been different.[1]

In the appendix of this book, readers will find a list of the fifteen possible presidents of the United States, and it is worth spending some time examining the lives and potential leadership of these fifteen individuals, who came close to being elevated to the presidency. These fifteen men will be discussed next in chronological order.

If Abraham Lincoln, whom Andrew Johnson succeeded, had been killed in the "Baltimore Plot" before his inauguration in 1861, or had been killed later by a sniper in 1864, Vice President Hannibal Hamlin would have been president. Also, if Hamlin had not been dropped by Lincoln in the 1864 presidential election contest for Andrew Johnson, he would have been Lincoln's successor.

Hamlin (1809–1891) was a Democrat until 1856, when he became a member of the recently created Republican Party. He served in the House of Representatives from 1843 to 1847 and as senator from Maine from 1847 to 1861, when he became the first Republican vice president. He was always a prominent opponent of the expansion of slavery into the western territories and was a strong supporter of the Wilmot Proviso of

1846, as the Mexican War began. He continued his opposition to the expansion of slavery following the Compromise of 1850 and the Kansas-Nebraska Act of 1854. After the passage of the Kansas-Nebraska Act, the Republican Party was formed to prevent the further expansion of slavery. In 1857, Hamlin served for two months as governor of Maine, until his return to the Senate, as a Republican, having resigned from the Democratic Party, which had endorsed the repeal of the Missouri Compromise in the Kansas-Nebraska Act.

Hamlin had little impact as vice president under Lincoln, but he urged the Emancipation Proclamation and the arming of blacks to fight the South during the Civil War. He had a good working relationship with Lincoln, but did not attend cabinet meetings and was often home in Maine, likely because it was known that the First Lady, Mary Todd Lincoln, did not like Hamlin.

After being dropped as vice president, Hamlin returned for two more terms to the U.S. Senate from 1869 to 1881, having served a total of about twenty-five years in the upper chamber. He finished his public service as President James A. Garfield's minister to Spain for about a year from 1881 to 1882, and also served under President Chester Alan Arthur for a few months. He then retired to his home in Bangor, Maine, for the rest of his life and died at the age of eighty-one.

It seems reasonable to assume that Hamlin would not have faced the tragic, divisive times that Andrew Johnson faced, as he was in total agreement on the idea of Lincoln's move toward emancipation and equality for African Americans. Andrew Johnson did not hold those views, which caused him to have a very tempestuous relationship with the Congress made up primarily of Republicans, unhappy with a president who had been a Democrat his whole political life, but he was put on the 1864 presidential ticket to help Lincoln win the election for a second term.[2]

If Vice President Andrew Johnson, who succeeded Lincoln, had been killed by George Atzerodt, as planned by John Wilkes Booth as part of the Lincoln assassination conspiracy, then there would have been no vice president. The president pro tempore of the Senate would have become president, as he was next in line under the Presidential Succession Law of 1792, in effect until changed in 1886. That man was Senator Lafayette S. Foster (1806–1880) of Connecticut, first a Whig and then a Republican, and a descendant of Miles Standish, the Pilgrim leader of the seventeenth-century Plymouth Colony in New England.

Foster served in the U.S. Senate from 1855 to 1867, had earlier been mayor of Norwich, and served in the Connecticut state legislature. After his time in the Senate, he served on the Connecticut Supreme Court as a judge from 1870 to 1876. His impact on the Senate was limited, as he was defeated for reelection in 1866. He remains the most obscure person on the list of potential presidents, and it is hard to know what his impact might have been in the presidency. But as a Northern Republican, he likely would have conducted himself differently than the confrontational Andrew Johnson.[3]

It was over thirty-five years before another individual could possibly have assumed the presidency due to assassination. William McKinley's first-term vice president, Garret Hobart (1844–1899), had he not died in office, most likely would have been kept on the presidential ticket for 1900, and therefore, would have succeeded McKinley upon his assassination in September 1901. Theodore Roosevelt would have remained governor of New York and war hero from the Spanish-American War, but would not have been president of the United States.

A New Jersey resident, Hobart was a Republican who served in local governmental positions, and then served in the New Jersey General Assembly and the state Senate, becoming speaker of the House and president of the Senate. He led a lucrative and comfortable life as a corporate attorney and was quite wealthy. He was a popular state official and was chosen as McKinley's running mate because his state was seen as significant in the upcoming presidential campaign.

As vice president, Hobart was seen as an important adviser to the president, but had major heart issues and died in November 1899 at age fifty-five. He was seen as very congenial and admired for his tact and charm. McKinley had a very close relationship with Hobart and his wife and visited their home, not far from the White House, on a regular basis; likewise, the Hobarts were frequent visitors for dinner with the McKinleys at the Executive Mansion. He was often called the "assistant president," and the "alter ego" of the president, and took on strong leadership in the Senate in getting legislation moved forward. His funeral attracted fifty thousand people to Paterson, New Jersey, to honor him, including the president and many other top government officials.

Hobart is seen as having expanded the powers of the vice presidency more than anyone before him, but is seldom recalled today. The shadow of his successor, Theodore Roosevelt, has made him little remembered, but it seems clear that he might have been a very effective president, although unlikely to be the progressive that TR became over time.[4]

When Theodore Roosevelt was president, and armed assailant Henry Weilbrenner was caught by the Secret Service trying to enter the president's home at Oyster Bay in 1903, again there was no vice president, since TR had succeeded McKinley upon his assassination in 1901. The Presidential Succession Law of 1886 had changed the succession from the president pro tempore of the Senate to the cabinet members, in order of the creation of the office, and that meant Secretary of State John Hay (1838–1905) would have succeeded TR in the presidency in 1903.

Hay was a very distinguished public servant, seen as an American statesman, diplomat, author, and journalist, and had been private secretary and assistant to President Abraham Lincoln during the Civil War. Hay, while working in the White House, lived in the northeast corner bedroom on the second floor of the White House, sharing it with his fellow secretary John G. Nicolay. He is the only secretary of state, other than Hillary Clinton, to have resided in the White House before being secretary of state. He was at Ford's Theatre when Lincoln was assassinated in 1865, and he and Nicolay wrote a ten-volume biography of Lincoln and published an edition of his collected works.

After Lincoln's death, Hay served in embassies in France, Spain, and Austria-Hungary, before being an editor for the *New York Tribune* for six years, and then was assistant secretary of state for President Rutherford B. Hayes for two years. Then, he became ambassador to Great Britain from 1897 to 1898, before becoming the leader of the State Department under William McKinley and then TR. Hay became notable for negotiating the Treaty of Paris, ending the Spanish-American War, and developed the Open Door policy toward China. The term "Splendid Little War," to describe the war against Spain, was coined by Hay. He also negotiated the agreements allowing for the building of the Panama Canal and was involved in treaty negotiations with other nations. It is thought that Hay would have been an excellent president had he been thrust into that position by fate.[5]

When Franklin D. Roosevelt faced an assassination threat as president-elect, and again when a plot was hatched against him by business interests, his vice president, John Nance Garner (1868–1967) of Texas, would have replaced him in the White House. Garner, the longest-lived vice president in American history, was a state representative from 1898 to 1902, and then served in the House of Representatives for the next thirty years from 1903 to 1933. He had the distinction of being the Speaker of the House from 1931 to 1933, and was a serious contender for the Democratic presidential nomination in 1932. Instead, he was put on the ticket with FDR to balance the interests of the party in the North and the South, similar to Lyndon B. Johnson being put on the ticket with John F. Kennedy in 1960 to balance the interests of both North and South.

Garner did not get along well with FDR on policy issues, as he was a conservative Southerner, so he opposed the sit-down strikes of labor unions, the deficit spending of the New Deal, and the attempted reorganization of the Supreme Court in 1937, better known as "the Court Packing Plan." Vice President Garner actually led active opposition to the court plan, and it was clear that FDR did not want him on his election ticket when he ran again for president in 1940. Garner himself had hoped to be the presidential nominee that year and actually declared for the presidency and openly broke with the president over his third-term bid. It is clear that there would never have been a New Deal had FDR died and Garner become president. The effect on the economic and social stability of the nation during the Great Depression might have been very different, and likely, more damaging and negative for the nation.[6]

When Roosevelt's ultimate successor, Harry Truman, was subjected to the possible threat of assassination by the Stern Gang in 1947, two individuals were eligible to succeed him had he become a victim of a mail bombing. The Presidential Succession Act of 1947, passed in July, changed the law from the cabinet members, beginning with the secretary of state, and put the order of succession into the hands of the Speaker of the House of Representatives.

In the first seven months of 1947, Secretary of State George C. Marshall (1880–1959) was a potential successor in case tragedy had befallen President Truman. Marshall was a very distinguished military leader, being one of five five-star generals of World War II, and also being chief of staff of the Army from 1939 to 1945, secretary of state from 1947 to 1949, and then secretary of defense from 1950 to 1951. He was the chief military adviser to FDR during World War II. Marshall had his name put on Truman's ambitious plan for the United States to rebuild Western Europe after the devastation of the war, and his promotion of the Marshall Plan gained him the Nobel Peace Prize in 1953.

Marshall devoted fifty-seven years of his life to military service, and he engaged on many battlefields, including the Filipino-American War of 1899–1902, World War I, World War II, and the Chinese Civil War. He was a distant relative of former Chief Justice John Marshall of the Supreme Court in the early nineteenth century. Marshall was responsible for the advancement in the military of famous Generals Dwight D. Eisenhower, George Patton, and Omar Bradley. He laid the plans for the D-Day invasion of Europe on June 6, 1944, at Normandy, France, although Eisenhower had been given the responsibility for the actual invasion. Marshall became the "Man of the Year" for *Time* magazine in 1943, and again in 1947.

One issue that might have ended up differently with a President Marshall was his strong opposition to the recognition of Israel in 1948. While he was secretary of state, he was so strong in his opposition to Israeli recognition that he told Truman he would vote against him in the presidential election of 1948 if Truman recognized Israel, which Truman proceeded to do, anyway, on May 14. It is not known if Marshall voted against Truman, but he left the cabinet in 1949, although later rejoining as head of the Pentagon in 1950.

Despite this disagreement on Israel, after retirement Truman said Marshall was the American who had made the greatest contribution of the previous thirty years. Sadly, Marshall was attacked as "soft on communism" by Wisconsin Senator Joseph McCarthy in the early 1950s, and presidential nominee Eisenhower in 1952 refused to come to his defense and refute McCarthy's outrageous charges of treason. It is unknown whether these scurrilous charges of McCarthy undermined Marshall's health and shortened his life. But Marshall had worldwide acclaim and lots of awards and honors, and is seen as one of the greatest American public figures of the twentieth century, despite these unfortunate personal attacks. Many buildings and streets in the United States and other nations are named after him, and awards and scholarships bear his name as well.[7]

In the second half of 1947, Speaker of the House Joseph William Martin Jr. (1884–1968) of Massachusetts, the only Republican Speaker from 1931 to 1995, could have succeeded if Truman had been assassinated by the Stern Gang. It is not clear if the Stern Gang had Republican supporters who would have wanted a Republican president to replace Democrat Truman.

Martin was a member of the House of Representatives for forty-two years, 1925–1967, and was House Minority Leader in 1939–1947, 1949–1953, and 1955–1959. He was Speaker of the House in 1947–1949 and 1953–1955. Originally a conservative, opposing internationalism under FDR, as well as his New Deal programs, he became a moderate under President Eisenhower, became an internationalist, backed federal aid for school construction, and backed the War on Poverty of President Lyndon B. Johnson in 1964. Martin was ousted as Republican leader of the House of Representatives in 1959, but remained in Congress until being defeated in a primary in 1966, and retiring at the beginning of 1967. He published a memoir on his first fifty years in politics in 1960 and died in 1968. Despite his long service, Martin is not looked upon as true presidential material.[8]

Alben Barkley (1877–1956) was vice president in President Truman's full term of office, so he would have succeeded Truman if the attack by Puerto Rican nationalists in 1950 at Blair House had succeeded in killing Truman. Barkley had a long, distinguished career in Congress from the state of Kentucky. He served in the House of Representatives from the time of Woodrow Wilson, having fourteen years in the lower chamber from 1913 to 1927, gaining a reputation as a liberal Democrat and strong promoter of Wilson's New Freedom domestic agenda. Then, he served in the U.S. Senate from 1927 to 1949, and was a strong supporter of Franklin D. Roosevelt's New Deal. He became Senate Majority Leader in 1937, and kept that position over the next decade, becoming Senate Minority Leader from 1947 to 1949, when the opposition Republicans gained control of the Senate.

He had a total of thirty-six years in Washington, D.C., when he became vice president, being seven and a half years older than Truman. He had been considered for the vice presidency when Alfred E. Smith was the presidential nominee in 1928, and again for FDR in his fourth-term bid in 1944. He was also considered a possible presidential nominee in 1940, before FDR decided to run for a third term. Additionally, he was considered as a possible Supreme Court nominee, but FDR did not choose him.

Barkley's keynote speech at the Democratic National Convention in 1948 aroused the delegates, and he was picked as Truman's running mate. As vice president, he played a more active role than any typical vice president, being invited to all cabinet meetings, and becoming a member of the newly formed National Security Council. He became Truman's spokesman on many issues when the Korean War intervention began in 1950. Had he been younger, Barkley might have been the Democratic presidential nominee in 1952, but instead, his distant cousin, Adlai E. Stevenson, became the candidate against Dwight D. Eisenhower. He returned to the Senate for a little more than a year from 1955 to 1956, when he died of a heart attack at the age of seventy-eight.[9]

The one possible president who might be considered the longest shot of all was Senator Robert F. Kennedy of New York, who many surmise would have defeated Vice President Hubert H. Humphrey for the Democratic presidential nomination in 1968, had he not been assassinated in June 1968 by Sirhan Sirhan. There is, however, no certainty about this, but the fact that Humphrey only trailed Richard Nixon by about a half million popular votes nationally, and the popularity of the Kennedy name, makes many observers believe that if RFK had been the opponent of Nixon, he would have overcome the deficit, and even undermined some of the white-working-class support for third-party nominee George C. Wallace. But this is all speculation, worthy of pondering, but impossible to prove.

The one point that does stand out, however, is that RFK was the only one of the three serious presidential candidates victimized by assassins who would have had a reasonable chance to be president, as that is clearly not the case for Huey P. Long or George C. Wallace. Both were Southern regional candidates, who could win electoral and popular votes support in theory (and reality for Wallace), but could not have won a national election.[10]

Vice President Spiro T. Agnew (1918–1996) would have become president in 1972 had Arthur Bremer, who stalked Richard Nixon and shot George C. Wallace, succeeded in killing Nixon. Agnew had been county executive of Baltimore County, Maryland, before becoming governor in the 1966 state elections. He served less than two years as governor, but was noticed for his condemnation of riots in his state and nationally after the assassination of Martin Luther King Jr. in April 1968. He made a strong case for "law and order," and came to the attention of Nixon as a result of his rhetoric, and was chosen as Nixon's running mate over many better-known Republican leaders. He was seen as having the ability to go for the "jugular vein" against opponents. Many began to call him "Nixon's Nixon," a term used during the presidential campaign of 1968, and in his almost five years as vice president.

Agnew, never personally close to Nixon, nevertheless, did the president's bidding, going after the "liberal' news media, including the *New York Times*, *Washington Post*, CBS, NBC, ABC, *Time* magazine, and *Newsweek* magazine, as well as campaigning against liberal Democrats in the midterm Congressional elections of 1970, and attacking other critics of the Nixon administration. In so doing, Agnew gained the enmity and disdain of liberal political observers, but was seen as effective in his attacks short term, and many speculated that he would be the successor to Nixon in 1976.

However, what was not uncovered until the second term of the Nixon presidency came to light in 1973, that Agnew had been involved in accepting cash bribes as Baltimore County executive, as Maryland governor, and even in the vice president's office. Once discovered and revealed, Nixon abandoned him, as he was himself enmeshed in the Watergate scandal. Agnew agreed to resign to avoid prosecution, but lost his law license, and was disgraced by his corrupt behavior. Many sighed relief that he never had the opportunity to become president, which would have occurred when Nixon resigned in 1974, if the Agnew scandal had not come to light. This reality made many observers greatly appreciate Gerald Ford as a far better successor to Nixon than Agnew would have been.

Had Agnew's scandal been uncovered after becoming president, the likelihood is that he would have faced impeachment and prosecution at a crisis-ridden time, after Nixon had already left the presidency. That would have probably led to Speaker of the House Carl Albert of Oklahoma becoming president, unless Agnew had already chosen a replacement vice president under the Twenty-fifth Amendment, and that person had been confirmed by both houses of Congress. The thought of this scenario is a nightmare, not good for the nation in the Cold War era, when strong, determined, and honest leadership was needed. Certainly, Spiro Agnew represented the worst possible nightmare scenario we have, probably, ever faced in our history.[11]

In September 1975, twice in seventeen days, if Lynette "Squeaky" Fromme or Sara Jane Moore had succeeded in killing President Gerald Ford, Vice President Nelson Rockefeller (1908–1979) would have succeeded to the presidency. Few people who have come to the vice presidency have been as prominent and successful as Rockefeller, who had been a leading presidential possibility three times, in 1960, 1964, and 1968. Each time, he was perceived as simply "too Northeastern" and "too liberal" for the Republican Party. It has often been thought that had he been the nominee of his party in 1960 and 1968, he might have defeated John F. Kennedy and Hubert H. Humphrey.

Instead, Rockefeller would serve fifteen years, almost four complete terms, as New York governor from 1959 through 1973, one of the longest periods of service of any governor in American history since the implementation of the Constitution. He transformed the state of New York's education and infrastructure and promoted its economic growth. He made enemies along the way, of course, but is seen historically as an outstanding state leader.

Rockefeller had alienated many conservatives with his strong attacks against his rival and successful nominee for president in 1964, Senator Barry Goldwater of Arizona. So there were suspicions when Rockefeller was selected by President Ford, under the provisions of the Twenty-fifth Amendment, to be his vice president. His confirmation hearings took four months as a result, compared to Ford's two months. Rockefeller was one of the wealthiest people in America, and his family was under suspicion, due to its great influence over economics, politics, and foreign policy. Ultimately, however, Rockefeller was confirmed, and served twenty-five months as vice president from December 1974 to January 1977.

Ford gave Rockefeller many responsibilities, making the vice presidency a more influential office, as it had started to become when Nixon was vice president under Eisenhower. With Rockefeller "in the loop" on policy decisions and cabinet meetings, this angered and worried conservatives in the party, who remained highly suspicious of the vice president's influence. They were very alarmed when the two assassination attempts took place in September 1975, and had a collective sigh of relief when Ford emerged unhurt from both assassination attempts. This motivated former California Governor Ronald Reagan to decide to run for the 1976 Republican presidential nomination against President Ford with renewed zeal. When Ford barely made it past Reagan for the nomination at the Republican National Convention, he was brought under pressure by political insiders to replace Rockefeller with a more conservative and acceptable choice for vice president for the full term, and chose Kansas Senator Bob Dole. However, when Ford lost the election to Jimmy Carter, the conclusion of many observers was that if Ford had retained Rockefeller on the ticket, he might have won the election.

What kind of president would Rockefeller have made, had Ford been assassinated? Probably he would have attempted to be an activist president immediately, as Lyndon B. Johnson was after the John F. Kennedy assassination. But he would have had only two and a half months more of the term he was finishing than LBJ had. The odds are that he would have been strongly challenged by Reagan immediately, and might have ended up being simply a caretaker president of sixteen months duration.[12]

When President Jimmy Carter was stalked by Raymond Lee Harvey in 1979 and John Hinckley in 1980, had events turned tragic, Vice President Walter F. Mondale (1928–) would have become president. If he had been president for about a year, or even for a few weeks, he would have had the advantage to be elected to a full term, similar to Lyndon B. Johnson after JFK's death in 1963. It is possible, therefore, to imagine that Ronald Reagan might never have been president as a result, and that Mondale, who lost a landslide to Reagan in 1984, might have had two terms plus in the White House. Shock and sympathy for a wounded or murdered Carter at the hands of John Hinckley could have transformed the presidential election of 1980, even with just weeks to the actual vote. It could have meant no Conservative Revolution in the 1980s.

Mondale, who had been Minnesota attorney general, and served in the U.S. Senate from 1964 to 1976, before becoming vice president under Carter, had the kind of experiences and connections in Washington, D.C., which made him a very useful asset to Carter, who had never even visited the capital. A protégé of former Vice President and Senator Hubert H. Humphrey, Mondale was congenial, was clearly a Washington insider, and gained the full trust and friendship of Carter. The two men worked very well together as a team, in a manner no previous vice president had ever experienced. This was a tribute to Carter, who saw Mondale as a "co-president," in on all decision making, spending more time with the president on a constant basis than any previous vice president. Mondale's vice presidency is perceived by experts as having "grown" the job in a major way.

A scenario of Mondale as president can imagine an activist, liberal presidency, more than Jimmy Carter ever was, and possibly an expansion of the New Deal–Great Society vision of FDR and LBJ, and the vision of his mentor, Hubert H. Humphrey. Carter and Mondale have continued their close association in the more than a third of a century since they were in the center of power. Every day, as of 2015, they have added to the record of the longest-lasting presidential–vice presidential team in retirement in American history, having surpassed John Adams and Thomas Jefferson, in that regard, in 2006.[13]

If President Bill Clinton, the next Democratic president after Carter, had been the victim of several plots in his first term as president in the years 1994 to 1996, Vice President Albert Gore Jr. (1948–) would have become president of the United States, and likely would have had the advantage for a full term in the presidential election of 1996, and potentially 2000. It is certainly ironic that Gore won the national popular vote for president in the presidential election of 2000, but lost the electoral vote and the election after intervention by the Supreme Court in the case of *Bush v. Gore* in December 2000.

Gore, whose father of the same first name had been a leading figure in Congress as a member of the House of Representatives from Tennessee from 1939 to 1953 and as senator from 1953 to 1971, served, like his father, in the House of Representatives from 1977 to 1985, and in the Senate from 1985 until 1993, when he became vice president for two terms until January 2001.

Gore was a very active vice president in the Mondale mode, promoting the development of the internet, and advocating environmental activism, influencing President Clinton to take significant action on an area of policy mostly ignored by Clinton when he was Arkansas governor. Gore was intimately involved on all major issues, and his experience in Congress was seen as a plus for another Southern governor, Clinton, who had never served in national government, similar to Jimmy Carter. Gore added stature to the growth of the vice presidency. It was clear that if Gore had to take over the presidency in case of a tragedy that he would have been able to do so in a very positive manner.[14]

If George W. Bush had been a victim in 2001 or 2005 of assassination attempts, Vice President Dick Cheney (1941–) would have succeeded to the Oval Office. When Cheney was selected for the vice presidency, many thought of him as better qualified on experience and background to be president than Bush, a similar feeling perceived about Al Gore and Walter Mondale as being more experienced and better qualified than Bill Clinton and Jimmy Carter to serve as president.

Cheney had been a Washington insider during the 1970s, having been chief of staff to President Gerald Ford from 1975 to 1977; Wyoming congressman from 1979 to 1989; and then secretary of defense under President George H. W. Bush from 1989 to 1993. Cheney never seriously thought of being president, although briefly a candidate in 1996, but he came to the vice presidency with tremendous national defense and national security experience. He had a great impact after the September 11 attacks by al Qaeda on the World Trade Center and the Pentagon, advocating war against the Taliban in Afghanistan, and against Saddam Hussein of Iraq. Cheney had waged war against Hussein in the Persian Gulf War under the first President Bush in 1991. Cheney was also an advocate of the PATRIOT Act, a highly contested challenge to civil liberties and civil rights, but deemed necessary to fight terrorism.

Cheney had no problem dealing with critics, within and outside the George W. Bush administration, and he was often thought to be the "real" president, rather than Bush. But in the second term, Bush started to distance himself from Cheney, who many thought should not be a heartbeat away from the presidency, considering his own major health issues related to his heart. But Cheney, even when rejected on some of his advice and counsel, remained loyal until the end of his tenure as vice president under Bush. In his memoirs, however, he would be critical of his colleagues; be a center of controversy in his criticisms of the Obama administration; and have a well-advertised heart transplant, and continue his public engagement on many issues and controversies. While Cheney may have been unpopular to many people, there was no question of his ability and talents to be president of the United States had tragedy befallen George W. Bush, and that was certainly comforting.[15]

Finally, the thirty-five and mounting threats against President Barack Obama, constantly developing before and during his presidency, has brought attention to his vice president, Joseph Biden (1942–), who came to the second-highest office with one of the most extensive records of experience, in years served more than any previous vice president, having served thirty-six years in the U.S. Senate from the state of Delaware, since first elected at age thirty in 1972. Biden had actually been elected a couple of weeks before his thirtieth birthday, and was, therefore, one of the youngest ever to take the oath to be a U.S. senator.

Biden would become chairman, at different times, of the Senate Judiciary Committee and the Senate Foreign Relations Committee, and thus would have a major impact on Supreme Court and other judicial nominations and on foreign policy issues. Having attempted twice to be the nominee of his party for president (in 1988 and 2008), he was seen as very bright, very knowledgeable, and an excellent balance to an inexperienced senator, nearly a generation younger than himself.

Biden was an active, engaged vice president, involved in every major issue of the Obama administration, similar to what Mondale, Gore, and Cheney had been under their presidents. President Obama would often applaud the loyalty and support of his vice president, and express his appreciation of his contributions, and his respect for his abilities. It was clear that were an untoward event to occur, the nation would be in good, well-experienced hands, with a well-respected, competent, and also likeable man in Vice President Biden. Because of his long history with many members of the Senate and the House of Representatives, if he were to become president, he might not be viewed with the contempt and fevered partisan obstruction, as President Obama faced from the day of his first inauguration.[16]

As one examines these fifteen men, the question arises which of this group would have been competent and safe to be president, if an emergency had arisen. In that regard, there are twelve men who would seem to have been the best to assume the office, with political views not to be considered, but the effect on the nation of their ascendancy. This list would include chronologically: Hannibal Hamlin; Lafayette S. Foster; Garret Hobart; John Hay; George C. Marshall; Alben Barkley; Robert F. Kennedy; Nelson Rockefeller; Walter Mondale; Al Gore; Dick Cheney; and Joe Biden.

The list of three other potential presidents would, likely, not have been good for the nation, and they are chronologically: John Nance Garner; Joseph William Martin Jr.; and Spiro Agnew.

Garner is perceived as highly unlikely to have promoted the New Deal visions of FDR, and to most scholars, that would have been a tragedy of major proportions.

Martin, the only Republican Speaker of the House from 1931 to 1995, was seen as not of presidential timber, but then again, most Speakers of the House are not seen in that vein.

It seems clear that Spiro Agnew, however, would have been by far the worst of the fifteen potential presidents, as his criminality that led to his resignation from the vice presidency plus his divisive rhetoric and actions in that office make just about any observer relieved that Gerald Ford succeeded to the presidency upon the resignation of Richard Nixon.

Overall, in most cases of potential presidents, it is believed that they would have conducted themselves well and would have been good for the nation, with some possibly better, maybe a few possibly worse, but with the impossibility of being able to be certain on the impact of the "Might Have Been" presidents.

APPENDIX

Table 17.1 Presidents and Presidential Candidates Who Faced Direct Assassination Threats

Year	*Person*	*Age*	*Political Party*	*City*	*Assassin/ Attempted Assassin*	*Age*	*Impact of Attack*
1835	Andrew Jackson	67	Democrat	Washington, D.C.	Richard Lawrence	34	Unhurt
1865	Abraham Lincoln	56	Republican	Washington, D.C.	John Wilkes Booth	26	Killed
1881	James A. Garfield	49	Republican	Washington, D.C.	Charles Guiteau	39	Killed
1901	William McKinley	58	Republican	Buffalo, New York	Leon Czolgosz	28	Killed
1912	Theodore Roosevelt	53	Progressive	Milwaukee, Wisconsin	John Flammang Schrank	36	Injured
1933	Franklin D. Roosevelt	51	Democrat	Miami, Florida	Giuseppe Zangara	32	Unhurt
1935	Huey P. Long	42	Democrat	Baton Rouge, Louisiana	Dr. Carl Austin Weiss	28	Killed
1950	Harry S. Truman	66	Democrat	Washington, D.C.	Oscar Collazo	36	Unhurt
					Griselio Torresola	25	

Table 17.1 Presidents and Presidential Candidates Who Faced Direct Assassination Threats

Year	*Person*	*Age*	*Political Party*	*City*	*Assassin/ Attempted Assassin*	*Age*	*Impact of Attack*
1963	John F. Kennedy	46	Democrat	Dallas, Texas	Lee Harvey Oswald	24	Killed
1968	Robert F. Kennedy	42	Democrat	Los Angeles, California	Sirhan Sirhan	24	Killed
1972	George C. Wallace	52	Democrat	Laurel, Maryland	Arthur Bremer	21	Injured
1974	Richard M. Nixon	61	Republican	Baltimore, Maryland	Samuel Byck	44	Unhurt
1975	Gerald R. Ford	62	Republican	Sacramento, California	Lynette "Squeaky" Fromme	26	Unhurt
				San Francisco, California	Sara Jane Moore	45	Unhurt
1981	Ronald Reagan	70	Republican	Washington, D.C.	John Hinckley Jr.	25	Injured

Table 17.2 Fifteen Who Might Have Been President if Circumstances Were Different

Date	*Potential Successor*	*Position*	*Potential Successor for*	*Years in Office*	*If Event Occurred*
1861	Hannibal Hamlin	First-Term Vice President	Abraham Lincoln	1861–1865	Lincoln Assassinated in Baltimore Plot
1864					Lincoln Assassinated by Sniper Shot
1865	Lafayette S. Foster	President Pro Tempore of Senate	Andrew Johnson	1865–1869	If Vice President Andrew Johnson Killed in Lincoln Assassination Conspiracy
1901	Garret Hobart	First-Term Vice President	William McKinley	1897–1901	Hobart Lived until McKinley's Assassination
1903	John Hay	Secretary of State	Theodore Roosevelt	1901–1909	Roosevelt Assassinated

Table 17.2 Fifteen Who Might Have Been President if Circumstances Were Different

Date	*Potential Successor*	*Position*	*Potential Successor for*	*Years in Office*	*If Event Occurred*
1933	John Nance Garner	Vice President Elect	Franklin D. Roosevelt	1933–1934	Roosevelt Assassinated at Bayfront Park
1933–1934		Vice President			Roosevelt Assassinated from “Business Plot”
1947	George C. Marshall	Secretary of State	Harry S. Truman	1945–1953	Truman Assassinated by Stern Gang
	Joseph William Martin Jr.	Speaker of House of Representatives			
1950	Alben Barkley	Vice President			Truman Assassinated at Blair House
1968	Robert F. Kennedy	Senator, Democratic Presidential Favorite	Presidency in 1968 Election		Kennedy Survived Assassination at Ambassador Hotel in Los Angeles
1972	Spiro Agnew	Vice President	Richard M. Nixon	1969–1974	Arthur Bremer Assassinated Nixon instead of Attacking George C. Wallace
1974					Agnew Scandal Had Not Arisen Until after Nixon’s Resignation

Table 17.2 Fifteen Who Might Have Been President if Circumstances Were Different

Date	*Potential Successor*	*Position*	*Potential Successor for*	*Years in Office*	*If Event Occurred*
1975	Nelson Rockefeller	Vice President	Gerald R. Ford	1974–1977	Ford Assassinated at Capitol Park, Sacramento
					Ford Assassinated outside St. Francis Hotel, San Francisco
1979	Walter Mondale	Vice President	Jimmy Carter	1977–1981	Carter Assassinated by Raymond Lee Harvey
1980					Carter Assassinated by John Hinckley Jr.
1994–1996	Albert Gore Jr.	Vice President	Bill Clinton	1993–2001	Clinton Assassinated Based on Numerous Threats
2001–2009	Dick Cheney	Vice President	George W. Bush	2001–2009	Bush Assassinated Based on Numerous Threats
2009–Present	Joseph Biden	Vice President	Barack Obama	2009–2017	Obama Assassinated Based on Numerous Threats

Table 17.3 Conspiracy Theories Surrounding Assassinations of Presidents and Presidential Candidates

Individual	*Conspiracy Theory/ Potentially Targeted by*	*Reasoning for Theory*
Abraham Lincoln	Catholic Church	Nativism – Anti-Catholic Sentiments in America
	Secretary of War Edwin Stanton	Alienated from Lincoln
	Confederate President Jefferson Davis and Confederate Vice President Alexander Stephens and Secretary of State Judah P. Benjamin	Confederate Leadership Targeted American President
Franklin D. Roosevelt	Italian Mafia	Assassination Attempt from Italian Giuseppe Zangara (Connection to Mafia)
	American Liberty League (Comprised of American Business Leaders, including DuPont Family, Prescott Bush, 1924 Democratic Presidential Nominee John W. Davis, 1928 Democratic Presidential Nominee Alfred E. Smith, Leaders of US Steel, General Motors, Standard Oil, Chase National Bank, and Goodyear Tire and Rubber Company)	Opposed Roosevelt's Economic Programs
	Nazi Germany, Fascist Italy, and Imperial Japan	World War II Enemies of United States
	Joseph Stalin	World War II Ally, but Ideological Opponent
	Winston Churchill	Opposed Loss of British Empire as Part of the Atlantic Charter
Huey P. Long	Shot by Bodyguard	Shot from a Different Gun than Gun Possessed by Dr. Weiss
	Roosevelt Administration	Vocal Critic of Franklin D. Roosevelt
John F. Kennedy	Fidel Castro	Response to Bay of Pigs Invasion
	Cuban Exiles	Angered by Kennedy's Inability to Overthrow Fidel Castro
	Lyndon B. Johnson	Became President Following Kennedy's Death
	Richard M. Nixon	Left Dallas Hours before Kennedy Arrived (Bitter over 1960 Presidential Defeat)
	Gerald R. Ford	Warren Commission Member Allegedly Covered Up Evidence
	George H. W. Bush	Possible CIA Agent with Connection to E. Howard Hunt

Individual	*Conspiracy Theory/ Potentially Targeted by*	*Reasoning for Theory*
	Watergate Burglar E. Howard Hunt	Photographic Evidence Shows Him Present in Dallas (Associated with CIA)
	Witness Tampering, Intimidation, and Foul Play	Some Witnesses Killed within One Year
	"Grassy Knoll" Theory (Multiple Gunmen)	Based on Number of Shots Fired and Location of Shots
	"Magic Bullet Theory"	One Bullet Shot Kennedy and Texas Governor John Connally
	Clay Shaw	New Orleans District Attorney Jim Garrison Put Him on Trial for Involvement (Found Not Guilty)
	CIA	Kennedy Reduced Power of CIA after Failed Bay of Pigs Invasion
	"Shadow Government"	Wealthy Industrialists and Right-Wing Politicians Opposed Kennedy's Policies
	Defense and Intelligence Interests	American Military Feared Reduction in Defense Expenditure (Military-Industrial Complex)
	Secret Service	Accidentally Shot Kennedy in Response to Attack on Presidential Motorcade
	FBI Director J. Edgar Hoover	Unhappy with Treatment of FBI and Kennedy's Scandalous Affairs
	Soviet Premier Nikita Khrushchev	Cold War Opponent of United States
	Right-Wing Extremist Groups (Southern Segregationists, Texas Oilmen, the Ku Klux Klan, the John Birch Society, and Right-Wing Christian elements)	Opposed Civil Rights
	Kennedy Accidentally Killed by Oswald; Texas Governor John Connally was Oswald's Intended Target	Oswald was Angry at Connolly for Not Helping Him with Issue
Robert F. Kennedy	Second Gunman	More Shots Fired (13) than Contained in Sirhan's Gun (8)
	Thomas Eugene Cesar	RFK Security Guard Withdrew Gun during Exchange with Sirhan Sirhan
	Manchurian Candidate Syndrome	Based on Popular Movie –Sirhan Programmed to Kill (No Memory of Assassination)

Individual	*Conspiracy Theory/ Potentially Targeted by*	*Reasoning for Theory*
	CIA Agents, in Conjunction with Angry Cubans	President Kennedy Reduced Powers of CIA after Failed Bay of Pigs Invasion
	FBI Director J. Edgar Hoover	Clashed with Kennedy when Kennedy Served as Attorney General
	Teamsters Union President Jimmy Hoffa (American Mafia)	RFK Fought against Organized Crime
	Lyndon B. Johnson	Mistreated by RFK as JFK's Vice President
	Defense and Intelligence Interests	Feared an End to Cold War (End of Military-Industrial Complex)
	Ku Klux Klan	Opposed Civil Rights Promoted by JFK and RFK
	Richard M. Nixon	Feared Losing to Another Kennedy
George C. Wallace	Richard M. Nixon	Concerned about His Effect on 1972 Presidential Election

Table 17.4 Notable Victims of Assassination Attempts against Presidents and Presidents-Elect

Date	*Individual*	*Position*	*Type of Injury*	*Under President*
04/14/1865	William Seward	Secretary of State	Stabbed with Knife	Abraham Lincoln
02/15/1933	Anton Cermak	Chicago Mayor	Assassinated from Gunshot	President-Elect Franklin D. Roosevelt
11/01/1950	Leslie Coffelt	Secret Service Agent	Assassinated from Gunshot	Harry S. Truman
	Joseph Downs	White House Police Officer	Injured from Gunshot	
	Donald Birdzell	Washington, D.C., Police Officer	Injured from Gunshot	
11/22/1963	John Connally	Texas Governor	Injured from Gunshot	John F. Kennedy
03/30/1981	Timothy McCarthy	Secret Service Officer	Injured from Gunshot	Ronald Reagan
	Thomas Delahanty	Washington, D.C., Police Officer	Injured from Gunshot	
	James Brady	White House Press Secretary	Injured from Gunshot; Died from Resulting Injuries in 2014	

NOTES

INTRODUCTION

1. The subject of presidential assassination has been examined in several studies over the years. These include: Robert J. Donovan, *The Assassins* (New York: Harper & Brothers, 1955); James W. Clarke, *American Assassins: The Darker Side of Politics* (Princeton, NJ: Princeton University Press, 1982); and Oliver M. Willard and Nancy E. Marion, *Killing the President: Assassinations, Attempts, and Rumored Attempts on U.S. Commanders-In-Chief* (Santa Barbara, CA: Praeger, 2010). Still, there are gaps in the literature. My work seeks to examine areas not covered by anyone else, including presidential candidates and those who "might have been" president, as well as covering presidential threats up to late 2014, against the living American presidents as of that year.

Stephen Sondheim and John Weidman, *Assassins* (New York: Theatre Communications Group, 1991) is a book published to accompany the play produced for off-Broadway by these two authors, includes music and lyrics, and looks at famous presidential assassins, including those involved in attempts against Abraham Lincoln, James A. Garfield, William McKinley, Franklin D. Roosevelt, John F. Kennedy, Richard Nixon, Gerald R. Ford, and Ronald Reagan. The Broadway cast recording of *Assassins* remains available and gives listeners a sense of the popular music of the different periods of time when presidents faced assassination. There have been several productions on Broadway, and in Los Angeles, London, Toronto, and Capetown, South Africa.

The interaction of the various presidential assassins of different eras lends a sense of uniqueness to the productions. At the end of the production, after a total of eleven musical numbers, the group of assassins load their guns and open fire on the audience. The play won five Tony Awards and two nominations in 2004, and also won three Drama Desk Awards and four nominations that same year. Although originally produced in 1990, with an off-Broadway production and then a West End production in London in 1992, the awards won in 2004 were based on the judgment that the production of that year was a revival, not an original musical.

There have been many scholarly articles attempting to assess the reality of violence in American history that have led to presidential assassinations becoming a serious threat. Among them are: *Political Assassination: The Violent Side of American Political Life* (www.digitalhistory.uh.edu/topic_display.cfm?tcid=98); Robert T. M. Phillips, "Assessing Presidential Stalkers and Assassins," *Journal of the American Academy of Psychiatry and the Law* 34 (2006): 154–64; and Frederick M. Kaiser, *Direct Assaults against Presidents, Presidents-Elect, and Candidates* (Washington, DC: Congressional Research Service, Library of Congress, 2008).

A book that gives the Secret Service perspective on protecting the life of the president of the United States is Ronald Kessler, *In the President's Secret Service: Behind the Scenes with Agents in the Line of Fire and the Presidents They Protect* (New York: Crown Archetype, 2009).

I. ANDREW JACKSON AT THE U.S. CAPITOL

1. The story of Andrew Jackson's assassination threats is well covered in several major studies of his presidency. Among them are: H. W. Brands, *Andrew Jackson: His Life and Times* (New York: Doubleday, 2005), 503–5; Jon Meacham, *American Lion: Andrew Jackson and His Times* (New York: Random House, 2008), 298–301; Sean Wilentz, *Andrew Jackson* (New York: Times Books, 2005), 113; and Donald B. Cole, *The Presidency of Andrew Jackson* (Lawrence: University Press of Kansas, 1993), 189, 221–22.

2. The Robert Randolph assault on Jackson in 1833 is documented in *The Microcosm, American and Gazette, Providence, Rhode Island, May 11, 1833* (www.rarenewspapers.com/view/575685), 2–3, available from Timothy Hughes: Rare and Early Newspapers. It is also covered in *The American Literary Blog* (http://americanliteraryblog.blogpost.com/2010/04/assassination-attempt), which also describes the Richard Lawrence attempt in 1835. Also, both attempts are discussed on the website: http://bgpappa.hubpages.com/hub/The-First-Presidential-Assassination-Attempt.

3. The Lawrence assassination attempt is also covered on the following website: http://winningherwaytofame.blogpost.com/2011/12/would-be-assassinations-of-President-Andrew-Jackson, as is the written threat of Junius Brutus Booth, father of Lincoln assassin John Wilkes Booth, on July 4, 1835. The

surprise that the father of Booth had threatened to kill Jackson thirty years earlier was authenticated by the staff of the Andrew Jackson plantation, the Hermitage, in Nashville, Tennessee, and reported in the *Knoxville, Tennessee News Sentinel* in 2009, as follows: Katie Freeman, "Letter Threatening Jackson's Life Determined to Be Written by Father of Man Who Killed Lincoln" (www.knoxnews.com/news/2009/jan/25/).

2. ABRAHAM LINCOLN AT FORD'S THEATRE

1. The earlier "Baltimore Plot" before Lincoln's inauguration in 1861 has two full-length studies: Michael J. Kline, *The Baltimore Plot: The First Conspiracy to Assassinate Abraham Lincoln* (Yardley, PA: Westholme Publishing, 2008) and Daniel Stashower, *The Hour of Peril: The Secret Plot to Murder Lincoln before the Civil War* (New York: Minotaur Books, 2013).

2. Full-length studies of the events surrounding the assassination include: Jim Bishop, *The Day Lincoln Was Shot* (New York: Harper & Row, 1955); and Edward Steers, *Blood on the Moon: The Assassination of President Abraham Lincoln* (Lexington: University Press of Kentucky, 2001). Also see the chapter in Harold Holzer, *Lincoln, President-Elect: Abraham Lincoln and the Great Secession Winter, 1860–1861* (New York: Simon and Schuster, 2008), 361–96. Studies of Booth include: Michael W. Kaufmann, *American Brutus: John Wilkes Booth and the Lincoln Conspiracy* (New York: Random House, 2004); James Swanson, *Manhunt: The Twelve Day Chase for Lincoln's Killer* (New York, William Morrow, 2006); and Nora Titone, *My Thoughts Be Bloody: The Bitter Rivalry That Led to the Assassination of Abraham Lincoln* (New York: Free Press, 2010).

3. JAMES A. GARFIELD AT THE D.C. RAILROAD STATION

1. The assassination of James A. Garfield has drawn recent interest, as one realizes the potential of this president, the belief that he might have been the standout president of the Gilded Age, had he not been murdered by Charles J. Guiteau.

The *New York Times*, *Harper's Weekly*, and *Frank Leslie's Illustrated Newspaper* cover the assassination in their usual fine fashion. The James A. Garfield Papers in the Manuscript Division, Library of Congress, offer primary sources, and the Garfield National Historic Site in Mentor, Ohio, gives a lot of attention to the death and its effect on the nation and his widow and children. Allan Peskin's

Garfield: A Biography (Kent, OH: Kent State University Press, 1978) is a full-length study. A good discussion on Garfield's assassination and the medical malpractice involved is in Ira Rutkow, *James A. Garfield* (New York: Times Books, 2006), 1–4, 82–139. Also see Justus D. Doenecke, *The Presidencies of James A. Garfield and Chester A. Arthur* (Lawrence: University Press of Kansas, 1981), 53, 95–96.

Online sources include: "Alexander Graham Bell and the Garfield Assassination," http://www.historybuff.com/library/refgarfield.html; "The Death of President Garfield, 1881," http://www.eyewitnesstohistory.com/gar.html; "The Charles Guiteau Trial: A Chronology," http://law2.umkc.edu/faculty/projects/trials/guiteau/guiteauchrono.html; and "Past Imperfect: The Stalking of the President," http://blogs.smithsonianmag.com/history/2012/01/the-stalking-of-the-president. For the medical report on President Garfield, see "Official Bulletin of the Autopsy on the Body of President Garfield, September 20, 1881," http://www.presidency.ucsb.edu/ws/?pid+69142.

2. Two full-length studies of Garfield and his assassination are: Kenneth D. Ackerman, *Dark Horse: The Surprise Election and Political Murder of President James A. Garfield* (Cambridge, MA: Da Capo Press, 2003), especially 371–446; and the magnificent study of Candace Millard, *Destiny of the Republic: A Tale of Madness, Medicine and the Murder of a President* (New York: Doubleday, 2011).

3. The trial of the assassin, Charles J. Guiteau, is covered in all of these named books here, and also in Charles E. Rosenberg, *The Trial of the Assassin Guiteau: Psychiatry and the Law in the Gilded Age* (Chicago: University of Chicago Press, 1995). A PBS documentary on the assassination of James A. Garfield is planned for 2015, as part of *The American Experience* series.

4. WILLIAM MCKINLEY AT THE BUFFALO PAN-AMERICAN EXPOSITION

1. The assassination of William McKinley has received growing attention as McKinley's reputation as a significant president has grown, plus with Theodore Roosevelt as his successor in the White House.

The assassination is well covered in the *New York Times*, *Harper's Weekly*, and *Frank Leslie's Illustrated Newspaper*. The William McKinley Papers in the Manuscript Division, Library of Congress, provide primary sources, and the William McKinley Presidential Library and Museum in Canton, Ohio, offers valuable insights into his life and death.

McKinley's assassination was much ignored in gaining attention, especially with the prominence of his successor, Theodore Roosevelt. Fortunately, the two full studies of that event in the past decade have brought him to the attention of students of assassination, in a way that should have been rectified long ago. Also, with Leon Czolgosz a declared anarchist, that made him more interesting in the age of terrorism, which became much more evident in the aftermath of September 11, 2001.

2. The assassination is fully analyzed in two works: Eric Rauchway, *Murdering McKinley: The Making of Theodore Roosevelt's America* (New York: Hill & Wang, 2003), especially 3–53; and Scott Miller, *The President and the Assassin: McKinley, Terror, and Empire at the Dawn of the American Century* (New York: Random House, 2011), especially 300–30. Lewis L. Gould, *The Presidency of William McKinley* (Lawrence: University Press of Kansas, 1980), 251–52, briefly deals with the assassination.

5. THEODORE ROOSEVELT AT THE MILWAUKEE GILPATRICK HOTEL

1. Studies on the presidential election of 1912, during which the assassination attempt took place, include: George E. Mowry, *Theodore Roosevelt and the Progressive Movement* (Madison: University of Wisconsin Press, 1946), 276; Francis L. Broderick, *Progressivism at Risk: Electing a President in 1912* (New York: Greenwood Press, 1989), 189–92; James Chace, *1912: Wilson, Roosevelt, Taft, and Debs: The Election That Changed the Country* (New York: Simon & Schuster, 2004), 230–35; Lewis L. Gould, *Four Hats in the Ring: The 1912 Election and the Birth of Modern American Politics* (Lawrence: University Press of Kansas, 2008), 170–72; Sidney Milkis, *Theodore Roosevelt, the Progressive Party, and the Transformation of American Democracy* (Lawrence: University Press of Kansas, 2009), 245–48; and the magnificent recent work of Doris Kearns Goodwin, *The Bully Pulpit: Theodore Roosevelt, William Howard Taft, and the Golden Age of Journalism* (New York: Simon & Schuster, 2013), 732–35.

2. The study of Theodore Roosevelt's presidency is massive, but not very much attention had been paid to the attempted assassination, when he was running on the third-party Progressive Party line in 1912, and none on the earlier assassination threat in 1903 at his Oyster Bay, Long Island, New York, home at Sagamore Hill.

Online sources on the 1912 assassination attempt include: "Teddy Roosevelt Shot by Anarchist, Manuscript of Speech Saves His Life," http://www.historybuff.com/library/refteddy.html; "Theodore Roosevelt's Assassination Attempt," http://www.historybyzim.com/2012/10/; "The Time Teddy Roosevelt Got Shot in the Chest, Gave Speech Anyway," http://mentalfloss.com/

article/12789/; “The Speech That Saved Teddy Roosevelt’s Life,” http://www.smithsonianmag.com/history-archaeology/; “Past Imperfect: Theodore Roosevelt’s Life-Saving Speech,” http://blogs.smithsonianmag.com/history/2012/04/; “Justice Story: Teddy Roosevelt Survives Assassin When Bullet Hits Folded Speech in His Pocket,” http://www.nydailynews.com/news/justice-story/takes-kill-bull-moose; “Shot in the Chest 100 Years Ago, Teddy Roosevelt Kept on Talking,” http://www.history.com/news/; “The Attempted Assassination of Theodore Roosevelt,” http://milwaukee.about.com/od/historylandmarks/a/Roosevelt.html; “Health and Medical History of President Theodore Roosevelt: Assassination Attempt, 1912,” http://www.doctorzebra.com/prez/z_x26a_g.htm; “Glass Used by Teddy Roosevelt after Assassination Attempt,” http://www.wisconsinhistory.org/museum/artifacts/archives/001692.asp; and “Murderpedia: John Flammang Schrank,” http://murderpedia.org/male.S/s/schrank-john.html.

3. The *New York Times* and other major newspapers in New York and Washington, D.C., covered the second, more direct threat, but only local newspapers on Long Island seem to have mentioned, without much attention, the earlier threat. The Theodore Roosevelt Papers in the Manuscript Division, Library of Congress, offer primary sources, along with the Theodore Roosevelt National Historic Site at Sagamore Hill.

4. The 1903 Henry Weilbrenner assassination threat at TR’s home in Oyster Bay, while TR was president, has been well hidden and is not mentioned in any work on the twenty-sixth president. Information about this was found at the following sites: “Assassination Attempt against Theodore Roosevelt,” http://suite101.com/a/; “The Syosset Farmer Who Would Have Shot Theodore Roosevelt?” http://www.oysterbayhistorical.org/submissions-summer-2011.html; also posted on “Syosset Jericho Tribune: It Happened in Syosset!—April 2, 2010,” http://www.antonnews.com/syossetjerichotribune/opinion/7055/.

5. The major study in depth of the 1912 attempt by John Flammang Schrank is Gerard Helferich, *Theodore Roosevelt and the Assassin: Madness, Vengeance, and the Campaign of 1912* (Guilford, CT: Lyons Press, 2013). An immediate study of the 1912 assassination attempt is that of Oliver E. Remey et al., *The Attempted Assassination of Ex-President Theodore Roosevelt* (New York: Ulan Press, JPS Norton, 2012)—originally published in 1912, and including photos of the event. Other major studies on the life of T. R. cover the event in less detail, including H. W. Brands, *T. R.: The Last Romantic* (New York: Basic Books, 1997), 720–24; Edmund Morris, *Colonel Roosevelt* (New York: Random House, 2010), 243–51; Patricia O’Toole, *When Trumpets Call: Theodore Roosevelt after the White House* (New York: Simon & Schuster, 2005), 217–22, 232–34; and Kathleen Dalton, *Theodore Roosevelt: A Strenuous Life* (New York: Knopf, 2002), 404–6.

6. FRANKLIN D. ROOSEVELT AT MIAMI BAYFRONT PARK

1. The Franklin D. Roosevelt presidency is the most written about of any twentieth-century president, and only Abraham Lincoln and George Washington have more published about them than FDR. But with all that has been published, it is only in recent years that much attention has been paid to the Giuseppe Zangara assassination attempt in 1933 and to the "Business Plot" of 1933–1934. The best sources for these events are the *New York Times* coverage, along with the Franklin D. Roosevelt Presidential Library and Museum in Hyde Park, New York, which has all of his presidential papers and great museum exhibits, including on the conspiracies against FDR.

The specialized studies on this assassination are: Blaise Picchi, *The Five Weeks of Giuseppe Zangara: The Man Who Would Assassinate FDR* (Chicago: Academy Chicago Press, 1998); and Sally Denton, *The Plots against the President: FDR, a Nation in Crisis, and the Rise of the American Right* (New York: Bloomsbury Press, 2012), 66–114.

Online sources include: "Attempted Assassination of FDR in Bayfront Park," http://miami-history.com/; "Joe Zangara Interview: Attempted Assassination of FDR," http://www.awesomestories.com/assets/; "The Strange Surroundings of the FDR Assassination Attempt," http://politicsreport.com/article/; "The Assassination Attempt on President-Elect Franklin Roosevelt," http://www.examiner.com/article/; "Lou Hutt and the FDR Assassination Attempt," http://www.newsphotog.com/2012/04/; "1933: FDR Escaped an Assassin's Bullet" (*Coronet Magazine* 1960), http://www.oldmagazinearticles.com/FDR_Assassination_Attempt/; "Murderpedia: Giuseppe Zangara," http://murderpedia.org/male.Z/z/zangara-giuseppe.htm; "The Attempted Coup against FDR," http://www.ctka.net/pr399-fdr.html; "The Real Plot to Overthrow FDR's America," http://www/dailykos.com/2005/02/27/95580/; and "The Plot against FDR," http://economistsview.typepad.com/economistsview/2007/07/.

2. For the Zangara assassination attempt against FDR, the available sources include: Frank Freidel, *Franklin D. Roosevelt: A Rendezvous with Destiny* (Boston: Little, Brown, 1990), 87–88; Arthur M. Schlesinger Jr., *The Age of Roosevelt: The Crisis of the Old Order, 1919–1933* (Boston: Houghton Mifflin, 1957), 464–66; James MacGregor Burns, *Roosevelt: The Lion and the Fox* (New York: Harcourt, Brace, 1956), 147; Jean Edward Smith, *FDR* (New York: Random House, 2007), 296–98; Conrad Black, *Franklin D. Roosevelt: Champion of Freedom* (New York: Public Affairs, 2003), 263–64; and H. W. Brands, *Traitor to His Class: The Privileged Life and Radical Presidency of Franklin Delano Roosevelt* (New York: Doubleday, 2008), 277–81.

3. On the Business Plot of conservatives and corporate leaders and Smedley Butler, a full study was done by Jules Archer, *The Plot to Seize the White House:*

The Shocking True Story of the Conspiracy to Overthrow FDR (New York: Skyhorse Publishing, 2007). Also, Sally Denton, *The Plots against the President: FDR, a Nation in Crisis, and the Rise of the American Right* (New York: Bloombury Press, 2012), 175–221, thoroughly covers the same ground. Only Arthur M. Schlesinger Jr.'s *The Age of Roosevelt: The Politics of Upheaval, 1935–1936* (Boston: Houghton Mifflin, 1960), 82–83, 85, covers the Business Plot, of any of the standard works on FDR, but only briefly as indicated.

7. HUEY P. LONG AT THE LOUISIANA STATE CAPITOL

1. The controversial life and career of Huey P. Long has gained the attention of only a few scholars, but he remains a person of great fascination and wonderment whether he could have been a serious presidential candidate, and even nominee of the Democratic Party in 1940, if not 1936.

The best sources for Huey Long are the files of the *New York Times* and the two outstanding scholarly biographies: T. Harry Williams, *Huey Long* (New York: Knopf, 1969), which won the Pulitzer Prize and National Book Award in 1970; and the more recent shorter study by Richard D. White Jr., *Kingfish: The Reign of Huey P. Long* (New York: Random House, 2006). Their coverage of the assassination is found as follows: the Williams biography on pages 862–76; and the White study on pages 260–72. There are lots of interesting materials on Long, and on his assassination, at the official Huey Long website: http://www.hueylong.com/, including original documents and photographs.

2. As years have passed, the controversy about Long's medical treatment after he was shot, and the issue of whether Dr. Carl Weiss actually was the gunman rather than Long's own bodyguards, who used Weiss as a "patsy," has raged, and there are online sources that demonstrate this debate. On Long's surgery and medical treatment, the following is valuable: "Huey P. Long's Last Operation: When Medicine and Politics Don't Mix," http://www.ncbi.nlm.nih.gov/pmc/articles/PMC3307515/. In 1992, the Louisiana State Police compiled a final investigative report on Huey Long, published on June 5, 1992, including documents that stated the belief that Dr. Carl Weiss had been the assassin of Long. This document was found online and is available from the State of Louisiana, Department of Public Safety and Corrections, Public Safety Services, and includes a case report, crime lab information, a preliminary report, and a final report.

Despite this work done fifty-seven years after the Long assassination, the subject of Dr. Carl Weiss as the assassin continues to fascinate many scholars, journalists, and ordinary citizens including the following: "Controversy, mystery still surround the death of Huey P. Long," www.nola.com/politics/index.ssf/2010/09/; "Who Killed the Kingfish Remains Unanswered," http://www.thepineywoods.com/HueyLongJan11.htm; "Assassination of Huey P. Long—Baton Rouge, Louisiana," http://www. exploresouthernhistory.com/hueylong2.html; "Who Killed the Kingfish?" http://www.law.uga.edu/dwilkes_more/other_4kingfish.html; "Researchers Exhume Doctor's Grave to Resolve Part of Huey Long Legend," http://www. nytimes.com/1991/10/21/us/; "Carl Austin Weiss," http://murderpedia.org/male.W/w/weiss-carl-austin.htm.

The memory of Huey P. Long is honored in the Louisiana State Capitol in Baton Rouge, and in the National Statuary Hall in the U.S. Capitol in Washington, D.C.

Finally, there is an excellent documentary by Ken Burns on PBS, *The American Experience: Huey Long*, 1985.

8. HARRY S. TRUMAN AT BLAIR HOUSE

1. The Truman presidency is well covered in the pages of the *New York Times* and the *Washington Post*, and the Harry Truman Presidential Library and Museum in Independence, Missouri, has all of the manuscripts of his presidency, including information about the assassination attempts against Truman. Online sources on the Truman assassination attempt in 1950 include: "President Harry S. Truman: Survived Assassination Attempt at the Blair House," http://www.historynet.com/harry-s-truman/; and "Assassination Attempt on President Truman's Life," http://www.trumanlibrary.org/trivia/assassin.htm/.

2. On the Zionist Stern Gang threat, see the following: "Jews Tried to Kill Truman in 1947," http://www.dcdave.com/article5/120510.htm/; and "The Attempted Assassination of President Truman," http://ariwatch.com/OurAlly/AttemptedAssassinationOfTruman.html. There is controversy, to be noted, about these two sites, as many would consider them anti-Semitic in nature, but the author thought they should be listed and judged by the reader, as to their veracity, on an attempt only noted by Margaret Truman, and no other Truman scholar to date.

3. The major studies of Truman cover the assassination attempt by Puerto Rican nationalists Griselio Torresola and Oscar Collazo in 1950 as follows: David McCullough, *Truman* (New York: Simon and Schuster, 1992), 809–13; Robert H. Ferrell, *Harry S. Truman: A Life* (Columbia: University of Missouri Press, 1994), 327–28; Robert Dallek, *Harry S. Truman* (New York: Times Books, 2008), 110–11; Donald R. McCoy, *The Presidency of Harry S. Truman* (Lawrence: University Press of Kansas, 1984), 242; Margaret Truman, *Harry S. Truman* (New York: Morrow, 1973), 486–89. Truman's daughter is the only

person to state that the Zionist Stern Gang attempted to kill her father, discussing it in her biography of her father on pages 489–90.

The only full-length study of the 1950 Puerto Rican nationalist attack at Blair House is Stephen Hunter and John Bainbridge Jr., *American Gunfight: The Plot to Kill Harry Truman, and the Shootout That Stopped It* (New York: Simon & Schuster, 2005).

9. JOHN F. KENNEDY AT DEALEY PLAZA

1. The Richard Pavlick 1960 assassination threat is covered in "The Kennedy Assassin Who Failed," Smithsonianmag.com/history/the-kennedy-assassin-who-failed-153519612/; and mentalfloss.com/article/30444/1960-retired-postal-worker-almost-killed-jfk/2013/11/11/.

2. The Chicago plot of early November 1963 is covered in 22november1963.org/uk/jfk-assassination-plot-chicago.

3. The standard studies of the assassination were published within a few years, most notably that of Jim Bishop, *The Day Kennedy Was Shot* (New York: Harper Perennial, 2013), and William Manchester, *The Death of a President: November 20–November 25, 1963* (New York: BBS Publishing, 1967).

4. The torrent of works on the Kennedy assassination, with the belief that there was a conspiracy, multiplied very quickly, and has continued to do so over the past fifty years, and to attempt a listing is pointless. But the rejection and destruction of all conspiracy theories is well covered in two studies: Gerald Posner, *Case Closed: Lee Harvey Oswald and the Assassination of JFK* (New York: Random House, 1993); and the massive work by Vincent Bugliosi, *Reclaiming History: The Assassination of President John F. Kennedy* (New York: W. W. Norton, 2007).

10. ROBERT F. KENNEDY AT THE LOS ANGELES AMBASSADOR HOTEL

1. The controversy surrounding the life and death of Senator Robert F. Kennedy continues, as many feel that he would have been the thirty-seventh president of the United States had he not been assassinated in June 1968.
The life and career of RFK is well covered in the files of the *New York Times* and *Washington Post*, as well as the *Los Angeles Times*, the city in which he was assassinated. The Robert F. Kennedy manuscripts are in the archives of the John F. Kennedy Presidential Library and Museum in Boston, Massachusetts, al-

though there is the possibility of them being deposited elsewhere in the future, as there are family members, including his widow, Ethel Kennedy, who feel that RFK has been overshadowed by his brothers, President Kennedy and Senator Edward Kennedy, in the attention and space given to both of them, much greater than RFK. See "Family of Robert F. Kennedy Rethinks His Place at Library," http://www.nytimes.com/2011/07/12/us/12rfk.html.

Two significant studies of the assassination contradict each other. William Klaber and Philip H. Melanson, *Shadow Play: The Murder of Robert F. Kennedy, the Trial of Sirhan Sirhan, and the Failure of American Justice* (New York: St. Martin's Press, 1997) sees contradictions and a conspiracy to cover up the truth about the events. But Mel Ayton, *The Forgotten Terrorist: Sirhan Sirhan and the Assassination of Robert F. Kennedy* (Washington, D.C.: Potomac Books, 2007) argues the guilt of Sirhan, and the act as the forerunner of present-day terrorism.

Finally, PBS produced a great documentary on RFK, *The American Experience: RFK*, in 2004.

2. The major scholarly study of RFK, the standard for RFK, Arthur M. Schlesinger Jr., *Robert Kennedy and His Times* (Boston: Houghton Mifflin, 1978) does not mention Sirhan Sirhan, and only spends three pages on the last moments before he was shot, and the funeral, on pages 914–16. C. David Heyman, *RFK: A Candid Biography of Robert F. Kennedy* (New York: Dutton, 1998), 486–509, covers the background, the scene, and the impressions, in interviews, of the tragic events, and of course, mentions Sirhan by name.

11. GEORGE C. WALLACE AT LAUREL, MARYLAND, SHOPPING CENTER

1. The controversial life and career of George C. Wallace, including the assassination attempt against him in 1972 by Arthur Bremer, which paralyzed him for life, causing great pain and suffering, until his death in 1998, has drawn the attention of a few journalists and scholars.

The *New York Times* and the *Washington Post* are, as usual, the best sources for the events surrounding Wallace and the events he was involved in, including the assassination attempt. The George C. and Lurleen B. Wallace Collection of manuscripts are located in the Alabama Department of Archives and History in Montgomery, Alabama, the state capital. An exceptional documentary from PBS, titled *The American Experience: George Wallace: Settin' the Woods on Fire* (2000), demonstrates Wallace as he was, for those who did not witness the phenomenon of the Alabama governor.

Online sources about the Wallace shooting abound, including: "Portrait of an Assassin: Arthur Bremer," http://www.pbs.org/wgbh/amex/wallace/sfeature/assasin.html; "George C. Wallace," http://www.encyclopediaofalabama.org/face/Article.jsp?id=h-1676; "Bremer and Wallace: It's Déjà vu All Over Again," http://www.ctka.net/pr599-bremer.html; "The Wallace Shooting: 40 Years Later," http://www.gazette.net/article/20120511/NEWS/705119655/1122/; "The Day George Wallace Was Shot," http://opensalon.com/blog/david_goodloe/2012/05/15/; "George Wallace's Assassination Attempt: FBI Agent Reflects, 40 Years Later," http://articles.washingtonpost.com/2012-05-09/local/35454828_1_arth; and "Witness to Wallace Assassination Attempt Speaks," http://www.wsfa.com/story/7339114/.

2. The three major studies of Wallace and coverage of the Bremer assassination attempt are: Marshall Frady, *Wallace: The Classic Portrait of Alabama Governor George Wallace* (New York: Random House, 1996), 252–83 (but this study stops in 1976, and only mentions the assassination scenario briefly); Stephan Lesher, *George Wallace: American Populist* (New York, Addison-Wesley, 1994), 479–87; and Dan T. Carter, *The Politics of Rage: George Wallace, the Origins of the New Conservatism, and the Transformation of American Politics* (New York: Simon & Schuster, 1995), 419–55 (the most detailed analysis of Bremer and the assassination attempt). Also, Arthur Bremer had compiled a diary, 142 pages when published in 1973 by Harper's Magazine Press, under the title *An Assassin's Diary*.

12. RICHARD M. NIXON AND THE BALTIMORE AIRPORT INCIDENT

1. Richard Nixon remains the most controversial modern president, but information about the potential threat of Arthur Bremer, who stalked Nixon in the spring of 1972, before wounding and paralyzing George C. Wallace, is hard to find. Even the Samuel Byck attempt to hijack a plane in the Baltimore-Washington Airport on February 22, 1974, resulting in his suicide after being shot, is not easy to document, as it was mostly ignored at the time.

The *New York Times* and *Washington Post* remain the best news sources available. The Richard M. Nixon Presidential Library and Museum in Yorba Linda, California, has all of the records and manuscripts of his life and presidency, and any available materials regarding these assassination threats.

2. For the incident involving former police officer Edwin Gaudet in New Orleans, reported on NBC News on August 20, 1973, see: "New Orleans/Nixon Trip/ Assassination Plot," http://tvnews.vanderbilt.edu/program.pl?ID=472120.

3. None of the major studies of Nixon mention Bremer or Byck. The best sources that exist are: "Samuel Joseph Byck," http://www.murderpedia.org/male.B/b/byck-samuel.htm; the History Channel documentary *The Plot to Kill Nixon* (2007); and the film from New Home Line Video *The Assassination of Richard Nixon* (2005), starring Sean Penn as Samuel Byck, with an excellent review of the film, as follows: http://www.dvdmg.com/assassinationofrichard-nixon.shtml.

4. For the Robert K. Preston White House helicopter incident, which occurred on February 17, 1974, before the Byck attempted airplane hijacking, see: "Protection of the White House Complex in the Twentieth Century," http://www.prop1.org/park/pave/rev9.htm.

13. GERALD R. FORD AT SACRAMENTO AND SAN FRANCISCO

1. Gerald R. Ford had an experience no other president faced while in office—two direct assassination attempts, both by women, and within seventeen days of each other in September 1975. These are well covered in the *New York Times*, *Washington Post*, and *Los Angeles Times*, with California being the state where both assassination attempts occurred. The Gerald R. Ford Presidential Library in Ann Arbor, Michigan, and the Gerald R. Ford Museum in Grand Rapids, Michigan, have documentation and exhibits about both such assassination events.

2. The small number of studies on Gerald Ford does not contain much, if any, information about these attempts. The one that gives two pages on the subject is Douglas Brinkley, *Gerald R. Ford* (New York: Times Books, 2007), 120–21. Otherwise, it is mostly ignored, or a very brief one paragraph mention.

3. However, there are studies done of both assassins worth investigating for more details. For Lynette "Squeaky" Fromme, see Jess Bravin, *Squeaky: The Life and Times of Lynette Alice Fromme* (New York: St. Martin's Press, 1997). For Sara Jane Moore, see Geri Spieler, *Taking Aim at the President: The Remarkable Story of the Woman Who Shot at Gerald Ford* (New York: Palgrave-Macmillan, 2009).

4. Information about "fence jumpers" during the Ford administration, including Marshal H. Fields, Gerald B. Gainous, Chester Plummer, and Steven B. Williams, is found in "White House Fence Jumpers," http://fencejumpers.blogspot.com/2004_02_25_fencejumpers_archive.html; and "White House Security Review: Protection of the White House Complex in the Twentieth Century," http://www.prop1.org/park/pave/rev9.htm.

14. RONALD REAGAN AT THE WASHINGTON HILTON HOTEL

1. Ronald Reagan has been much written about, and his being seriously wounded by John Hinckley in March 1981 has drawn the attention of scholars and journalists. The major newspapers, the *New York Times*, *Washington Post*, and *Los Angeles Times*, covered the news surrounding the assassination in their usual, thorough fashion. The Ronald Reagan Presidential Library and Museum in Simi Valley, California, offers manuscript sources and exhibits that cover the event, and all others of the Reagan presidency.

2. Two detailed studies of the Reagan assassination attempt are: Del Quentin Wilber, *Rawhide Down: The Near Assassination of Ronald Reagan* (New York: Holt, 2011); and Jerry Parr and Carolyn Parr, *In The Secret Service: The True Story of the Man Who Saved President Reagan's Life* (Carol Stream, IL: Tyndale House Publishers, 2013).

3. The major books on Reagan cover the assassination event as follows: Steven F. Hayward, *The Age of Reagan: The Conservative Counterrevolution, 1980–1989* (New York: Crown Forum, 2009), 136–49; Edmund Morris, *Dutch: A Memoir of Ronald Reagan* (New York: Random House, 1999), 427–39; Lou Cannon, *President Reagan: The Role of a Lifetime* (New York: Simon and Schuster, 2000), 115, 123, 141–42, 145, 155–56, 158, 188, 198–99; Richard Reeves, *Ronald Reagan: The Triumph of Imagination* (New York: Simon and Schuster, 2005), 34–51, 115; and John Patrick Diggins, *Ronald Reagan: Fate, Freedom, and the Making of History* (New York: W. W. Norton, 2008), 34, 183–87.

4. For information about "fence jumper" David Mahonski, see "A History of White House Attacks," http.www.history.com/news/a-history-of-white-house-attacks/; and for "fence jumper" Robert Latta, see http://en/wikipedia.org/wiki/Robert_Latta.

15. LATE TWENTIETH-CENTURY PRESIDENTS AND ASSASSINATION THREATS

1. The assassination threats against presidents Jimmy Carter, George H. W. Bush, and Bill Clinton are well covered in major newspapers, including the *New York Times*, *Washington Post*, and *Los Angeles Times*. The Jimmy Carter Presidential Library and Museum in Atlanta, Georgia; the George H. W. Bush Presidential Library and Museum in College Station, Texas; and the Bill Clinton

Presidential Library and Museum in Little Rock, Arkansas, have relevant documentation and exhibits.

2. On Carter and Raymond Lee Harvey, Anthony Henry, and Michael John Strickland, see: “Bizarre 1979 Plot to Assassinate President Jimmy Carter,” http://www.dailykos.com/story/2007/07/04/353992/; “Protection of the White House Complex in the Twentieth Century: White House Security Review,” http://www.prop1.org/park/pave/rev9.htm; “White House Fence Jumpers,” http://fencejumpers.blogspot.com/2004_02_25_fencejumpers_archive.html; “Raymond Lee Harvey,” http://en.wikipedia.org/wiki/Raymond_Lee-Harvey; and “White House Intruders,” http://en.wikipedia.org/wiki/White-House-intruders.

3. For Carter’s statement to Larry J. Sabato about assassination attempts, see: “Book: Jimmy Carter Targeted by U.S. and Foreign Assassins,” http://washingtonexaminer.com/. Also, see: “Jimmy Carter Has Had up to Three Assassination Plots against Him since Leaving Office Making Him the Most Targeted Former President,” http://www.dailymail.co.uk/news/article-2378257/Jimmy-Carter-assassination-plots. Finally, on the assassination plot against Jimmy Carter in the Middle East in 2009, see: “Hamas Says It Foiled Carter Assassination Attempt,” http://blogs.ajc.com/political-insider-jim-galloway/2009/06/16/.

4. On George H. W. Bush, the only major threat reported was after his presidency when he visited Kuwait in 1993 and is well reported in: “U.S. Strikes Iraq for Plot to Kill Bush,” http://washingtonpost.com/wp-srv/inatl/longterm/iraq/timeline/062793.htm.

5. The number of threats against Bill Clinton became much more noticeable, as compared to Carter and Bush. On Ronald Gene Barbour, see: “Unemployed Man Is Charged with Threat to Kill President,” http://www.nytimes.com/1994/02/19/us/; and “United States of America v. Ronald Gene Barbour,” http://theorlandosentinel.blogspot.com/2006/11/.

6. On Frank Eugene Corder, see: “The September 12, 1994 Plane Crash,” The White House Security Review Public Report, http://www.fas.org/irp/agency/ustreas/usss/tlpubrpt.html.

7. On Francisco Martin Duran, see “The October 29, 1994 Shooting,” The White House Security Review Public Report, http://www.fas.org/irp/agency/ustreas/usss/tlbpubrpt.html.

8. For Leland William Modjeski, see: “Shooting at White House/Fence Jumper, Agent Hit, Clinton Safe,” http://wwwsfgate.com/news/article/PAGE-ONE-Shooting-at-White-House-Fence-3032180; “Officials Doubt Intruder Meant President Harm,” http://www.nytimes.com/1995/05/25/us.html; “Investigators Sift History of White House Intruder,” http://articles.baltimoresun.com/1995-05-25/news/1995145004_1_modjeski-pizza-hust-town; “Man Held as Intruder Is on Suicide Watch,“ http://articles/latimes.com/1995-05-31/news/mn-

7963_1_suicide-watch; and "White House Intruder's Bid For Release Fails," http://articles.latimes.com/1995-06-02/news/mn-8516_1_.

9. For the attempt against Clinton in the Philippines in 1996, see "Osama bin Laden Came within Minutes of Killing Bill Clinton," http://www.telegraph.co.uk/news/worldnews/asia/philipppines/6867331; and "The Assassination Attempts against George W. Bush and Bill Clinton," http://swampland.time.com/2011/02/08/.

16. TWENTY-FIRST-CENTURY PRESIDENTS AND ASSASSINATION THREATS

1. The assassination threats against the twenty-first-century presidents, George W. Bush, and Barack Obama, have multiplied as compared to earlier presidents. The major newspapers, the *New York Times*, *Washington Post*, and *Los Angeles Times*, are again the best sources of information regarding these threats, along with online sources, cable news, and the major television networks. The George W. Bush Presidential Library and Museum in Dallas, Texas, has the major documents and information regarding all aspects of the Bush presidency.

2. On Robert W. Pickett in 2001, see: "A History of White House Attacks," http://www.history.com/news/; "10 U.S. Presidents on Whom Assassination Attempts Failed," http://www.tiptoptens.com/2011/12/04/10; "U.S. Presidential Assassinations and Attempts," http://timelines.latimes.com/; and "2001 White House Shooting," http://wn.wikipedia.org/wiki/.

3. On Vladamir Arutyunian, see: "10 U.S. Presidents on Whom Assassination Attempts Failed," http://www.tiptoptens.com/2011/12/04/10; "Vladamir Arutyunian," http://en.wikipedia.org/wiki/; and "The Assassination Attempts against George W. Bush and Bill Clinton," http://swampland.time.com/2011/02/08/.

4. On Shawn Cox, see: "White House Fence Jumper Was Looking for Chelsea Clinton," http://www. foxnews.com/story/2005/12/09/; and "Arkansas Man Scales White House Fence," http://www.washingtonpost.com/wp-dyn/content/article/2005/12/04/AR2005120400459.html.

5. On Brian Patterson, see: "Man Apprehended on White House Grounds," http://www.nbcnews.com/id/12239161/ns/us_news-security/t/; "Intruder Captured Near White House," http://www.nytimes.com/2006/04/10/washington/10whitehouse.html; and "White House Fence Jumpers," http://fencejumpers.blogspot.com/2004_02_25_fencejumpers_archive.html.

6. On Roger Witmer, see: "White House Fence Jumper Caught," http://articles.chicagotribune.com/2006-06-05/news/0606050237.

7. On Alexis Janicki, see: "Man Apprehended Near White House," http://seattletimes.com/html/nationworld/2003305413_ndig15.html.

8. On Catalino Lucas Diaz, see: "66-Year Old Man Leaps White House Fence," http://usatoday30.usatoday.com/news/washington/2007-03-16-white-house-jumper_N.htm; and "Storming the House,' http://www.miaminewtimes.com/2007-03-29/news/storming-the-house/full/.

9. On Muntadhar al-Zaidi, see: "Muntadhar al-Zaidi," http://en.wikipedia.org/wiki/.

10. On Benjamin Smith, see "Man Allegedly Decides the Way to George W. Bush's Daughter's Heart Is to Kill Her Father," http://freakoutnation.com/2014/02/01/.

11. On Barack Obama being the most threatened modern president, see: "President Barack Obama Is the Most Threatened President in History," http://www.dailykos.com/story/2012/11/25/1164628/; and "Obama Faces 30 Death Threats a Day, a 400 Percent Increase over Those against George W. Bush," http://www.abovetopsecret.com/forum/thread499773/pg1.

12. On Jerry Blanchard and Raymond H. Geisel, see: "Assassination Threats against Barack Obama," http://en.wikipedia.org/wiki; and "Man Held for Obama Assassination Threat," http://www.cbsnews.com/news/ (on Geisel).

13. On Tharin Robert Gartrell, Shawn Robert Adolf, and Nathan Dwaine Johnson, see: "Barack Obama Gets Threats Online," http://ireport.cnn.com/docs/DOC-441180; "Assassination Threats against Barack Obama," http://en.wikipedia.org/wiki/; and "Barack Obama Assassination Plot in Denver," http://en/wikipedia.org/wiki/.

14. On Paul Schlesselman and Daniel Cowart, see: "Assassination Threats against Barack Obama," http://en.wikipedia.org/wiki; "Barack Obama Gets Threats Online," htti://ireport.cnn.com/docs/DOC-441180; "Barack Obama Assassination Plot in Tennessee," http://en.wikipedia.org/wiki; and "White Supremacist Daniel Cowart Pleads Guilty in Plot to Kill Obama," http://www.huffingtonpost.com/2010/03/30/518408.html.

15. On Alfred Brock, see: "Barack Obama Gets Threats Online," http://ireport.cnn.com/docs/DOC-481180.

16. On the Turkish assassination attempt against Obama, see: "Plot to Assassinate Obama Foiled in Turkey," http://edition.cnn.com/2009/POLITICS/04/06/turkey.assassination.plot/; and "Barack Obama Gets Threats Online," http://ireport.cnn.com/docs/DOC-481180.

17. On Pamela Morgan, see: "Fence-Jumper Immediately Apprehended at White House," http://www.washingtontimes.com/weblogs/potus-notes/2009/jun/09/.

18. On Kristy Lee Roshia, threat against First Lady Michelle Obama, see: "Assassination Threats against Barack Obama," http://en.wikipedia.org/wiki.

19. On Robert Anthony Quinones, see: "Robert Anthony Quinones, Georgia Army Base Gunman, Threatened to Kill Obama, Bill Clinton, Federal Prosecutors Say," http://www.huffingtonpost.com/2010/09/07/.

20. On Michael Stephen Bowden, see: "Threats Against Obama: Michael Stephen Bowden Is Just the Latest," http://www.csmonitor.com/USA/2010/1126/.

21. On the major threat that was presented by Oscar Ramiro Ortega-Hernandez, see "Man Charged with Obama Assassination Attempt," http://www.aljazeera.com/news/americas/2011/11/2011111719561027922l.html; "Oscar Ramiro Ortega-Hernandez Thought He Was Jesus, Obama Was Antichrist," http://www.huffingtonpost.com/2011/11/18/; "Oscar Ramiro Ortega-Hernandez, Accused White House Shooter, Considering Plea Deal," http://www.huffingtonpost.com/2013/09/06/; "Man Who Shot at White House Sentenced to 25 Years," http://www.cbsnews.com/news/; "Idaho Man Who Fired at White House in 2011 Sentenced to 25 Years," http://blogs.rollcall.com/hill-blotter; and "Assassination Threats against Barack Obama," http://en.wikipedia.org/wiki/.

22. *Washington Post* and *New York Times* of September 28, 2014.

23. On Ulugbek Kodirov, see: "Ulugbek Kodirov Sentenced to More Than 15 Years in Prison for Plot to Kill President Obama," http://www.huffingtonpost.com/2012/07/13/; and "Muslim Gets 15 Years for Obama Assassination Plot," http://atlasshrugs2000.typepad.com/atlas_shrugs/2012/07/.

24. On the plot by an anarchist militia within the U.S. Army (Michael Burnett, Christopher Salmon, and Isaac Aguigui), see: "4 U.S. Soldiers Accused in President Obama Assassination Plot," http://hiphopwired.com/2012/08/28/4; and "Assassination Threats against Barack Obama," http://en.wikipedia.org/wiki.

25. On the Albany death ray plot of Glen Scott Crawford and Eric J. Feight, see: "2013 Albany Death Ray Plot," http://en.wikipedia.org/wiki/; and "Assassination Threats against Barack Obama," http://en.wikipedia.org/wiki.

26. On Larry Klayman, see: "Crazy Larry Klayman Joins Melee at White House, Demands Obama Put Down Koran, Surrender," http://crooksandliars.com/karoli/; and "Desperate Right Winger Launches a Treasonous Plot to Overthrow President Obama," http://www.politicsusa.com/2013/09/19/.

27. On Mario Edward Garnett, see: "Man Shot Dead after Bank Robbery Convicted of Threatening Obama in 2010," http://www.cnn.com/2013/12/29/justice/.

28. On retired Army General Paul E. Vallely, see: "Retired General Wants March on White House and Citizens Arrest of Obama," http://www.politicsusa.com/2013/12/31/.

29. On Georgetown University professor Michael Scheuer, see "Georgetown University Professor/Fox News Expert Calls for Obama's Assassination," http://m.dailykos.com/story/2014/01/03/1267011/.

30. *Washington Post* and *New York Times*, September 29, 2014.

31. *New York Times*; and *Washington Post*, September 20, 2014.

32. *New York Times* and *Washington Post*, January 13, 2015; and *New York Times* and *Washington Post*, January 19, 2015.

17. FIFTEEN "MIGHT HAVE BEEN" PRESIDENTS IN HISTORY

1. The fifteen "Might Have Been" presidents are a fascinating group, and sources are available for all of them.

2. For Hannibal Hamlin, see: Harry Draper Hunt, *Hannibal Hamlin of Maine, Lincoln's First Vice President* (Syracuse, NY: Syracuse University Press, 1969).

3. For Lafayette Foster, see: Thomas Vogt and Darla Shaw, *Lafayette Foster: A Heartbeat Away from the Presidency* (Shelbyville, KY: Wasteland Press, 2010).

4. For Garret Hobart, see: David Magie, *Life of Garret Augustus Hobart* (New York: G. P. Putnam, 1910), which has been reproduced in 2010 by Kessinger Publishing in Whitefish, Montana, and is available on Amazon.com.

5. John Hay is a major public figure and much was published by him, including a ten-volume study of Abraham Lincoln, his "boss" during the Civil War, when Hay was his private secretary and lived in the White House, coauthored by fellow secretary John G. Nicolay, in 1890. Hay has been the center of attention in two very recently published books: John Taliaferro, *All the Great Prizes: The Life of John Hay, from Lincoln to Roosevelt* (New York: Simon and Schuster, 2013), and Joshua Zeitz, *Lincoln's Boys: John Hay, John Nicolay, and the War for Lincoln's Image* (New York: Viking, 2014). These recent studies add much to the reputation of Hay.

6. For John Nance Garner, see: O. C. Fisher, *Cactus Jack: A Biography of John Nance Garner* (Waco, TX: Texian Press, 1978); and Marquis James, *Mr. Garner of Texas* (Indianapolis, IN: Bobbs Merrill, 1939).

7. George C. Marshall is another giant figure in military and political history, and much has been published about his distinguished career in the military and in government. The best studies are Ed Cray, *General of the Army: George C. Marshall, Soldier and Statesman* (New York: W. W. Norton, 1990); Mark A. Stoler, *George C. Marshall: Soldier-Statesman of the American Century* (New York: Twayne Publishers, 1989); and Forrest Pogue, *George C. Marshall: Statesman, 1945–1959* (New York: Viking Press, 1987).

8. For Joseph William Martin Jr., see his autobiography: Joseph Martin, *My First Fifty Years in Politics* (New York: McGraw-Hill, 1960); and James J. Kenneally, *A Compassionate Conservative: A Political Biography of Joseph W. Martin, Jr., Speaker of the U.S. House of Representatives* (Lanham, MD: Lexington Books, 2003).

9. For Alben Barkley, see his autobiography: Alben W. Barkley, *That Reminds Me: Autobiography of the Veep* (New York: Doubleday, 1954); and James K. Libbey, *Dear Alben: Mr. Barkley of Kentucky* (Lexington: University Press of Kentucky, 1979).

10. For Robert F. Kennedy, see: Arthur M. Schlesinger Jr., *Robert Kennedy and His Times* (Boston: Houghton Mifflin, 1978); and Evan Thomas, *Robert Kennedy: His Life* (New York: Simon & Schuster, 2000).

11. For Spiro Agnew, see: Jules Witcover, *White Knight: The Rise of Spiro Agnew* (New York: Random House, 1972); Richard Cohen and Jules Witcover, *A Heartbeat Away: The Investigation and Resignation of Vice President Spiro T. Agnew* (New York: Bantam Books, 1974); and Jules Witcover, *Very Strange Bedfellows: The Short and Unhappy Marriage of Richard Nixon and Spiro Agnew* (New York: Public Affairs Press, 2007).

12. For Nelson Rockefeller, see: Cary Reich, *The Life of Nelson Rockefeller* (New York: Doubleday, 1996); Joseph Persico, *Imperial Rockefeller: A Biography of Nelson Rockefeller* (New York: Simon & Schuster, 1982); and Richard Norton Smith, *On His Own Terms: A Life of Nelson Rockefeller* (New York: Random House, 2014).

13. For Walter Mondale, see: Finlay Lewis, *Mondale: Portrait of an American Politician* (New York: Harper & Row, 1980); Steven M Gillon, *The Democrats' Dilemma: Walter F. Mondale and the Liberal Legacy* (New York: Columbia University Press, 1992); and Walter Mondale and David Hage, *The Good Fight: A Life in Liberal Politics* (New York: Scribner, 2010).

14. For Albert Gore Jr., see: Bill Turque, *Inventing Al Gore: A Biography* (Boston: Houghton Mifflin, 2000); David Maraniss and Ellen Y. Nakashima, *The Prince of Tennessee: Al Gore Meets His Fate* (New York: Simon and Schuster, 2000); and Troy Gipson, *From Carthage to Oslo: A Biography of Al Gore* (CreateSpace, 2012). Additionally, Gore has published a number of books on his favorite pursuit: the environment.

15. For Dick Cheney, see his autobiography: Dick Cheney and Liz Cheney, *In My Time: A Personal and Political Memoir* (New York: Threshold Publishing, 2011); Stephen F. Hayes, *Cheney: The Untold Story of America's Most Powerful and Controversial Vice President* (New York: HarperCollins, 2007); Barton Gellman, *Angler: The Cheney Vice Presidency* (New York: Penguin Press, 2008); Lou Dubose and Jake Bernstein, *Vice: Dick Cheney and the Hijacking of the American Presidency* (New York: Random House, 2006); and Peter Baker,

Days of Fire: Bush and Cheney in the White House (New York: Doubleday, 2013).

16. For Joe Biden, see his autobiography *Promises to Keep: On Life and Politics* (New York: Random House, 2007); and Jules Witcover, *Joe Biden: A Life of Trial and Redemption* (New York: William Morrow, 2010).

SELECT BIBLIOGRAPHY

GENERAL WORKS ON ASSASSINATIONS

Clarke, James W. *American Assassins: The Darker Side of Politics*. Princeton, NJ: Princeton University Press, 1982.

Donovan, Robert J. *The Assassins*. New York: Harper and Brothers, 1955.

Kessler, Ronald. *In The President's Secret Service: Behind the Scenes with Agents in the Line of Fire and the Presidents They Protect*. New York: Crown Archetype, 2009.

Oliver, Willard M., and Nancy E. Marion. *Killing the President: Assassinations, Attempts, and Rumored Attempts on U.S. Commanders-In-Chief.* Santa Barbara, CA: Praeger, 2010.

ANDREW JACKSON (1829–1837)

Cole, Donald B. *The Presidency of Andrew Jackson*. Lawrence: University Press of Kansas, 1993.

Schlesinger, Arthur M., Jr. *The Age of Jackson*. Boston: Little, Brown, 1945.

Wilentz, Sean. *Andrew Jackson*. New York: Times Books, 2005.

ABRAHAM LINCOLN (1861–1865)

Bishop, Jim. *The Day Lincoln Was Shot*. New York: Harper and Row, 1955.

Kauffman, Michael W. *American Brutus: John Wilkes Booth and the Lincoln Conspiracy*. New York: Random House, 2004.

Kline, Michael J. *The Baltimore Plot: The First Conspiracy to Assassinate Abraham Lincoln*. Yardley, PA: Westholme Publishing, 2008.

McGovern, George S. *Abraham Lincoln*. New York: Times Books, 2008.

Paludan, Philip Shaw. *The Presidency of Abraham Lincoln*. Lawrence: University Press of Kansas, 1994.

Stashower, Daniel. *The Hour of Peril: The Secret Plot to Murder Lincoln before the Civil War*. New York: Minotaur Books, 2013.

Steers, Edward. *Blood on the Moon: The Assassination of President Abraham Lincoln*. Lexington: University Press of Kentucky, 2001.
Swanson, James. *Manhunt: The Twelve-Day Chase for Lincoln's Killer*. New York: William Morrow, 2006.
Titone, Nora. *My Thoughts Be Bloody: The Bitter Rivalry That Led to the Assassination of Abraham Lincoln*. New York: Free Press, 2010.

JAMES A. GARFIELD (1881)

Ackerman, Kenneth D. *Dark Horse: The Surprise Election and Political Murder of President James A. Garfield*. Cambridge, MA: Da Capo Press, 2003.
Doenecke, Justus D. *The Presidencies of James A. Garfield and Chester A. Arthur*. Lawrence: University Press of Kansas, 1981.
Millard, Candice. *Destiny of the Republic: A Tale of Madness, Medicine and the Murder of a President*. New York: Doubleday, 2011.
Rosenberg, Charles E. *The Trial of the Assassin Guiteau: Psychiatry and the Law in the Gilded Age*. Chicago: University of Chicago Press, 1995.
Rutkow, Ira. *James A. Garfield*. New York: Times Books, 2006.

WILLIAM MCKINLEY (1897–1901)

Gould, Lewis L. *The Presidency of William McKinley*. Lawrence: University Press of Kansas, 1980.
Miller, Scott. *The President and the Assassin: McKinley, Terror, and Empire at the Dawn of the American Century*. New York: Random House, 2011.
Philips, Kevin. *William McKinley*. New York: Times Books, 2003.
Rauchway, Eric. *Murdering McKinley: The Making of Theodore Roosevelt's America*. New York: Hill and Wang, 2003.

THEODORE ROOSEVELT (1901–1909)

Auchincloss, Louis. *Theodore Roosevelt*. New York: Times Books, 2001.
Gould, Lewis L. *The Presidency of Theodore Roosevelt*. Lawrence: University Press of Kansas, 1991.
Helferich, Gerard. *Theodore Roosevelt and the Assassin: Madness, Vengeance, and the Campaign of 1912*. Guilford, CT: Lyons Press, 2013.
Remey, Oliver E. *The Attempted Assassination of Ex-President Theodore Roosevelt*. New York: Ulan Press, JPS Norton, 2012.

FRANKLIN D. ROOSEVELT (1933–1945)

Archer, Jules. *The Plot to Seize the White House: The Shocking True Story of the Conspiracy to Overthrow FDR*. New York: Skyhorse Publishing, 2007.
Denton, Sally. *The Plots against the President: FDR, a Nation in Crisis, and the Rise of the American Right*. New York: Bloomsbury Press, 2012.

Jenkins, Roy. *Franklin Delano Roosevelt*. New York: Times Books, 2003.
Leuchtenberg, William E. *Franklin D. Roosevelt and the New Deal*. New York: HarperCollins, 1963.
Picchi, Blaise. *The Five Weeks of Giuseppe Zangara: The Man Who Would Assassinate FDR*. Chicago: Chicago Review Press, 1998.
Schlesinger, Arthur M., Jr. *The Age of Roosevelt*. 3 volumes. Boston: Houghton Mifflin, 1957–1960.

HUEY P. LONG

Brinkley, Alan. *Voices of Protest: Huey Long, Father Coughlin, and the Great Depression*. New York: Knopf, 1982.
White, Richard D., Jr. *Kingfish: The Reign of Huey P. Long*. New York: Random House, 2006.
Williams, T. Harry. *Huey Long*. New York: Knopf, 1969.

HARRY S. TRUMAN (1945–1953)

Dallek, Robert. *Harry S. Truman*. New York: Times Books, 2008.
Hunter, Stephen, and John Bainbridge Jr. *American Gunfight: The Plot to Kill Harry Truman, and the Shootout That Stopped It*. New York: Simon and Schuster, 2005.
McCoy, Donald R. *The Presidency of Harry S. Truman*. Lawrence: University Press of Kansas, 1984.
McCullough, David. *Truman*. New York: Simon and Schuster, 1992.
Truman, Margaret. *Harry S. Truman*. New York: Morrow, 1973.

JOHN F. KENNEDY (1961–1963)

Bishop, Jim. *The Day Kennedy Was Shot*. New York: Harper Perennial, 2013.
Brinkley, Alan. *John F. Kennedy*. New York: Times Books, 2012.
Bugliosi, Vincent. *Reclaiming History: The Assassination of President John F. Kennedy*. New York: W. W. Norton, 2007.
Giglio, James. *The Presidency of John F. Kennedy*. Lawrence: University Press of Kansas, 1991.
Manchester, William. *The Death of a President: November 20–November 25, 1963*. New York: BBS Publishing, 1967.
Posner, Gerald. *Case Closed: Lee Harvey Oswald and the Assassination of JFK*. New York: Random House, 1993.
Sabato, Larry J. *The Kennedy Half Century: The Presidency, Assassination, and the Lasting Legacy of John F. Kennedy*. New York: Bloomsbury, 2013.
Schlesinger, Arthur M., Jr. *A Thousand Days: John F. Kennedy in the White House*. Boston: Houghton Mifflin, 1965.
Sorensen, Theodore. *Kennedy*. New York: Harper and Row, 1965.

ROBERT F. KENNEDY

Ayton, Mel. *The Forgotten Terrorist: Sirhan Sirhan and the Assassination of Robert F. Kennedy*. Omaha, NE: Potomac Books, 2007.

Klaber, William, and Philip H. Melanson. *Shadow Play: The Murder of Robert F. Kennedy, the Trial of Sirhan Sirhan, and the Future of American Justice*. New York: St. Martin's Press, 1997.

Schlesinger, Arthur M., Jr. *Robert Kennedy and His Times*. Boston: Houghton Mifflin, 1978.

Thomas, Evan. *Robert Kennedy: His Life*. New York: Simon & Schuster, 2000.

GEORGE C. WALLACE

Carter, Dan T. *The Politics of Rage: George Wallace, the Origins of the New Conservatism, and the Transformation of American Politics*. New York: Simon and Schuster, 1995.

Frady, Marshall. *Wallace: The Classic Portrait of Alabama Governor George Wallace*. New York: Random House, 1996.

Lesher, Stephan. *George Wallace: American Populist*. New York: Perseus Books, 1994.

RICHARD M. NIXON (1969–1974)

Ambrose, Stephen E. *Nixon: The Triumph of a Politician, 1962–1972*. New York: Simon and Schuster, 1989.

———. *Nixon: Ruin and Recovery, 1973–1990*. New York: Simon and Schuster, 1991.

Drew, Elizabeth. *Richard M. Nixon*. New York: Times Books, 2007.

Small, Melvin. *The Presidency of Richard Nixon*. Lawrence: University Press of Kansas, 1999.

GERALD R. FORD (1974–1977)

Bravin, Jess. *Squeaky: The Life and Times of Lynette Alice Fromme*. New York: St. Martin's Press, 1997.

Brinkley, Douglas. *Gerald R. Ford*. New York: Times Books, 2007.

Greene, John Robert. *The Presidency of Gerald R. Ford*. Lawrence: University Press of Kansas, 1995.

Spieler, Geri. *Taking Aim at the President: The Remarkable Story of the Woman Who Shot at Gerald Ford*. New York: Palgrave Macmillan, 2008.

JIMMY CARTER (1977–1981)

Bourne, Peter G. *Jimmy Carter: A Comprehensive Biography from Plains to Post-Presidency*. New York: Scribner, 1997.

Kaufman, Burton I., and Scott Kaufman. *The Presidency of James Earl Carter, Jr*. 2nd ed. Lawrence: University Press of Kansas, 2006.

Zelizer, Julian E. *Jimmy Carter*. New York: Times Books, 2010.

RONALD REAGAN (1981–1989)

Cannon, Lou. *President Reagan: The Role of a Lifetime*. New York: Simon and Schuster, 2000.
Hayward, Steven F. *The Age of Reagan: The Conservative Counterrevolution: 1980–1989*. New York: Crown Forum, 2009.
Parr, Jerry, and Carolyn Parr. *In the Secret Service: The True Story of the Man Who Saved President Reagan's Life*. Carol Stream, IL: Tyndale House Publishers, 2013.
Wilber, Del Quentin. *Rawhide Down: The Near Assassination of Ronald Reagan*. New York: Holt, 2011.

GEORGE H. W. BUSH (1989–1993)

Greene, John Robert. *The Presidency of George Bush*. Lawrence: University Press of Kansas, 1999.
Naftali, Timothy. *George H. W. Bush*. New York: Times Books, 2007.

BILL CLINTON (1993–2001)

Evans, Harold. *Bill Clinton*. New York: Times Books, 2014.
Harris, John F. *The Survivor: Bill Clinton in the White House*. New York: Random House, 2005.

GEORGE W. BUSH (2001–2009)

Draper, Robert. *Dead Certain: The Presidency of George W. Bush*. New York: Free Press, 2007.
Zelizer, Julian E. *The Presidency of George W. Bush: A First Historical Assessment*. Princeton, NJ: Princeton University Press, 2010.

BARACK OBAMA (2009–)

Maraniss, David. *Barack Obama: The Story*. New York: Simon and Schuster, 2012.
Todd, Chuck. *The Stranger: Barack Obama in the White House*. New York: Little, Brown, 2014.

INDEX

ABOUT THE AUTHOR

Ronald L. Feinman has taught American history, government, and politics for more than four decades, including the past twenty-five years at Florida Atlantic University in Boca Raton, Florida. He received his PhD from the City University of New York Graduate School under the tutelage of Professor Arthur M. Schlesinger Jr., who served in the John F. Kennedy White House. Feinman is the author of *Twilight of Progressivism: The Western Republican Senators and the New Deal* (Johns Hopkins University Press, 1981). His historical and political blog, *TheProgressiveProfessor.com*, has been active since 2008. He loves traveling to historical sites and lecturing before groups in the South Florida area on topics such as the presidency, the U.S. Senate, and contemporary political controversies.